The Heart and the Island

SUNY series in Italian/American Culture

Fred L. Gardaphe, editor

The Heart and the Island

A Critical Study of Sicilian American Literature

Chiara Mazzucchelli

Cover image of Sicily with heart from Fotolia.

Published by State University of New York Press, Albany

© 2015 State University of New York

For information, contact State University of New York Press, Albany, NY
www.sunypress.edu

Production, Diane Ganeles
Marketing, Fran Keneston

Library of Congress Cataloging-in-Publication Data

Mazzucchelli, Chiara
    The heart and the island : a critical study of Sicilian American literature /
Chiara Mazzucchelli.
        pages cm. — (SUNY series in Italian/American culture)
    Includes bibliographical references and index.
    ISBN 978-1-4384-5923-3 (hardcover : alk. paper)
    ISBN 978-1-4384-5922-6 (paperback : alk. paper)
    ISBN 978-1-4384-5924-0 (e-book)
    1. American literature—Sicilian American authors—History and criticism.
2. American literature—20th century—History and criticism.   3. Sicilian
Americans—Intellectual life.   I. Title.

    PS153.S23M39 2016
    810.9'851073—dc23   2015006733

10 9 8 7 6 5 4 3 2 1

Damien, always keep the island in your heart.

Contents

Preface

When I arrived at the Miami airport in 2003, I had two big suit-cases with me, one of which was full of books, mostly nineteenth- and twentieth-century Italian novels. When I moved into my first apartment in Boca Raton, I just arranged all my books neatly in a bookcase in alphabetical order. As I started my PhD in Comparative Studies at Florida Atlantic University, I also started collecting books I needed for my courses, but it was not difficult to separate them on my shelves from the ones I had brought with me from Italy. After all, my new readings were all in English. So they started forming the "American" shelves of my bookcase. However, when I started taking classes on ethnic literature, I felt that, as different as they were, Toni Morrison's *Beloved*, Saul Bellow's *Herzog*, and Gloria Anzaldúa's *Borderlands/La Frontera* needed a space of their own, separate from, say, Samuel Huntington's *The Clash of Civilizations*. So now my bookcase was tripartite: It had a canonical Italian, a mainstream American, and an ethnic American section.

Little by little, my Italian American novels and books started to take over the ethnic space in my bedroom. Helen Barolini sat next to Sandra Cisneros and *Umbertina* was looking to buy *The House on Mango Street*, while Mari Tomasi's *Lesser Gods* bought the lot previously owned by *The Joy Luck Club* run by Amy Tan. Not too long after, I had to buy another bookcase to give John Fante a space of his own, purportedly because Fante wrote many books, but really because Arturo Bandini didn't get along with anyone.

Around that time, I also started working on my dissertation topic. I knew that writers such as Giovanni Verga, Luigi Pirandello, Vitaliano Brancati, Maria Messina, Giuseppe Tomasi di Lampedusa, and more recently, Leonardo Sciascia, Vincenzo Consolo, Dacia Maraini, and

Andrea Camilleri had infused their works with a sense of a distinct *sicilianità*—or Sicilianness. Many of these authors' books had been assigned readings in high school, and later in college. Several of them made the trip to the United States with me, packed in my red Samsonite. But the more I read, the more obvious it became to me that the same thing had happened within the broader field of Italian American literature. Many U.S. writers, such as Jerre Mangione, Ben Morreale, Tony Ardizzone, Nat Scammacca, Vincenzo Ancona, Gioia Timpanelli, Rose Romano, and others, have focused their works on their experiences as Sicilian Americans. These authors, I concluded, have produced Sicilian American literature.

Following this realization, I got on my knees one Sunday afternoon, rearranged all my Italian and Italian American books together in alphabetical order, and then I started writing my dissertation, which later became this book.

Acknowledgments

This book has been in the making for some time. Some colleagues have especially been critical to its completion. With deepest gratitude I thank, first and foremost, Anthony Tamburri and Fred Gardaphé for their encouragement and guidance through all the stages of this project and of my academic career in the United States. Special acknowledgment also goes to Paolo Giordano for his support, Keith Folse for his precious advice, and all my colleagues in Italian American studies, whose work on all aspects of the Italian American experience has been crucial to my intellectual and scholarly formation. Amy Barnickel carefully read my manuscript and provided much needed copyediting advice. I also thank this book's reviewers for their serious critique of my work. I could not have wished for better anonymous readers. I am grateful to James Peltz and Fred Gardaphé at State University of New York Press for believing in this book since its inception and to my production editor Diane Ganeles for helping me bring this project to a conclusion. An early and condensed version of chapter 1 was published with the title "Ethnic Regionalism in American Literature: The Case of Sicilian/American Writers," in *Tamkang Review* 38.1 (2007): 119–142. Chapter 3 appeared, in a slightly different form, as " 'The Scum of the Scum of the Scum': Rose Romano's Search for Sisterhood," in *Journal of Lesbian Studies* 18.3 (2014): 298–309. I thank the editor of the *Tamkang Review* and Taylor and Francis for their prompt help in securing permission to reprint.

Infine, tra le altre persone cui sono debitrice per il supporto intellettuale ed emotivo, un ringraziamento speciale va a Silvia Giagnoni e Alessandra Senzani, che mi sono vicine a distanza.

Questo libro è dedicato alla mia famiglia in Italia e to my family here in the United States.

Introduction

Io non ho che te
cuore della mia razza.

—Salvatore Quasimodo, *Tutte le poesie*

Odio, detesto la Sicilia nella misura stessa in cui l'amo,
e in cui non risponde al tipo d'amore che vorrei nutrire per essa.

—Leonardo Sciascia, *La Sicilia come metafora*

Generally, Sicilians feel strongly about their birthplace. Due to a combination of geographical and historical factors, and social and cultural identity, Sicilians develop a strong bond with their mother(is)land and build on their own perceived uniqueness. In fact, the bond is so strong that it survives even the separation brought about by emigration. And so it happens that the sense of a distinct Sicilian Americanness—or, as I call it here, *sicilianamericanità*—has surfaced in a corpus of texts, which, although subsumed under the broader rubric of (Italian) American literature, have distinguished themselves as examples of an exquisitely Sicilian American literary experience. In their works, many American authors of Sicilian descent derive inspiration from their ethnic milieu and lay out a recognizable set of Sicilian cultural markers; these authors have produced Sicilian American literature. This book is about these writers and their works.

Here, I explore issues of identity and Sicilian Americanness, paying special attention to the literary production of four well-known Italian American authors who have elaborated their own unique perspectives on Sicily and being Sicilian in the United States. Regardless of their different personal (his)stories, interests, and careers, the four authors on whom I focus, namely, Jerre Mangione, Rose Romano, Ben Morreale, and Gioia Timpanelli, are all so thoroughly conscious of their sicilianamericanità that they capitalized on it and turned it into a writing asset. I also suggest that a similar process of identity construction is at the core of Sicilian literature in Italy and Sicilian American literature in the United States. In both contexts, Sicily has managed to carve out a space in the heart and works of writers who have defined their identity in relation to the island.

The main factors responsible for the construction of such uniqueness in literary traditions an ocean apart, I argue, are intrinsically geographical as well as historical. Sicily's island status combined with centuries of conquests and foreign rule have shaped its people and culture in many distinct and distinguishable ways. Especially after the 1861 unification of Italy, the island's spatial disjunction from the mainland caused a great lack of knowledge about it, which tended to be filled with sociological as well as literary fantasies about how to best understand and interpret the nature of Sicilians. Travelogues, novels, essays, pseudoscientific studies, among others, all attempted to solve the dilemma that Sicily and its people posed to the newborn Italian state. Perhaps in response to what they perceived as inaccurate and misleading accounts of the "Sicilian ways," and in an effort to provide a more informed insider's view of the island and its people, many Sicilian and, later, Sicilian American writers started to write back, so to speak, and to reflect on this perceived diversity. Ironically enough, these writers' compulsion to meditate on, explain, and justify Sicily has also helped to reinforce the idea of a separate and, in many ways, distinct Sicilian identity.

Critics have largely ignored questions of regionalism as they surface in Italian American literature. By focusing on the specific critical significance of just one of the many regional components of Italian America, I hope to challenge the belief that to emphasize specific differences in the ethnic experience relating to gender, sexual preference, class, or geographical origins, just to mention a few variables in the social equation, complicates matters by fragmenting even more the already vulnerable position of ethnic minorities in society. In fact, the notion of ethnicity conceived as an essentially constructed category has been increasingly contested from the inside, and more and more attention has been paid to the groups' internal differences that had been previously glossed over. It is now essential for ethnic critical communities to bring new and diverse perspectives to bear on the field of multicultural literary studies.

One of the main ideas supporting this book is that the complex fabric of the Italian American community is reflected in its literature, and diversity within both domains, the social and the literary, should be recognized and valorized rather than silenced or suppressed. In the field of Italian American studies, a critical ethnic discourse in literature came into being conspicuously later than most of the larger (in terms of number) groups that constitute the cultural tapestry of the United States. The 1990s, especially, was the decade that witnessed a booming critical production thanks to the works of scholars such as Helen Barolini, Fred Gardaphé, Robert Viscusi, Mary Jo Bona, Edvige Giunta, and Anthony Tamburri, just to mention a few.[1] As far as literary debates over the last decades are concerned, Italian American ethnic identity has generally been constructed discursively on the historical consideration that its culture was shaped by immigrants from the Mezzogiorno, an area that extends south and east of Rome, and which includes the Abruzzi region, Campania, Puglia, Basilicata, Calabria, and the two islands of Sicily and Sardinia. Most critical discourses have focused on the experience of the forsaken South as a whole, thus equating the sociocultural background of an immigrant peasant of the area immediately south of Rome with that of a fisherman of the southwest coast of Sicily. The common denominator for such different experiences is the status of second-class citizenship from which most of the immigrants from southern Italy tried to flee en masse. Also, by and large, the economic and political disenfranchisement of *meridionali*—or Southern Italians—continued in the United States, where the immigrant status per se has historically forbidden a fuller political and economic participation. All this has led to the tendency in Italian American studies to couch its literature in terms of the social and economic marginality that meridionali experienced both in the "old country" and in the "new world," and to conceive of and represent them as a homogenous and coherent category of historically muted subjects.

Admittedly, since the unification, the Italian southern masses as a whole have experienced various degrees of difficulty to access the decisional spheres of institutional power. The Kingdom of Italy was, in fact, constituted under the rule of the Piedmontese House of the Savoy at a time when the North of Italy was trying to keep pace with the European first-comers of the industrialization process, that is, England, France, and Germany. In this historical juncture, the Mezzogiorno, with a traditional economy based on the agrarian system, could hardly participate in the hegemonic project of newborn

Italy. At the beginning of the twentieth century, Italian intellectual and political theorist Antonio Gramsci provided a most lucid analysis of the problems engendered by economic inequalities in relation to geographic distribution in Italy, and of the subaltern condition of Italian southern peasant masses. In his all-too-famous 1926 article "Alcuni temi sulla questione meridionale," the economic developmental paradigm that Italy had chosen to adopt at the moment of unification generated what Gramsci notoriously baptized as the "southern question."[2] Six years earlier, in 1920, in a series of considerations on the effects of the First World War on the dramatically unequal economic growth of Italy, Gramsci lamented in the pages of the communist daily publication *L'Ordine Nuovo*:

> People often talk about the lack of initiative in the southerners. It is an unjust accusation. The fact is that capital always seeks the most secure and fruitful forms of employment. . . . Where the factory already exists, it continues to develop through savings. . . . So . . . all the national productive potentiality engaged in the war industry clusters more and more in Piedmont, Lombardy, Emilia and Liguria thus further weakening that little life that existed in the Southern regions. (Cavalcanti and Piccone 102–103)

According to Gramsci, the Mezzogiorno had been reduced to a reserve of natural resources for the industrial North, to a supply of cheap labor, and, finally, to a market for the North's finished products in order to serve the needs of the capitalistic system. Early enough in history, then, Southern Italy gave its share to what has become a commonplace expression that turns the South from a geographical location into a metaphor of slow advancement and economic backwardness: the "World's South."[3] With the programmatic recrimination "the Northern bourgeoisie has subjugated the South of Italy and the Islands, and reduced them to exploitable colonies" (*The Southern Question* 16), Gramsci managed to bridge the chronological gap between the Italian post-unification and the postcolonial struggles in other parts of the world.

Publicized as a "national" venture, the Italian unification was, in fact, supported by an imperial ideology that even resorted to the disturbingly familiar rhetoric of a civilizing enterprise that continues to inform current neo-imperialist projects. According to many, the rural South lacked cultural and social sophistication, while the Northern stock, eager to embrace the industrial model set up by the most powerful European countries, proved to be superior. In Italy, the Manichean polarization that characterizes any imperialistic project, which is based on dichotomies such as rationality versus irrationality, modernity versus backwardness, progress versus obsolescence, and the like, followed territorial criteria: the category "good Italians" was occupied by Northerners, while Southerners were "bad Italians." At the beginning of the last century, Italian socialist Camillo Prampolini condensed the unhappy situation with a sentence that has become a common expression in Italy: "L'Italia si divide in nordici e sudici."[4]

The anthropological doctrines of racial superiority and inferiority that saw the light at the end of the nineteenth century also played a distinct role in the construction of relations between the North and the South of Italy. Through the works of the School of Positivist Criminology of Cesare Lombroso, Alfredo Niceforo, Giuseppe Sergi, and Enrico Ferri, the racial theory of the social and moral inferiority of the meridionali vis-à-vis Northerners became the dominant mode of understanding the problem of the "two Italies."[5] An example of this pernicious line of thought can be found in Niceforo's 1901 study *Italiani del nord, italiani del sud*, in which he insisted on the differences between Northerners, belonging to the Germanic or Aryan race, and Southerners, representing the Mediterranean or African stock. According to Niceforo, racial differences accounted for the more advanced "psychology" of Northerners, which bred a superior civilization in terms of economy, industrialization, education, social structure, and political behavior. The main characteristic of the "psychology" of "dark Mediterraneans," on the other hand, was the "excessive excitability of the *self*" (116),[6] which was responsible for all kinds of genetic ills, such as a general impossibility for Southerners to concentrate on a task, a lack of volubility and practicality, unrestrained emotions and imagination, and impulsivity (118–120).[7] Unlike most of his colleagues, Niceforo was ready to grant Southerners an unexpected and rather flattering quality: "quick wit" (120).[8] However, this concession was more apologetic than anything else, being that Niceforo was himself from Sicily. It is unnecessary to point out how much these theories helped to absolve those who enjoyed the privilege of decisional power from any responsibility as to the unequal economic development of the country. Despite the opposition of some of the most influential scholars of the time, the pseudoscientific discourses elaborated by "social Darwinists" managed to take root in Italy, and they are at the origins of a series of prejudices and divisions that continue to trouble the country today.[9]

In his aforementioned article "Alcuni temi," Antonio Gramsci tackled not only the economic aspects of the unification but also the ideological propaganda that served as a justification for the exploitation of Southern masses. In a tone that calls to mind the postcolonial discourses of our times, Gramsci thus deplored the Northern hegemonic ideology:

> It is well known what kind of ideology has been disseminated in innumerable ways by the propagandists of the bourgeoisie among the masses of the North: the South is the ball and chain that prevents a more rapid progress in the civil development of Italy; Southerners are biologically inferior beings, either semi-barbarians or out and out barbarians by natural destiny; if the South is underdeveloped it is not the fault of the capitalist system, or any other historical cause, but of the nature that has made Southerners lazy, incapable, criminal and barbaric. This harsh fate has been only slightly tempered by the purely individual explosion of a few great geniuses, like isolated palms in an arid and sterile desert. (*The Southern Question* 20)

One point to emphasize is that, despite the provisional title given to his incomplete article, Gramsci never thought of the Southern question as a problem circumscribed to a given geographical area for which that area only was responsible. Rather, he read it as the ineludible effect, on a national level, of the economic inequalities generated by the capitalistic system. Indeed, the solution proposed by Gramsci to the Southern question was of national importance, accomplished through the constitution of a Comintern, or a "governo operaio e contadino" made up of Northern proletarian and Southern peasant masses in an anticapitalistic perspective. However, the "revolutionary bloc" theorized by Gramsci to counter the "historic bloc" made up by Southern agrarian elites and Northern industrialists never had the much-hoped-for political weight. The proletarian revolution never took place, and the Southern question in Italy is still awaiting an answer.

In light of the considerations presented, then, a reading of Italian American literature as mostly "Southern Italian" could be a rather plausible representational model. In fact, using this model has also proven to be a successful initial strategy for the construction of ethnic difference in the U.S. multicultural context. In other words, in order to promote the study and understanding of the history, culture, and literature of Americans of Italian descent, scholars felt it necessary to present a cohesive front in its most simplified version, that is to say, different enough to be recognized as "Italian" but not so differentiated as to confuse mainstream America. However, some Italian American critics have already suggested that the field needs to do away with any essentialist definitional strategy because it limits the possibilities born out of a sense of the concrete political, social, and cultural discontinuities of the country of departure. As literary critic and writer Edvige Giunta pointed out in her 2002 study of Italian American women's literature, *Writing with an Accent*, "What must be emphasized is that Italian Americans do not constitute a homogenous group in any way—in terms of regional origins, social and economic status, or political perspective" (23). In the field of sociological studies, Donna Gabaccia points out that a politics that constructs meridionali as a homogenous class of subaltern subjects is, at best, a scholarly construction. In her essay "Two Great Migrations: American and Italian Southerners in Comparative Perspective," Gabaccia writes:

> No matter how defined, the southern provinces of Italy shared no common language. They did not acknowledge the collective leadership of a single regional elite, and neither did traditional ties of marriage, common agricultural practices, or commercial exchange bind the southern provinces into a single region. Regional identities meant *siciliani* and *napolitani*, not *meridionali*. (221)

Gabaccia's sociological analysis disproves the assumption that Southern Italian culture is a monolithic culture. In fact, if on the one hand Italian American literature at large purports to speak for the experience of all Italians in the United States, on the other hand, many of its texts are exemplary sites of cultural particularities in a regional sense. Oftentimes, the literature's finest portraits of Italian American life are highly localized, and they depend on the author's knowledge and description of local features on the historical, social, cultural, and linguistic levels. A focus on the regional facets of Italian

American literature at large would serve the purpose of an intraethnic decentering project. A regional analysis, in fact, challenges the totalizing notion of Italianness as it has been conceived and articulated so far in the field of Italian American studies. Starting from these observations, we can work to identify and study the construction of Sicilian Americanness in Italian American literature.

In fact, the existence of a distinctive Sicilian American literature has already been acknowledged on the critical front in the United States. In a 2003 essay, tellingly titled "Re-Inventing Sicily in Italian American Writing and Film," Fred Gardaphé writes:

> Sicily, the setting for many famous myths such as those we know from Homer's *The Odyssey*, has proven to be equally fertile soil for the mythology of Italian Americans . . . the offspring of Sicilian immigrants have created an eruption of writing that testifies to the power that the island has on the artists it creates. (55)

Also, two anthologies have been compiled and published by Venera Fazio and Delia De Santis: the 2004 *Sweet Lemons: Writing with a Sicilian Accent*, and the 2010 *Sweet Lemons 2: International Writings with a Sicilian Accent*. These collections feature, for the most part, contributions by or on Sicilian, Sicilian American, and Sicilian Canadian authors. If anything, the editors' wide-ranging selection testifies to the unifying role that the island plays for Sicilians of the diaspora.

Therefore, the first task at hand is to attempt a definition of Sicilian American literature. Some of the questions to address are: What is Sicilian American about these texts? Also, must the writer be entirely of Sicilian descent, or is it sufficient that the characters be Sicilian Americans for a text to be defined as Sicilian American? Must the writer and the characters perform their Sicilian Americanness overtly and ostensibly? Within the context of this book, I understand Sicilian American literature as the literature written by U.S. authors of Sicilian descent that explicitly deals with the Sicilian American experience. These restrictive criteria find a raison d'être in the literary fortune that Sicily has enjoyed as a source of inspiration for Italian American writers in general as well as in the avowed intentions of this study.[10] Were I, in fact, to include all Italian American accounts of *Siciliana* in the category of Sicilian American literature, the Neapolitan American Mario Puzo would stand out as one of the most prominent authors in terms of both productivity and fame. In fact, after the best-selling success of his 1969 novel *The Godfather*, Puzo devoted the rest of his literary career to the depiction of what he portrayed as the "Sicilian ways" through a rather unskilled use of much-exploited topoi about Sicily and its people in *The Sicilian* (1984), *The Last Don* (1996), and the posthumous *Omerta* (2000). Whether Puzo helped or did a disservice to Sicilians, Sicilian Americans, and the Italian American community at large with his highly controversial novels is a question that has been debated since the publication of *The Godfather* and Francis Ford Coppola's cinematographic trilogy. But this seemingly endless *querelle* transcends the scope of this study, for its avowed purpose is, instead, to analyze the narrative construction of self and group identity in some Sicilian American texts. Therefore, I can carry out this project only by focusing on the acts of representation and self-representation by Sicilian Americans.

As for the second criterion for inclusion, which limits the content of my analysis to works that openly deal with the Sicilian American experience, it is, once again, determined by the purpose of this study. In this book, I am more concerned with the deliberate articulation of sicilianamericanità as identity politics rather than a semiotic reading devoted to the detection of Sicilian signs in Italian American literature. As not all ethnic writers engage in ethnic literature, not all Italian American writers of Sicilian origins have made their texts ideal contexts for the reading I undertake here. For example, when I considered these texts chronologically, Sicilian-born Francesca Vinciguerra was the first Italian American woman writer to reach notoriety at the beginning of last century, so much so that Olga Peragallo included her in her posthumously published dissertation, *Italian American Authors and Their Contribution to American Literature* (1949). Writer and critic Helen Barolini also stated that Vinciguerra "went on to become a successful, prolific writer, not unaided by the anglicization of her name which, she has related, was a condition to the publication of her first book, *The Ardent Flame* (1927)" (*The Dream Book* 9). Thus, Francesca Vinciguerra became Frances Winwar, and she sacrificed any trace of her ethnic heritage at the altar of the Anglo-based literary hegemony of the beginning of the last century.

Similarly, there is no trace of any regional particularity in Philip Lamantia's works either. The only son of Sicilian immigrants from Palermo and Ustica, Lamantia pursued a poetic path that led him to be the visionary and surrealist voice of the San Francisco Renaissance and, later, the Beat movement. Despite the fact that, purportedly, "among Philip's earliest memories were the Sicilian folktales [his paternal grandmother] told him in her backyard rose garden" (Caples, Joron, and Peters xxiv), this self-styled "high poet" was, since a young age, drawn more to the marvelous in the world, which he continuously pursued in his poetry as well as in his life, through the use of substances that would enhance his dreamlike visions. As a teenager in the early 1940s, surrealism in the arts and literature struck Lamantia as the most suitable mode to express himself. He even earned the admiration of André Breton himself, who published some of Lamantia's early poems in the New York–based surrealist magazine *VVV*. Following the demise of surrealism in the post-WWII period, which coincided with Lamantia's own disillusionment with the movement, the Sicilian American poet began his association and personal friendship with the younger generation of Beat writers who were taking over the literary scene in the Bay Area. In the early 1960s, the poet eventually returned to his first source of poetic inspiration. Lamantia's interests were as varied as his travels, and they materialized in repeated trips to Mexico to study its history and culture, to Spain and Egypt to study Egyptology, to France, Morocco, Greece, and even Italy. However, Lamantia never turned his Sicilian origins into a source of personal or poetic inspiration. The poet's Sicilian Americanness was seemingly apparent only in the way he talked. Garrett Caples, Andrew Joron, and Nancy Joyce Peters, editors of a most recent collection of Lamantia's poetry, the 2013 *The Collected Poems of Philip Lamantia*, quote Jack Kerouac commenting on the poet's diction as follows:

> [T]hat accent he talks in I do not know where he picked it up—It's like a Moor educated at Oxford. . . . it's a distinctly flavored accent made up of (apparently) American Italian second-generation but with strong Britishified overlays upon his Mediterranean elegance, which creates an excellent and strange new form of English I've never heard before. (xxxv)

Surrealist poet Franklin Rosemont also noted that Lamantia joined the anarchist scene of the Bay Area, and that "he made his way into the largely Italian-language anarchist group in his hometown, and soon he was good friends with several Italian and Sicilian old-timers" (124). However, except for his thick "American Italian second-generation" accent, his deep-seated anarchism, and a couple of episodes of late, brief, and intense embracing of Catholicism, I suppose that Lamantia's sicilianamericanità was a latent variable in his poetic inspiration that never explicitly came into being.

If Lamantia chose not to address his Sicilian Americanness in his poetry, another Beat poet, Diane di Prima, frequently raised issues pertaining to her origins. In *Recollections of My Life as a Woman*, di Prima's Sicilian roots morph into the seeds of her "Arabic" self. In fact, in her autobiography, the quest for her roots takes the form of a dream that the writer reportedly had in 1987:

> I am in an ancient church in Sicily. In the dream I think that it is "like a mosque." . . . My uncle Joe has died. . . . The funeral service is going on, and it is mainly music, incredibly beautiful vocal music, Arabic in its modulations, but polyphonic, with one voice joining another. In the dream, it is very important for me to understand how "Arabic" my people are (the Sicilian side of my family). It will help me to understand my life. (15–16)

The beatnik poet also recalls the identity conflicts she experienced as a child when pressured by her Neapolitan relatives to take distance from the Sicilian side of her family:

> The Mallozzis, I was given to understand, were everything desirable. (These matters were discussed only by my mother and her sisters, and usually in Neapolitan.) Mallozzis were smarter, thinner, more ambitious. "Upwardly mobile" we might say but there wasn't that term then. All the Mallozzi women had gone to college. The one male Mallozzi sibling had rebelled and refused: but of course, that is different from not being able to, because of lack of money or of brains. Each of the kids in the family was often under discussion: was s/he a Mallozzi or a Di Prima? . . . I felt it as a moral imperative. Mallozzi or bust. They were more "northern," too, the Italian snobbery. . . . *Oh built-in Manicheanism, very stuff of the Tao! Of Yin and Yang, though I can't say which was which. All dichotomies in the world were laid out for me, and before my birth. Mallozzis and Di Primas. Cosmology.* . . . Everyone knew Sicilians were outré. (46–47)

However, other than these scattered considerations on her origins and family, di Prima did not contribute much to a discourse on sicilianamericanità, and her literary career evolved following a passion for transgression and uncompromising freedom of individual expression that made her a representative of the Beat generation.

The son of immigrants from Sicily, Guido D'Agostino, rising to literary notoriety in the 1940s, took a different path from the authors mentioned earlier. In his first and most famous novel, namely, the 1940 *Olives on the Apple Tree*, D'Agostino chose to feature mostly "Italiano" characters, thus earning a reputation for being one of the earliest Italian American novelists, along with his contemporaries John Fante, Pietro di Donato, and Jerre Mangione. However, unlike Fante, di Donato, and Mangione, D'Agostino in his novel completely suppresses any reference to regional identities.[11] The main protagonist, a hobo who goes by the name of Marco, has reportedly left Italy to escape Mussolini's dictatorship. However, nothing in the novel indicates his original provenance, and the fact that he can hum Pietro Mascagni's masterpiece 1890 opera *Cavalleria rusticana*, adapted from Sicilian writer Giovanni Verga's short story and play by the same title, is more a way to announce the development of the story than a commentary on Marco's origins. The many Italian immigrants who populate the novel, living in shacks in the poor section of the town up the hill known under the derogatory name of Wop-Roost, or the more upwardly mobile Gardellas, all remember and talk about Italy without revealing any specific details regarding their native places. We can safely assume the immigrants are aware of each other's home places. In fact, toward the end of the novel, when Federico Gardella invites Marco to stop wandering around and stay in town to take care of his farm for him, he tells him: "I show you how to make the sausage from my part of the country" (D'Agostino 296). But we do not get to learn from what part of Italy Gardella, or anyone else in the novel, hails. Some critics have suggested that we could read the writer's recurrent theme of the clash between rural Italy and urban America as an expression of his sicilianamericanità. As Mary Jo Bona and JoAnne Ruvoli point out, "In his allegiance to rural antecedents, D'Agostino ably embraced both his Sicilian peasant origins and the American landscape, which he claims as his own" (*By the Breath of Their Mouths*, 118). But with the characters from *Olives on the Apple Tree*, Guido D'Agostino makes a case for the peaceful integration of all "Italiano" immigrants in the United States, whether they are from the islands or peninsular Italy.[12]

However, many other Sicilian American authors chose to paint their characters with Sicilian colors. For instance, the hardship and loss brought about by emigration, along with a strong sense of place, are at the heart of the moving and poetic novel by Tony Ardizzone *In the Garden of Papa Santuzzu* (1999). Also, the protagonists of some of Rita Ciresi's novels, such as *Blue Italian* (1997), and *Sometimes I Dream in Italian* (2000), and of Kenny Marotta's 1985 debut, the humorous novel *A Piece of Earth*, are immigrants from the island and their mostly, but not entirely, Americanized children. Unmistakably Sicilian are also the protagonists of Josephine Gattuso Hendin's 1988 novel *The Right Thing to Do*, Rachel Guido De Vries's 1986 *Tender Warriors*, and of two novels written by Dodici Azpadu, namely, *Saturday Night in the Prime of Life* (1983) and the more recent *Living Room* (2010). Other Sicilian American prose writers, such as Diana Cavallo, Anthony Valerio, Renée Manfredi, and Nancy Caronia, have sometimes dealt with sicilianamericanità in some of their works.

In the multidimensional aspects of her work, feminist critic and poet Sandra Mortola Gilbert has crafted some of the most lyrically intense lines on Sicilian American belonging. Sicily and Sicilian American themes feature prominently in the dialect poetry of first-generation immigrants Vincenzo Ancona and Antonino Provenzano.[13] They also surface in the poetry of Nat Scammacca, Maria Famà, Rosette Capotorto, Phyllis Capello, Diane Raptosh, Grace Cavalieri, Mary Russo Demetrick, Emanuel di Pasquale, Lewis Turco, Louisa Calio, Marisa Frasca, among others.

Several Sicilian American writers have made significant contributions to the field of memoirs. Both set in Sicily, the two memoirs by third-generation Sicilian American Theresa Maggio, *Mattanza* in 2001, and *The Stone Boudoir* in 2003, show a fascination with the place, its people, and the culture so intense that the writer herself wondered:

> Maybe I am so drawn to Sicily because I am half Sicilian and the island is hard-wired into my genes. Or maybe Sicily is a vortex that pulls some people in—a center of the universe, like the Omphalos at Delphi, a navel stone that connected some inner world to the outer. . . . Sicily is hard to leave. (*The Stone Boudoir* 7)

However, despite the confessional nature of the memoir, the writer's reflections on her own sicilianamericanità rarely interrupt the flow of the narration and do not extend beyond the assertion of her heritage.

Like Theresa Maggio, Nat Scammacca also inverted the immigration trajectory of his forebears by moving from the United States, where he was born, to Sicily, where he died in 2005. In Sicily, Scammacca joined the Antigruppo Siciliano, a populist movement, which expressed its antiestablishment attitudes by bringing free public poetry readings to small towns' piazzas. In his numerous poems as well as his autobiographical works—such as the collection of short stories *Bye Bye America*, first published in Italian in 1972 with the subtitle *Ricordi di un Wop*; the 1979 novel *Due Mondi*; and the 1989 *Sikano l'Amerikano!*—Scammacca took to writing about what it means to be a Sicilian American in Italy.

In her 2007 book *Unto the Daughters: The Legacy of an Honor Killing in a Sicilian-American Family*, Karen Tintori digs into her family secrets to discover the truth behind the disappearance of her grandmother's sister. Several other Sicilian American authors explore the possibilities offered by memoir and confessional writing. Most recently, Domenica Ruta laid bare her dysfunctional life, and, especially, her problematic relationship with her addicted-to-anything mother in her best-selling 2013 debut *With or Without You*. Before her, Sicilian American women writers such as Mary Cappello, Kym Ragusa, and Carol Maso published memoirs inspired by their own personal experience as Sicilian Americans without engaging, though, in the identity politics that I investigate in this study.[14] While this general survey in no way should be considered an exhaustive, let alone complete, inventory of Sicilian American authors who have already received some critical attention, I believe it nevertheless conveys a sense of the importance of the phenomenon and the criteria I have adopted in this book.

I chose to focus on those authors and writings that most consistently deal with questions of Sicilian Americanness. For Morreale, Mangione, Romano, and Timpanelli, their ethnic identity is a salient and relevant aspect of their selves, and their being of Sicilian descent plays a role as significant as their being American. Most importantly, these writers undertook not only to represent the Sicilian American *Weltanschauung* but also to study it and understand it. These writers could not resist the urge of exploring and discussing their sicilianamericanità in their works, thus establishing a tradition at the textual level. These four authors embody the belief that while the branches can reach far, the roots are firmly planted in the island's soil.

There is also another reason why I chose to discuss these four specific writers, and this is related to Sicilian writer Gesualdo Bufalino's concept of "isola plurale," or "plural island." In his collection of short essays *Cere perse*, Bufalino explains:

> We know that Sicily is plural, that the Kingdom of the Two Sicilies should have been called of the Ten, of the Hundred Sicilies. The ambiguous crossroad and bellybutton of the world, a blend of different races and events, Sicily has never stopped being a great geographical and anthropological oxymoron made up of dark and light, lava and honey. (50)[15]

As there are many Sicilies, there are also many Sicilian Americas, so to speak, and if these authors reveal a shared preoccupation with heritage and place, their literary projects are not monolithic and homogenous; rather, their arena is composed of different subject positions, and it is multidimensional in its scope and forms. Thus, if the works of these four writers celebrate Sicilian Americanness, they do so in a way that frustrates any attempt to reduce the concept to a single, representative way of being Sicilian American and writing about it. Combined together, they create a melodious cacophony of voices.

In fact, each of these authors deals in his or her own way with the question of sicilianamericanità, endeavoring, in different manners, to present, understand and explain, challenge, and reinvent it. Each of them attempts a conceptual reorientation of some of the most pressing issues of being an American of Sicilian descent. Depending on the writer, these issues can relate to social concerns for ethnic minorities, the sociological and cultural factors influencing the Sicilian American communities, gender and sexual orientation, and more. The variety inherent in this ethnic literary milieu is also reflected in these writers' genres of choice. While Morreale's literary production is primarily made up of fictional novels, Mangione engaged in memoir writing. Romano also wrote highly personal accounts of her life as a Sicilian American, but as a confessional poet. Finally, tying herself to the principle that in the beginning was the Word, Timpanelli wove together traditional Sicilian storytelling with modern ways of writing about social and gender equality. In other words, even though there are many more equally important and talented Sicilian American novelists, memoirists, poets, and essayists, the four on whom I focus inspire an appreciation of the diversity of perspectives, voices, styles, and genres of the Sicilian American literary (is)landscape.

This book testifies to the variety of ways in which Sicily informs the literature of these Sicilian American authors. Chapter 1 is an overview of the theoretical issues pertaining to Sicily as an island, and, especially, the concept of Sicilianness as it has been articulated so far. The arrangement of the following chapters follows a general progression from presenting, understanding, challenging, and, finally, recovering a distinct Sicilian American heritage. Building on what is discussed in the first chapter, chapter 2 focuses on the intertextual dimensions of Ben Morreale's novels. Personal, sociological, and political analyses intertwine in *The Seventh Saracen* (1958), *A Few Virtuous Men (Li Cornuti)* (1973), and *Monday, Tuesday . . . Never Come Sunday* (1977), which present sicilianamericanità in a way that makes Morreale an ideal bridge between Sicily and Sicilian America and their respective literary traditions. Chapter 2 provides an in-depth review of Morreale's work, and I identify its relations with Sicilian literature.

Understanding and articulating a sense of Sicilian Americanness proved to be the most distinctive trait and a crucial factor in Jerre Mangione's literary career. With the publication in 1943 of his memoir *Mount Allegro*, and his subsequent studies on what he defined as "the Sicilian Way"—*Reunion in Sicily* (1950), *A Passion for Sicilians* (1968), and *An Ethnic at Large* (1978)—Mangione set out to understand the roots and meaning of sicilianamericanità in literature. Chapter 3 addresses the works of the writer who, because of his indefatigable literary quest for his ethnic heritage, earned the honorary title of "dean of Sicilian American writers" (Gardaphé, "Re-Inventing Sicily" 56).

A whole different search for ethnic (af)filiation in literature comes from Rose Romano's poetry. Chapter 4 focuses on the poet's challenging and polemical stances on issues such as gender roles and homosexuality that serve as a counterpoint to the hetero- and male-oriented perspective of other Sicilian American writers, while her discussion on racial categorizations allows for an exploration of power dynamics within the multicultural community. In this chapter, I analyze Romano's two poetry collections, namely, *Vendetta* (1990) and *The Wop Factor* (1994), to show how sicilianamericanità overlaps with contestations of traditional gender roles, heterosexual scripts, and racial categorizations.

Finally, the work of storyteller Gioia Timpanelli shows an explicit recovery and resistance strategy. Drawing inspiration from Sicilian oral traditions, folklore, and legends for her works, Timpanelli reinvents them from the perspective of a modern American feminist. Timpanelli has dealt with Sicilian folktales most explicitly in her 1998 *Sometimes the Soul: Two Novellas of Sicily*. The paucity of her published production is consistent with the oral and performed nature of her work, as she imported to the United States the Sicilian tradition of the *novellatori/novellatrici*, or hearth tellers, who, in the old days, enchanted the listeners by weaving their own popular wisdom into tales and legends. In chapter 5, I address the importance of Timpanelli's work for the survival of the Sicilian oral traditions in the United States, which are recovered and rewritten with a modern and feminist twist.

The purpose of this book is to extend current research on and understanding of Italian America. The study of sicilianamericanità as it surfaces in Italian American literature should not be perceived as a further fragmentation of U.S. national literature, let alone a balkanization of the field of Italian American studies. Its goal, in fact, is not that of further dividing up categories into smaller units. Rather, this study is meant as a work parallel to that of scholars who look for intersections of ethnic, class, gender, and sexual identities in literature. In other words, as the Italian American works marked by feminist or working-class concerns are still Italian American works within the domain of American literature, what I have defined as Sicilian American literature is the literary manifestation of a specific process of identity construction that is part and parcel of Italian American identity and literature as well as multicultural Americana at large. The field of Italian American studies benefits from a number of good to excellent anthologies, edited collections, and monographs dealing with many aspects of Italian American culture and literature. The works of Italian American authors have been analyzed and dissected from the point of view of their ethnic content, feminist perspective, political message, gay and lesbian agenda, linguistic features, and so on. This book will complement all these studies and add a new perspective to the body of knowledge on Italian Americana.

However, the focus on Sicily as the island at the heart of many Sicilian and Sicilian American writers allows me to initiate an intriguing dialogue between the two literary traditions. Therefore, this study is also meant as part of a larger project whose underlying assumption is that U.S. ethnic literature would profit from a conversation with the literatures of the countries of origin with which it shares many characteristics. This book has been conceived as a first small step toward a wider process of inquiry and exploration of the common ground between Italian and Italian American literatures. As far as Italian American literature is concerned, an investigation of its connections with Italian literature promises to be as significant and legitimate a task as the study of ethnicity within the greater domain of American literature. Scholars of Italian literature, on the other hand, would derive further inspiration from the realization that the same forces that lead to a more insightful reading of American literature could make a crucial contribution to our understanding of Italian literature as well, because in matters of themes, symbols, and problematics, Italian American literature *is* germane to Italian literature. I hope that *The Heart and the Island* will allow for a more accurate characterization of Italian American literature at large, while at the same time opening a space for new discussions on what it means to be Italian on both sides of the ocean.

Of Sicily and Its Ripples

Sicilianamericanità and
Sicilian American Literature

'N jornu ca Diu Patri era cuntenti
e passiava 'n celu cu li Santi,
a lu munnu pinsau fari un prisenti,
e di la curuna si scippau 'n diamanti;
cci addutau tutti li setti elementi,
lu pusau a mari 'n facci a lu livanti:
lu chiamarunu "Sicilia" li genti,
ma di l'Eternu Patri è lu diamanti.

—Canto Popolare Siciliano

In 1918, writing about Sicilian actor Angelo Musco for the "Cronache Teatrali" of *Avanti!*, intellectual and political theorist Antonio Gramsci noted:

> For the past fifty years, our politicians have tried to create the appearance of a uniform *Italian* nation: regions should have disappeared in the country, and their dialects from the literary language. Sicily is the region that has most *actively* resisted this tampering with history and freedom. Sicily has shown on numerous occasions to have a national, more than regional character of its own. . . . The truth is that Sicily preserves its own spiritual independence. (*Letteratura e vita nazionale* 394)[1]

The political unification of Italy had not yet resulted in a blending of its people, the Italian *nation*. The integration might have taken place at the level of administration, but on all other levels—economic, social, cultural, and so on—the process had failed miserably. The more to the south one traveled, the more evident it became that the Italian regional identities worked against the homogenizing imperative of the newborn state. Of all the regions, the Sardinian Gramsci singled out Sicily as the one that challenged the imposed order at its core. In fact, even though Gramsci's analysis originally pertained to Sicilian dialect theater, it extended to identify its roots in a "spiritual independence" that he believed was a characteristic of Sicily and its people. The Italian nation's search for its soul had stopped at the tip of the boot.

Little has changed since Gramsci's observation, and Sicilians' allegiance to their mother(is)land is still very strong. Sometimes this bond transcends the boundaries of a *genius loci* to become, in its most perverse articulation, an ideology according to which Sicily *is* its people, the island defines its population in unequivocal ways, and the two are fused together in commonplace discourses. This way of "feeling" or "being" Sicilian has been the topic of seemingly endless analyses and unresolved controversies in Italy.

The pronounced self-view and the strong sense of identity are reinforced by an outsider's perception of Sicily, which is rarely neutral. The mere toponym, in fact, evokes in others either exotic pictures of sun, sea, history, and arts or else the crude images of a backward mafia-ridden land. Agrigento's Valley of the Temples, Taormina's Greek amphitheater and breathtaking views, the Baroque architectural beauty of towns like Modica and Noto, and the natural charm of some local pristine beaches, all contribute to creating an aura of magnificence for tourists. However, its endemic political corruption, the octopus-like grip of the mafia, a stunted economy, and staggering unemployment rates are only a few of the factors that might make anyone refrain from calling Sicily a paradise. All these factors together make Sicilians experience being Sicilian as either a blessing or a curse rather than mere happenstance.

To be sure, every Italian region has its own unique history, culture, traditions, dialects, foods, and the like, but there is something about Sicily that makes the claims to a distinct character echo louder: Sicily is an island. With a total area of almost ten thousand square miles and a population of about five million inhabitants, Sicily is both the largest island of Italy—and of the whole Mediterranean—and one of its most populated regions. I might be stating the obvious, but a study of *Siciliana* that underplays the "island factor" is, at best, incomplete, and at worst, misleading. The legacy of its geography cannot be overemphasized because living on an island forces one to think of it, first and foremost, in geographical terms. Sicily is part of the broader national Italian context and of the Italian South, as it is one of the twenty administrative regional entities that make up the Italian state. These are all perfectly sensible and valid perspectives from which anyone can view and consider Sicily. However, as an island, Sicily is detached though connected to the mainland, geographically separated but politically united to the state, and this feature warrants further consideration.[2]

The condition of being an island is, of course, not peculiar to Sicily alone. In fact, much of what is being and will be said here with regard to Sicily also applies to a discussion on Sardinia, just to stay in Italian waters, or any other Mediterranean and non-Mediterranean island. A whole field of scholarship, namely, island studies, or nissology, is devoted to the study of the world's islands on their own terms with a transdisciplinary research approach. In his article "The Geographical Fascination of Islands," Russell King focuses on islands as a geographical phenomenon that has inspired the scholarly attention of historians, anthropologists, sociologists, and literary critics. King writes: "An island is a most enticing form of land. Symbol of the eternal contest between land and water, islands are detached, self-contained entities whose boundaries are obvious; all other land divisions are more or less arbitrary" (14). According to this scholar, and many others, the geographical factor is at the core of an island's peculiarity and, at the same time, of the commonalities among islands. In fact, although nearly everyone agrees that many factors contribute to differentiating one island from another—among them, an island's scale, its population's size, its landscape and weather conditions, its location and degree of isolation and peripherality, and political and administrative systems, to mention just a few, island studies scholars adopt a methodological approach that seeks to uncover the common elements that bind together islands the world over. In sum, even though each island has its own specific identity, the fact itself of being an island influences the character of all islanders in similar ways.

On cultural and social levels, the "island factor" or "island way of life" produces what some have called *islandness*, which Godfrey

Baldacchino defines as "an intervening variable that does not deter-
mine, but contours and conditions, physical and social events in
distinct, and distinctly relevant, ways" ("The Coming of Age of
Island Studies" 278).[3] Baldacchino adds: "Geographical bounded-
ness, historical distinctiveness, floral and faunal speciation and
endemism, linguistic nuances, cultural specifics, jurisdictional adven-
turism . . . collectively, the evidence proclaims *islandness* as a com-
manding paradigm" (279). There is no fixed yardstick with which
to measure the scale of islandness, and there are, of course, extreme
variations among islands. The experiences of some islands are not
necessarily the experiences of all others, and there is no universal
Truth for all islands in the world. However, islandness is a key feature
that cannot be underestimated, and it is felt by islanders as well as
perceived and recognized by others.

As a case study, Sicily seems to confirm the idea that its clear
geographical limits influence the way its people think of themselves.
Sicilian writer Gesualdo Bufalino points out that "Sicily suffers from
an excess of identity, and I don't know whether it's a good or a bad
thing" (Bufalino and Zago v).[4] The island's specificity, Bufalino continues, "is not just a geographical segregation, but engenders other
types: of the province, of the family, of one's bedroom, of one's heart.
Hence, our pride, our mistrust, our modesty; and the sense of being
different" (vi).[5] Sicilians show thorough consciousness of being born
and living on an island and an exasperated sense of belonging that
engenders an amplified sense of community and identity, which is a
form of cultural-specific islandness.

However, this islandness is not the unilateral product of geographical conditions. In fact, an inherent contradiction generally
characterizes islands. If, on the one hand, their geography invites
closure, on the other, the history of most of the world's islands shows
connection. Islandness, Edward Warrington and David Milne write,

> may best be understood in terms of a characteristic set of
> tensions and ambiguities, opportunities and constraints aris-
> ing from the interplay of geography and history. *Geography
> tends towards isolation*: it permits or favors autarchy, distinc-
> tiveness, stability and evolution propelled endogenously.
> *History*, on the other hand, *tends towards contact*: it permits
> or favors dependence (or interdependence), assimilation,
> change and evolution propelled exogenously. An island's

character develops from the interplay of geography and history, evasions and invasions, the indigenous and the exotic. (383)

In fact, islands have always been, and still are, even in postcolonial times, hot spots of international political strains. Due to their usually modest size and scarcity of military and nonmilitary resources, most islands are vulnerable and have been overseas possessions for many colonizing countries and empires.[6] Sicily is no exception; it has been, for most of its history, a territory ruled by more or less distant political centers.

Sicily's island status is essential to its identity as is its troubled history. Especially because of its geographical location, embedded as it is between Europe and Africa, and, on the east-west axis, between western Europe and western Asia, Sicily has historically been the strategic epicenter of colonizing enterprises.[7] A "crossroad of civilizations" is the most common euphemistic definition for the island's past, for there met the interests of the Greeks, Romans, Byzantines, Arabs, Normans, and Spaniards, to mention just the most influential civilizations in chronological order. There was no standard form of colonization to which Sicily was subjected; it was a settler colony under Greek rule, the first province of the Roman Empire—and, famously, its breadbasket—and an administrative colony under the Bourbons. In November of 1860, following a popular plebiscite, Sicily was officially annexed to the Kingdom of Italy, thus becoming the southernmost part of the newborn country. To some, time-wise, Italy is only the most recent offshore colonizing power to conquer the island, so much so that in the aftermath of World War II, almost one hundred years after the unification, Sicilian nationalists coded their dissent to the Italian state in the language of a postcolonial struggle.[8] In short, armed conquest, expropriation of land, extortion of tributes, military occupation, and, most recently, *miseria*—or starvation—emigration, and high unemployment rates have played an almost uninterrupted role in the historical development of Sicily.[9]

According to some, most notably Sicilian intellectual/writer/literary critic Leonardo Sciascia, the Sicilian history of colonial suffering and exploitation, coupled with its geographical insularity—read, isolation—engendered a particular process of identity construction, as well as recognizable cognitive and behavioral patterns in the population. In his 1970 *La corda pazza: Scrittori e cose della Sicilia*, Sciascia speculated on the perpetual insecurity of the Sicilian people, which, according to him, was the primary legacy of a history of colonization:

> One can safely say that insecurity is the primary component of Sicilian history, and it affects the behavior, the way of being, the take on life—fear, apprehension, distrust, closed passions, inability to establish relationships outside of the private sphere, violence, pessimism, fatalism—of both the collectivity and single individuals. (13)[10]

This "historical fear," Sciascia continues, turned into an "existential fear," which, sociologically, manifests itself in

> a tendency in individuals, groups, and communities—and, finally, in the entire region to isolate and separate themselves. At a certain point, insecurity and fear have reverted to the illusion that such insularity, with all the conditionings, qualms, and rules that originate from it, is a privilege and a source of strength, when, in truth and experience, it engenders vulnerability and weakness. Hence a sort of alienation and madness, which, in terms of psychology and customs, induces attitudes of presumptuousness, haughtiness, and arrogance. (14)[11]

Borrowing the expression from Sicilian avant-garde and Antigruppo poet and painter Crescenzio Cane,[12] who, in his turn, drew inspiration from Senegalese poet and intellectual Léopold Senghor's concept of négritude, Sciascia baptized the sum of these attitudes as sicilitudine.[13]

Before the publication of La corda pazza, Sciascia had dealt with the concept of sicilitudine in the preface of an anthology of Sicilian writers edited in 1967 with Salvatore Guglielmino, namely, Narratori di Sicilia. He further developed the topic in the book-length interview La Sicilia come metafora (1989), which contains the all-too-famous chapter "Come si può essere siciliani?" ("How can one be Sicilian?"), and in Pirandello e la Sicilia, in which he insists on the "historical insecurity" of Sicilians to justify the "Sicilian ways" (30). Sciascia's sicilitudine is, to date, the most influential discourse on Sicilianness, the specific form that the islandness discussed earlier has taken for this particular island. No discussion about Sicily and Sicilians is possible today without questioning or concurring with

Sciascia's speculations. Sicilianness became, in his articulation, a "way of being," the inescapable condition of a population marked by "a history of defeats" (*La Sicilia come metafora* 6). With the concept of sicilitudine, Sciascia seemed to have pinned down the essence of Sicilians and unraveled their complex nature within the operative framework of cultural anthropology. Sicilitudine proved a most valuable grand narrative for Sicilians and non-Sicilians alike. While the former could finally resort to a well-articulated discourse to explain, in essentialist terms, their "nature," non-Sicilians found in sicilitudine a key to solving the riddles that the island posed—and continues to pose—to mainland Italy.

But much to Sciascia's dismay, a most complex discourse like sicilitudine has been readily misinterpreted by many and too often reduced to a learned source of stereotypes. Sicilitudine has, in fact, become so commonplace in contemporary discussions in Italy that in an article published in 2000 in the Italian national newspaper *La Repubblica,* entitled "Cent'anni di sicilitudine," critic and journalist Matteo Di Gesù invoked a sabbatical year during which all discussions about the Sicilian identity would be suspended. "To the difficulty of being Sicilian," Di Gesù explains, "one must add a certain intolerance that grows from being reminded of that so often" (10).[14] The concept has gained so much currency in popular culture that at this point, Di Gesù adds, "Sicilitudine explains everything: for the most strident contradictions, blatant messes, and even the most banal crimes, there is always a self-exculpatory 'sicilianological' analysis, always accompanied by learned quotations" (10).[15] Di Gesù was thus expressing his frustration over the inescapability of a situation in which a matter-of-fact statement such as "I'm (a) Sicilian" is automatically turned into an indulgent narrative.

In several academic and newspaper articles written throughout the years, Di Gesù has repeatedly questioned the presumed value of sicilitudine as a discourse to explain the consequences of Sicily's colonial past. The critic is especially worried about the sedimentation of what has become a cliché, "a falsely ethnographic stereotype," and a "huge 'cultural' encrustation, ahistorical and self-absolving" (*Dispatrie lettere* 72).[16] So much so that, Di Gesù continues, today what is encouraged is only "a selection of memories and collective history that omits anything that does not correspond to the paradigms of the presumed sicilitudine, and that updates, by reiterating them, the usual *topoi* on the ontology of Sicilians" (72).[17] Di Gesù, instead, proposes to create a counternarrative to the dominant paradigm of sicilitudine with its emphasis on Sicily's alleged immobilism, and fatalism, starting with an alternative reading of its history.

In fact, the history of Sicily is not one of consistently supine acceptance of foreign rule. For instance, the Sicilian Vespers of 1282 can be read as an early successful episode of indigenous rebellion to resist and topple foreign domination. After the death of Frederick II, aka Stupor Mundi, and following the demise of the Hohenstaufen, the Angevins ruled Sicily with an iron hand. The population did not appreciate the new French rulers. In his study *The Sicilian Vespers*, historian Steven Runciman describes Charles of Anjou as a king who "distrusted the Sicilians . . . He did practically nothing to help their economy. He never visited the island except when he was on his way to the Tunisian crusade; he never personally supervised its administration" (211).[18] Sicilians found an excuse to revolt on March 30, 1282, an Easter Monday, in Palermo. The Vespers were initiated by the now-legendary episode of Drouet, a French soldier who allegedly behaved inappropriately with a local woman. Runciman comments: "it was more than her husband could bear" (215). But it was actually more than the whole population could stand from the French. Soon Palermo, Messina, and other Sicilian cities and towns rebelled and declared their independence. Runciman points out that "the massacre [of Frenchmen] at Palermo and the gallant defence of Messina had been achieved by Sicilians alone. Their rising had been the result of a great conspiracy. . . . Their passionate hatred of the oppressor had given them strength enough so far" (228). Eventually, the Aragonese monarch Peter III seized the moment and, upon invitation by Sicilians themselves, entered the island, where he was declared king only a few months after the popular revolt. In sum, the Sicilian Vespers were an exemplary episode of a popular and spontaneous insurrection of a population ravaged by conquests but also willing and able to rebel.[19]

Di Gesù further points out that

> it would be very difficult to attribute certain characteristics to Sicilian identity such as immobilism, fatalism, and fear of the future if one considered that, at least during the first century after the Unification, its subaltern classes have been very vibrant, progressive, confrontational, and combative. (*Dispatrie lettere* 74)[20]

The critic briefly remembers the *fasci siciliani*, the socialist-inspired popular movements that spread around Sicily between 1888 and 1894. Originally formed in Messina, and later in Catania and, especially, Palermo, the *fasci dei lavoratori* created an important social and political platform for workers and small business owners with Marxist leanings but also, and especially, farmers. The adherence and active participation of the latter group is particularly important because, as historian Francesco Renda points out in his 1977 study *I fasci siciliani*, "the leading elements in the formative process of the organization are not the workers nor the artisans, but the farmers. The center of gravity moves from the city to the countryside" (10).[21] The involvement of farmers with the activities of the fasci should not come as a surprise. In fact, they were a direct product of the great Italian agrarian crisis of the end of the nineteenth century. In January of 1893, in Caltavuturo, a town in the province of Palermo, farmers had decided to protest against treatment and conditions. But their pacific demonstration met the bloody hostility of the king's soldiers, and the rally soon turned into a massacre. The solidarity to the farmers on the part of the fasci all over Sicily was immediate and uniform. Renda observes: "The proclamation of the doctrine of class struggle moved from words to facts, and the countryside revealed itself as fertile land for the penetration of the socialist message" (110).[22] The political nuances of the protest especially alarmed the government, which was pressured by many to restore public order. Following the issuance of a few new policies that did not please the fasci, in August of 1893, the movement organized in Corleone the first mass farmers' strike in the history of Italy. From there, the protest spread like wildfire. But once again, after Caltavuturo, in Giardinello, the soldiers met the farmers' demands with bullets. In an ironic and cruel twist of destiny, it was a Sicilian, Francesco Crispi, the newly appointed prime minister of Italy, who decided to repress the fasci, and to this end, he sent an army of thirty thousand soldiers to the island. The history of the fasci siciliani can be considered concluded with the proclamation of the state of siege in January of 1894. However, this chapter still represents the first time that "popular and socialist-inspired organizations, born in opposition to and rising up against constituted power" (Renda, *I fasci siciliani* 144),[23] were the protagonists of history, the first time in Italy that workers and farmers *made* history. The Sicilian Vespers and the fasci, along with other more or less organized movements of resistance to domination, however episodic, should be read as instances of assertion of an all-too-local identity, as well as strong statements for political self-determination enacted by the local population through spontaneous insurgence.

Based on what has been discussed so far, Sciascia's sicilitudine is certainly a controversial discourse. However, it is definitely more than a form of self-exoticism with little conceptual merit. In his 1993 *Culture and Imperialism*, Edward Said suggests the following:

> in Post-colonial national states, the liabilities of such essences as the Celtic spirit, négritude, or Islam are clear: they have much to do not only with the native manipulators, who also use them to cover up contemporary faults, corruptions, tyrannies, but also with the embattled imperial contexts out of which they came and in which they were felt to be necessary. (16)

In light of Sicily's colonial past, sicilitudine, too, like many other essentialist projects, has much to do with "the embattled imperial contexts out of which [it] came and in which [it was] felt to be necessary." Following in the footsteps of Frantz Fanon's 1952 analysis of the "black men of the Antilles" in *Black Skin, White Masks*, Sciascia shifted his interest from the political and economic effects of colonialism in Sicily to a psychoanalytic (or pseudo-psychoanalytic) analysis of its consequences on the population. He was, then, performing the role of the intellectual who diagnosed a colonial malaise in his fellow Sicilians, and pointed to its most obvious symptoms. Critic Roberto Dainotto offers a similar interpretation in his article "The Importance of Being Sicilian," in which he identifies Sciascia as the initiator of an Italian cultural studies discourse, and focuses on the role the intellectual assigned to Sicily as a subaltern cultural model. According to Dainotto, "through sicilitudine, Sciascia had then set the background to begin his work as a critic of the hegemonic, colonial Culture to which Sicily had been subjected" (211). In other words, by creating the notion of sicilitudine, Sciascia was bringing to the political fore again, after Gramsci, the Southern question, only this time from a Sicilian *and* postcolonial angle in essentialist terms.

Sciascia famously popularized the concept of sicilitudine in Italy, but he was not the only Sicilian writer to deal with questions of islandness. In fact, sicilitudine as a postcolonial discourse heavily informs the literature of many Sicilian authors. Since the end of the nineteenth century, there has been a constant effort on the part of islanders to reclaim their agency by attempting to look at themselves, rather than being looked at, and to articulate their own identity. The preferred realm where this investigation has taken place is literature.[24] Especially throughout the 1900s, the sense of a distinct Sicilianness informed the literature of some Sicilian-born authors, who have written on the variegated history of the island and its effects on their fellow islanders. Some of them, like Luigi Capuana, Federico De Roberto, Dacia Maraini, and Giuseppe Tomasi di Lampedusa, have depicted the lives of a select few aristocrats, while some others, like Luigi Pirandello and Giovanni Verga, have focused on the middle class and, also, the lowest echelons of the social ladder to tell stories about, to use Verga's own expression, the *popolo dei vinti*. Some others, most notably Vitaliano Brancati with his notion of *gallismo*, a form of Don Juanism, have cast ridicule on what they perceived to be some aspects of Sicilian culture.[25] In the post-WWII period, Sicily became a metaphor for the country's ravaged state in Elio Vittorini's and Gesualdo Bufalino's novels, while the island's history and culture inform the literary production of Vincenzo Consolo. Poetry and theater made in Sicily also reflect a preoccupation with all things Sicilian, as in the works of vernacular poet Ignazio Buttitta, Nobel Prize–winner Salvatore Quasimodo, Nino Martoglio, and Pirandello. More recently, Sicilian director/screenwriter/writer Andrea Camilleri has earned a prominent spot on the bookshelves of detective fiction enthusiasts as well as literary critics, having captivated legions of fans in Italy and also abroad thanks to his Montalbano stories set in Sicily.[26] These are but just a few of the most prominent Sicilian writers who have written about Sicily, and all of them have contributed to this sort of obsessive-compulsive self-investigation and, consequently, to the formation of a distinctly Sicilian literary production. Thanks to literature, geography has been turned upside down, and Sicily has moved from the fringe to the center, from the periphery of Italy to its very core.

To be sure, Sicilian literature can be framed within the larger domain of island studies and island literatures. As Pete Hay points out in his article "The Poetics of Island Place," writers from the islands often tend to engage in "an identity-claiming literature of place." According to Hay, "The impact of colonial power relationships has been, and still is, distilled, concentrated on islands. . . . Much island literature has to do with the politics of identity, with 'reclaiming the territory' " (553). The contestatory potential of Sicilian literature lies in its refusal of the forced process of "Northernization" or homogenization according to Northern Italian standards on a cultural and literary level. The aforementioned authors have managed to enter the Italian literary panorama without camouflaging, and, more often than not, by capitalizing on their distinctly Sicilian voices. It seems like Sicily is, by choice, and more often necessity, the favorite topic of the literary production of Sicilian writers, who have engaged in a particular and recognizable process of identity construction in literature.

In the past forty years, Sicilian literature has received plenty of critical attention in the form of scholarly and nonscholarly studies, and many anthologies have been compiled by critics.[27] Despite its local character, which takes the form of a constant preoccupation with all things Sicilian, realistic depictions of local scenes and situations, as well as recognizable linguistic features, Sicilian literature has managed to become part and parcel of the world's literary panorama.

Sicilianamericanità and Sicilian American Literature

Interestingly, a parallel phenomenon has emerged in the United States. Regardless of generational considerations, or interregional filiations, some ethnic American authors have taken imaginative possession of the island and fashioned a Sicilian American identity. Many of these authors' works specifically focus on their experience as Sicilian Americans and lay out a recognizable set of Sicilian cultural markers; these authors have produced Sicilian American literature.

The existence of a parallel process of identity construction in such distant places is due to both the perceived uniqueness of the island and the importance of its migratory movement toward the United States. Particularly during the course of the twentieth century, leaving became a significant part of the Sicilian life. It is easy to understand how the island's finite geography translates into a lack of economies of scale, of resources, and, in most extreme scenarios, of access to decent standards of living and quality of life, therefore encouraging emigration.[28] Since the unification of Italy in 1861, all of the aforementioned phenomena, exacerbated by the newborn state's failure to adequately address the different realities of the Italian mosaic, caused the whole Italian South to experience periods of intense emigration flows to the other side of the ocean, mainly to Brazil, Argentina, and the United States. The debate around the numbers of emigration from different regions of Italy is still open. The figures are controversial and vary according to different sources that take or fail to take into consideration important factors such as the quality of immigration—that is, temporary versus permanent—and the role that illegal immigration plays in the data, just to mention a couple of scenarios that ostensibly could alter the numbers. As for the regions that contributed the greatest numbers of emigrants to the Italian diaspora, it might be appropriate to keep in mind historian Piero Bevilacqua's description of the emigration from Sicily, Campania, and Calabria as an "authentic demographic earthquake" (*Breve storia dell'Italia meridionale* 37).

During the first three decades of the twentieth century, Sicily underwent a massive displacement of its people to the United States that resembles that of Ireland during the second half of the nineteenth century and Puerto Rico since World War II. The following lines from vernacular poet Domenico Azzaretto's 1906 poem "La partenza dell'operaio per l'America" invoke the full extent of the impact emigration to the United States had on the people of Sicily:

> What confusion in every town
> family and home
> since they started hearing about America,
> everyone is getting ready to leave
> some prepare their underwear and shirts
> the penniless ones mortgage their houses
> distressed, they all say good-bye to their families
> and off to America they go! (Qtd. in Franzina 116)[29]

In his 1963 study *L'emigrazione in Sicilia*, historian Francesco Renda reports that in 1900, about 29,000 emigrants left Sicily, of whom 21,000 left for the United States. Only six years later, in 1906, the number of Sicilians leaving the island had grown to more than 127,000, with 70 percent of them directed to the New World (48). What characterized the Sicilian emigration phenomenon and made it particularly worrisome, Renda continues, was

> its element of permanence, being mostly if not all transoceanic, and its extraordinary growth rate, which caused

more than one million men to leave within a few years,
all of whom were young men in the prime of life, in their
peak of moral and physical strength. (58–59)[30]

A hemorrhage of such proportions affected every aspect of the islanders' lives by bringing about substantial demographic, social, economic,
and cultural changes.

As a result, those who left had to reinvent a bond with their
mother(is)land. In his introduction to the 1967 edition of the anthology *Narratori di Sicilia*, Sciascia claimed that

> From Palmieri to Quasimodo, every Sicilian who flees from
> Sicily will be in the condition of the exile, of the man
> who *cannot return*. In some, this condition fuels painful
> memories, nostalgia, or myth; in others, it causes a willing-
> ness to forget, distress, bitterness. (10)[31]

Whether nostalgic, romantic, or bitter, these and many other less
famous exiles have passed their cultural legacy on to their offspring,
and some of their descendants have felt it keenly and have written
about it.

The work of Sicilian-born playwright, actor, and poet Giovanni
De Rosalia is an early form of Sicilian American literature. During
the first decades of the twentieth century, De Rosalia entertained
the Italian American immigrant community of New York City with
his farces. On stage, De Rosalia most notoriously played the role
of Nofrio, a dialect- and Italglish-speaking Sicilian bumpkin who,
with his antics, managed to build a large following of fans. After
De Rosalia, several Sicilian American immigrants themselves and
their children and grandchildren found a different kind of inspiration in their origins. In fact, in the works of Vincenzo Ancona,
Jerre Mangione, Rose Romano, Ben Morreale, Tony Ardizzone, Nat
Scammacca, Gioia Timpanelli, and others, Sicily plays a special role,
and these writers' connection to the island is as much an emotional
attachment as it is an aesthetic or inspirational source. This is not
just for those who, like Ancona, were born there, or like Morreale,
spent a significant part of their lives in Sicily; it is also for those who
visited it later in life, like Mangione and Romano; and it is even for
those who have never been there. Some of these authors, notably
Mangione and Scammacca, became personally involved in the civil

struggles of the island against the two related phenomena of political and economic stagnation and the mafia. For all these novelists, short-story writers, memoirists, playwrights, and poets, Sicily and the Sicilian (is)landscape represent not just the raw material for their works but a call of sorts to which they *need* to respond. For instance, the Brooklyn-born-and-raised Ignazio (Nat) Scammacca reversed his family's footsteps by settling in Sicily to live, work, and write until his death in 2005. There, in the early 1960s, he was one of the leaders and founders of the social and poetic movement Antigruppo Siciliano. As he explained to critic Fred Gardaphé in a 1988 interview, "It took me two decades to give up America and two families. The remorse is still great; tears come to my eyes for what I have had to give up." Scammacca continued: "I supply myself with ideological excuses for my choices and destiny. Like Odysseus, I had to return to Sicily if life had any meaning at all" (*Dagoes Read* 201). Odysseus is a recurring theme in Scammacca's work.[32] The writer identified closely with the legendary hero, the spirit of adventure that led him to his peregrinations, and finally, his journey back to his home island of Ithaca (Sicily). However, unlike Odysseus's journey back home, which lasted more or less a decade, Scammacca's took generations to accomplish. Sicily represented a strong magnet for this and many other U.S. authors who long for a home(is)land they only lived on through their Sicilian American families' legacies.

However, if on the one hand there is, on the part of these authors, an emotional identification with the island of their forebears, on the other there is a revisitation of the bond from the perspective of an ethnic American experience. Especially for second-, third-, and even fourth-generation writers, the island of Sicily had been mapped out and imagined in strict accordance to the authors' personal Sicilian American network but also in comparison to the United States. For instance, Sicily's natural beauty, orange groves, and patches of wild chicory made it the antithesis of metropolitan American cities, with their skyscrapers and pavement. The culture of the island's proud people, characterized by dignity, frugality, humility, and collectivism, clashed with the core principles of American culture that favor a more individualistic worldview and encourage rising through ambition and determination. Also, especially at the turn of the twentieth century, the acritical defense of everything Sicilian contrasted with the image conveyed by media and American society at large of Sicily as a land dominated by organized crime, whose people turned to private forms of justice to settle controversies, and whose intense bouts of jealousy and wrath were resolved with the use of a knife or, worse yet, a sinister organization that promised to "take care of it." With all of this information combined, the common denominator of many Sicilian American writers is a strong attachment to the island and, at the same time, a desire to reconcile their Sicilian origins with their American citizenship.

Therefore, sicilianamericanità is a self-ascriptive enterprise born out of discursive practices of both Italy and the United States. In this sense, it is not the answer but a response to, on the one hand, to paraphrase Gramsci, the "Sicilian question," and, on the other, the American ethnic question. Sicilian American writers feel the pull of roots, but they are the product of routes traveled by themselves or their immigrant families. The different, and at times conflicting, acts of representation, self-representation, and writing strategies of these Sicilian American authors allow for a multifaceted reading of the Sicilian American Self(ves). In fact, sicilianamericanità reveals, in all its weakness, the fallacy that a relative space can only subsume a relative identity, contained, and easily identifiable. In this sense, there is no such thing as a "representative," let alone "authentic," Sicilian American writer. Rather, each author has elaborated in his or her text(s) an all-too-personal notion of Sicilian ethnic identity within the context of Italian American literature at large.

Consequently, sicilianamericanità in literature can take many disparate forms. It can range from naturalistic depictions of local traditions and folklore to more lyrical representations that tend toward the (re)evocation, through memory or imagination, of the Sicilian socio-cultural dimensions both in Sicily and in Sicilian communities in the United States. The ethnic component of sicilianamericanità might allow some authors to achieve a critical distance from any essentialist discourse on identity, while others might perceive their American Self(ves) as threatening cultural disintegration, and therefore, they might reinforce the already-pronounced tendency to insularity. While some Sicilian American authors may succeed in questioning the values generally ascribed to Sicilians, others uncritically resort to the most stereotypical modes of representation and self-representation. Certain themes, concepts, symbols, and language features in their texts signal that a Sicilian American consciousness is at work, and questions of ethnicity and identity construction surface in the form of syntheses between Sicilian and American epistemological systems and literary traditions.

For instance, one of the characteristics of Sicilian literature is its oral substratum. Oral communication was for centuries the most immediate and valuable instrument of expression of the Sicilian population, and traces of orality surface in the works of Luigi Pirandello as they do, some eighty years later, in the most recent novels and short stories by Andrea Camilleri. Orality plays an important role in Sicilian American literature, too, especially for Mangione and Timpanelli, as well as for Ardizzone and Marotta, as it reflects that cultural system out of which Sicilian American authors operate. However, functioning as they do within a system reliant on the written word, Sicilian American writers must ultimately find a way to bridge the cultural gap they inhabit by creating new hybrid positions for themselves and their texts.

Also, the linguistic aspects of some texts reveal the construction of a hybrid Sicilian *and* American identity. Sicilianamericanità draws its material from the daily life of Sicilians in the United States, and, as such, it speaks Sicilian and American English. In his 1963 study, *Storia linguistica dell'Italia unita*, Tullio De Mauro calculated that at the moment of unification in 1861, only 2.5 percent of the Italian population was italophone, in the sense of being able to read and write in what was considered "standard" Italian without a significant effort (37). As for the rest, the greatest majority of Italians resorted to their own local dialects for everyday transactions as well as any form of artistic creation. De Mauro also adds that "in absolute and relative numbers emigration especially weighed upon the regions with the highest rates of illiteracy, and, therefore, upon dialect-speaking areas" (57).[33] The linguistic choices of Italian American writers place them in a specific position with regard to the sociological and regional varieties of the Italian language, and Sicilian American texts abound with words and expressions that are style markers of the Sicilian dialect. The poems of Vincenzo Ancona, Antonino Provenzano, Lewis Turco, Emanuel Di Pasquale, and Maria Famà betray at first glance their Sicilian roots.

Sicilianamericanità is, to some authors, a sort of political program through which they position themselves as commentators and critics of both the Italian and the U.S. power structures. The contestatory potential of Sicilian American literature lies in its refusal of the forced process of homogenization to Northern Italian standards and of conformity to mainstream American literature on a cultural and literary level. This one strategic aspect of sicilianamericanità is especially helpful, for it allows readers to reconsider Sicilian culture as a complex system within the Italian context, as well as Italian culture at large as a multiform ethnic alternative to Anglo-American mainstream culture. Rose Romano, along with Dodici Azpadu, Rachel Guido De Vries, Josephine Gattuso Hendin, and other Sicilian American writers challenge many of the assumptions of both Italian and American systems, especially regarding gender and sexuality issues.

One of the most common themes in many of these writers' works, not surprisingly, is the mafia. Since the mid-1800s, mafia is a word that has been used—and misused—with great frequency, and it takes on a multiplicity of meanings. Today, in its broad sense, it is used to refer to specific forms of corruption, especially in the presence of close ties between politics and criminality, made explicit by favoritism, clientelism, and so forth. It also is used when referring to the activities of other ethnic-specific forms of organized crime, as in the case of the Russian mafia, Chinese mafia, and so on. However, despite its international usage, when asked to locate on a world map the island of Mafia, anyone's finger would go to the Mediterranean and point at Sicily rather than wandering in the ocean waters off of Zanzibar, where a small island of approximately forty thousand people happens to bear that infamous name.

Interestingly, in Italy, the term first appeared in print around 1862/63, when Giuseppe Rizzotto and Gaetano Mosca wrote the drama I mafiusi della Vicaria, set in the cells of the famous jail in Palermo. In its early printed appearances, the term already carried negative connotations, as it was used to refer to bandits, to isolated individuals, who, for different reasons, refused the social and political orders—thieves, murderers, and so on.[34] Then, during the decades of social and political unrest that would eventually lead to the unification, especially on the western side of the island in and around Palermo, the mafia will acquire the profile of a network that unites the political, social, and criminal segments of society, namely, high- and low-profile politicians, landowners, sulphur mine owners, gabellotti—or middlemen of latifondi estates—and campieri—or field guards—brigands and the like.

However, only a couple of decades later, the word "mafia" made an early appearance in the United States in connection with the bloodiest episode of the history of Sicilian immigration in that country: the New Orleans lynching. The 1891 execution was carried out by a mob of several thousand people against eleven Sicilians who were accused of the assassination of New Orleans police chief David Hennessy. On that occasion, the American press printed the word in capital letters to warn against the dangers of including in its society members of a primitive civilization who could not easily adapt to modern forms of justice. The *Leslie's Weekly* reported:

> [P]robably no reasonable, intelligent, and honest person in the United States regrets the death of the eleven Sicilian prisoners in the New Orleans jail, Saturday, March 14. Whether they were members of the law-defying mafia or not, they belonged apparently to the lowest criminal classes, and on general principles deserved, and no doubt expected, to meet a violent death. (Qtd. in LaGumina, *WOP!* 84).

Subsequently, the decades following the murder of Hennessy were the most intense in terms of emigration numbers. Author of the 1993 *Storia della mafia: Dalle origini ai giorni nostri*, historian Salvatore Lupo writes: "The mafia families, just like the natural ones, separate and reunite again in a web of relations that cross the ocean in both directions" (151).[35] This is a crucial period for Sicilian American mafia, which found a profitable niche in U.S. society and built its business in connection with the island. Things have changed dramatically economically, socially, and politically in Sicily and in the United States since then, and the practices of mafia have adapted to the times and changes in both contexts. The various anti-mafia movements, especially those arising after the infamous killings of judges Giovanni Falcone and Paolo Borsellino in 1992, have done a lot to weaken its power, but the mafia still maintains a strong grip on the island and outside of it. Therefore, every discussion about Sicily and all things Sicilian calls for a consideration and deeper understanding of the consequences of this criminal organization on the local population and its offspring abroad.

In fact, if a history of the mafia and its developments transcends the scope of this study, its repercussions on American public opinion, and therefore, on the life, and especially the literature, of Sicilian Americans is at its core. The stereotype of an archaic society that resorts to violence and intimidation to resolve interpersonal conflicts and achieve its goals, whatever they might be, is still a difficult one to eradicate and one that Sicilian Americans have had to confront.[36] Many Sicilian American writers tried to fight this partially distorted and potentially self-damaging perception. Jerre Mangione and Ben Morreale were especially affected by the mere existence of the phenomenon and wrote about it. Sicilian American women writers have also felt the same sting. In her poem "Mafioso," Sandra Mortola Gilbert wonders:

> Frank Costello eating spaghetti in a cell at San Quentin,
> Lucky Luciano mixing up a mess of bullets and
> calling for parmesan cheese,
> Al Capone baking a sawed-off shotgun into a
> huge lasagna—
> are you my uncles, my
> only uncles?
> Mafiosi,
> bad uncles of the barren
> cliffs of Sicily—was it only you
> that they transported in barrels
> like pure olive oil
> across the Atlantic? (Barolini, *The Dream Book* 348–49)

Some Sicilian American writers were personally affected by the mafia and chose to write about it in a most candid way. It is the case, for instance, of Karen Tintori's 2007 *Unto the Daughters: The Legacy of an Honor Killing in a Sicilian American Family*. In this half-fictional, half-true story, Tintori tries to solve the mystery of the disappearance of her great aunt who, in 1919, had the courage to defy the rules of family, honor, and tradition by refusing to marry the man her father had chosen for her and eloping, instead, with a barber. The betrothed, Tintori would later find out, was the son a powerful mafia family in 1920s Detroit. The price of free will and disobedience was too high for this teenage Sicilian American girl, especially since the all-too-powerful Detroit mafia was involved. She was "taken care of," most likely raped and tortured before being drowned by her own two older brothers. Because of both its mediatic and real dimensions, the mafia plays an important role in the social, cultural, and literary discursive practices of Sicilian Americans.

Finally, correspondences can sometimes be detected between Italian and Italian American literatures. The Sicilian American literary experience echoes the material, psychological, and ideological reality of the social group from which it springs. Therefore, models and themes that are relevant for that group might surface as conscious or unconscious leitmotivs in the literature that the same inspires. In other words, it should not come as a surprise that Sicilian and Sicilian American literatures might share common themes, conventions, as well as literary strategies because the two share a common heritage. Particularly significant is the case in which the Sicilian American authors under examination in this book deliberately establish a dialogue with Sicilian sources. Through explicit intertextual references, some Sicilian American authors claim a cultural (af)filiation and present themselves as parts of a discourse developed through the centuries and across the ocean. Although my study is not a comparative study in the traditional sense, an attention to both Sicilian and Sicilian American traditions allows a channel of communication to open between the two, and it is the reading lens of the next chapter.

2
_____

From Sulphur Mines to Tenements

Sicilianamericanità in Ben Morreale's Novels

We must be careful to avoid, as it usually happens, that the clay vases break among the copper ones when the ship runs in the storms and rocks them.

—Antonio Gramsci, "The Mezzogiorno and the War," in Pedro Cavalcanti and Paul Piccone, *History, Philosophy and Culture in the Young Gramsci*

In a 1979 interview with French journalist Marcelle Padovani, Leonardo Sciascia, in a fit of *campanilismo*, declared: "We all love the place where we were born, and tend to praise it. But Racalmuto is really an extraordinary town" (*La Sicilia come metafora* 22).[1] Sciascia's hometown was, in fact, the source of literary inspiration for many of his works, most notably the 1956 *Le parrocchie di Regalpetra.*[2] This small town in the province of Agrigento also stimulated the literary imagination of Sicilian American writer Ben Morreale. Born in New York's Lower East Side, Morreale spent part of his life in Racalmuto, the town his parents left in 1910 in search of the American Dream, and to which they regularly returned, sometimes for long periods of time, while their American-born son was still a child.[3] The years spent in Racalmuto left an indelible mark on Morreale, which is especially evident in his literary production. In most of this writer's works there is a constant focus on Sicily and *Siciliana* that echoes, and, in many ways, amplifies the literary quest of the other Sicilian American writers considered in this study. In fact, his passion for the island is comparable to Jerre Mangione's unrelenting commitment to the advancement of the cause of Italian American studies. These writers' dedication culminated in 1992 in the joint publication of *La Storia: Five Centuries of the Italian American Experience*, defined by critic Robert Viscusi as "the grant-funded construction of a collective history as an act against collective forgetting" (*Buried Caesars* 97), and by Frank Gallo as "the best book available on the Italian American experience" (202).[4] But arguably more than any other Sicilian American writer, Morreale has built bridges with Sicilian literature, especially with Sciascia and his works. In his 2000 memoir *Sicily, the Hallowed Land*, Morreale recalls Sciascia first as the kid who was two years ahead of him at school in Racalmuto, and, later on, as the now-famous writer whom he "often interviewed informally while walking in the chiazza" (13). Sciascia also makes a cameo appearance in Morreale's *The Seventh Saracen* and features as one of the main characters of *A Few Virtuous Men* under the guise of writer Nardu Pantaleone. From a literary perspective, Morreale's novels are closer to Sciascia's early works—such as *Le parrocchie di Regalpetra*, *Gli zii di Sicilia*, and *Il giorno della civetta*—which are populated by farmers, sulphur miners, and workers, than to his later works, in which the protagonists are mostly middle-class doctors, attorneys, teachers, and the like. While the influence of Sciascia is too obvious to ignore, more generally, Morreale inscribes his own works in the literary tradition of the island at large. The author once stated in a 1986 interview with Gardaphé, "I read a lot of Sicilian history and discovered Vittorini and Pirandello" (*Dagoes Read* 163); later, he added: "I first wrote *The Seventh Saracen* as an imitation of Vittorini's *Conversations in Sicily*" (163). Therefore, I will demonstrate that Morreale infuses his works with many themes and motifs that recur in Sicilian literature. In this chapter, I look at how Morreale articulates his Sicilian Americanness in three of his novels: *The Seventh Saracen* (1958), *A Few Virtuous Men (Li Cornuti)* (1973), and *Monday, Tuesday . . . Never Come Sunday* (1977). I especially analyze how, through the use of a series of literary strategies—such as intertextual references and allusions as well as various themes and topoi—Morreale's Sicilian American texts reveal their literary (af)filiation with Sicilian literature. By turning sicilianamericanità into part of a greater discourse on Sicilianness enacted by Sicilian writers, Morreale's novels become an ideal bridge between the fields of Italian and Italian American studies.

Morreale's first novel, *The Seventh Saracen*, is entirely set in the "extraordinary town" of Racalmuto. Immortalized under the fictional name of Racalmorra, this predominantly mining and agricultural town in the southwest coast of the island is the real protagonist of the novel. As an American ethnic writer, Morreale tries to establish literary connections through ancestry with his Sicilian predecessors. Through the use of a series of images that appeal to the reader's five senses, Morreale places himself in relation to a tradition that reaches across the Atlantic Ocean and connects Sicilian American to Sicilian literature, thus turning Racalmorra from an actual place into a literary *locus*. In fact, Racalmorra is a microcosm that reflects the tangled threads and strains of the larger Sicilian culture that have been a constant source of literary inspiration for Sicilian writers since Giovanni Verga, through Luigi Pirandello and Leonardo Sciascia, to Andrea Camilleri. Morreale's fictional town is a miniature Sicily, characterized by *latifondi* and *zolfare*—big landed estates and sulphur mines—in the hands of a few who are ruthlessly indifferent to the living and working conditions of the working masses. Racalmorra also reflects the topography of a typical Sicilian town, where the remains of a Saracen fortress, known as *lu Castidruzzu*, overlook a cluster of cube-like houses, and the life of the villagers revolves around the sulphur mine—"quiet, still, the one tall chimney pouring a thick olive-oil-yellow ribbon of smoke" (11)—but also the church, the local tavern, and most importantly, the town's *chiazza*, or piazza.[5]

On one end of the *chiazza*, the pharmacy of Buruanu is the place where the self-styled intellectuals of the town gather to talk about literature and try to recreate a salon-like atmosphere through the occasional use of a few words in French. The intellectuals of Racalmorra are depicted by Morreale with bittersweet irony as follows: "lawyer so-and-so, who lived from his mother's pension; and the engineer this-and-that, who at night went gathering wild escarole and snails for the next day's meal; and the professor who gave lessons to the mine owner Farubi's son while he waited sixteen years for a post" (72). The list of pompous titles sharply contrasts with the description of the intellectuals' meager means of support to underscore the uselessness of such titles in a land where education alone does not guarantee employment. However, the intellectuals in Racalmorra are very few in number, for most of the people in town are illiterate farmers and miners. From the fields, and the subterranean tunnels of the mine, the men of the village emerge every evening to join others in the traditional *passeggiata*, the almost institutional leisure stroll along the town's main street. The narrator explains: "Walking in the *chiazza* was a tradition and had all the ceremonial quality of a thing done for thousands of years," and continues:

> A man chose his walking partners more carefully than his woman, for more confidences were exchanged in the *chiazza* than in a matrimonial bed. So that there were various pacing groups: those of the scholars, like the schoolteachers, the pharmacist, and all those laureated unemployed; those of the merchants; the religious group; and, of course, the Workers Party group that always walked faster than any other, in spite of the fact that once it reached one end of the *chiazza*, it only turned and then rushed back to the other. (21)

As this passage shows, life in Racalmorra is a complex system of hierarchies and relations, and harmony in town is maintained through collective observance of the unwritten rules of the community.

In this close-knit town, personal events become communal experiences. Thus, the routine of daily life in Racalmorra is shaken by the news of the arrival of an "American" in town. Gaetano, or, better, Guy Licata is, in fact, arriving from New York to claim his legacy as the only heir to the properties of his deceased grandfather Papa Giuliano. The arrival of the second-generation Sicilian American Guy, which coincides with the festival in honor of the town's patron saint, the Black Virgin of Racalmorra, sets in motion a series of events that will affect the life of all the townspeople.

Guy's two elderly aunts, Pipina and Rosa, are thrilled by the news of their nephew's visit. Knowing that Guy can inherit his grandfather's properties only on the condition that he marries a woman from the village, the two women see Grazia, the sweet and beautiful daughter of their neighbors, as the perfect wife for him. Also intrigued by the arrival of the American, for reasons that will become clearer later in the novel, is Carlu Spina. A most mysterious character, Carlu is a solitary man who works as a truck driver, bringing the workers to and from the mine. Having lost his wife, Carlu tends his sick son, an eight-year-old who needs surgery to save his leg. Because of his reserved manners, and, especially, his close friendship with Pitruzzella, the local mafia boss, Carlu is rumored to be a "man with mustaches," an expression used by the villagers to indicate mafia affiliates. Finally, the town priest, Father Jouffà, is particularly excited about Guy Licata's arrival in Racalmorra.

Those who are familiar with *Siciliana* understand that the priest's name in *The Seventh Saracen* recalls the legendary Giufà, the protagonist of a number of Sicilian folk legends. Sicilian oral tradition offers a rich reservoir of stories and characters from which some Sicilian American authors, most notably Morreale and Gioia Timpanelli, draw inspiration for their works. Akin to a Shakespearean fool, Giufà is a *babbu*, a simpleton whose apparent stupidity, in some cases, may hide an unexpected wisdom and bring him good fortune. In his 1875 *Fiabe, novelle e racconti popolari siciliani* (*Sicilian Fables, Stories and Popular Tales*), the Palermo-born physician-turned-folklorist Giuseppe Pitrè included thirteen stories with Giufà—alternatively, Giucà or Giuzà—as the protagonist.[6] Later, Italo Calvino chose six of Giufà's stories from Pitrè's collection and included them in his own monumental collection of Italian folktales, the 1956 *Fiabe italiane*. As a commentary to the stories, Calvino wrote:

> The large cycle about the fool, even if we are not dealing with the folktale properly speaking, is too important in popular narrative, Italian included, to be omitted. It comes from the Arabic world and is appropriately set, subsequently, in Sicily, which must have heard it directly from the Arabs. The Arabic origin is seen in the very name of the protagonist—Giufà, the fool for whom everything turns out well. (755)

In her 2001 book *Le storie di Giufà*, Italian Arabist Francesca Maria Corrao compiled a sort of Mediterranean anthology of this character's stories, thus showing that, in fact, Giufà is a direct heir and the Sicilian counterpart of, among others, the Arabic Ǧuhâ and the Turkish Nasreddin Hoca, whose origins can be traced back to the seventh century. The main problem with Giufà lies in his total lack of common sense, which leads him to interpret words literally, a tendency that provides many comic moments. For instance, in one of the most popular stories, before leaving the house, Giufà's mother reminds him to make sure to pull the door when he leaves later. Unable to understand the figurative meaning of his mother's words, Giufà ends up taking the door off its hinges. Seemingly disconnected from reality, the only way Giufà can make sense of it is through literal interpretation.

Morreale's Father Jouffà is similarly guilty of another kind of literality. To him, priesthood is less a divine calling than a worldly career that has allowed him to escape life as a mineworker. He has none of the attributes that one would expect from a priest. Father Jouffà is the caricature of a village priest infatuated with modernity. The greatest event in his life was a trip to the United States, where he toured the Italian American communities and raised funds in order to renovate his church.[7] From this trip, the priest returned to Racalmorra with a large sum of money, and, especially, with knowledge of the ways through which his Irish colleagues made money in their parishes. The story goes, "Being a man who never denied reality, [Father Jouffà] finally admitted that he must apply these modern ways if the village church were to prosper. And he thanked the Lord for showing him this truth" (22). This is when Morreale's Jouffà takes on the role of the Giufà we know from Sicilian folktales. He, in fact, is guilty of literal cultural translation when he believes he can import some American ideas and incorporate them to the letter in the daily life of his parish. His insistence on adopting American ways in the Sicilian town is an obvious, and ultimately comic, transgression of common sense. For instance, among the most radical innovations the priest introduced in his church was a series of neon tubes bought in Rome, which make the church look like a train station; various Christmas decorations imported from the United States that decorate the church all year long; and a phonograph on which he usually plays the "Ave Maria" sung by opera singer Beniamino Gigli. But his most egregiously foolish innovation since his return from the United States was

> a siren [installed] in his steeple which he sounded at seven in the morning, at twelve noon, at one, and at five, as a service to the villagers. He had made it automatic by connecting it to the steeple clock. But the clock was not always accurate, so that often at three in the morning the siren sounded and the roosters crowed, the chickens rustled and the donkeys brayed through the village, for they thought the new day had begun. At such times many

> a man reached for his shotgun, swearing to blow off the
> head of "that Father Jouffà." (23)

Father Jouffà's insistence on adopting the "modern ways" of his American Catholic counterparts destabilizes the life of the village, shaped by centuries-old natural rhythms. The confusion created by the father's "modern" siren foreshadows the disorder the "American" will bring to the village. Morreale's situating a second-generation Sicilian American in close contact with his Sicilian roots allows the reader to explore some of the most burning issues at the core of the gap between Sicily and the United States, and, finally, between sicilianità and sicilianamericanità.

The experience of New York–raised and Princeton-educated Guy in a Sicilian entourage allows Morreale to present, in all its complexity, the intricacies of a bicultural identity. Guy's process of identity ascription is characterized by the tension between pride and shame of having a Sicilian father, and, therefore, of being partly Sicilian himself. While crossing the island on a train headed to Racalmorra, Guy is enchanted by the pastoral (is)landscape: "Damn nice country, damn nice country," he repeatedly comments (27). An Arcadia of sorts, Sicily seems at first to hold the promise of a life closer to Mother Earth. Most importantly, the glories of the island's past work to strengthen Guy's connection to the island. The names of the towns the train passes "sounded ancient to Guy, ancient in his life, ancient in the life of the world. And suddenly a pride filled him; he came from this land" (32). The college-educated Guy, the narrator further explains, "had felt this pride at Princeton in class, when they spoke of Cyclops, of the Sirens, of Dionysius, of Archimedes, of a people who wrote their history when the rest of the world was still in infancy" (32). Guy's ethnic identity is the result of a selective process that favors the historical and mythical aspects of his ancestral heritage and weeds out the less glorious ones tied to immigration to the United States.

Guy, then, chooses to tie his sense of belonging to an image of Sicily he has derived from his studies. However, critic Anthony Tamburri notes that today's Italian Americans can pride themselves on the glories of Italy's past, even though

> a large number of their ancestors came to the United States
> as an escape from insufferable poverty and socio-political

oppression in Italy, especially in Southern Italy. In this respect, then, Southern Italy and the Italian/American sense of Italianness may bring to the fore contrasting sentiments of pride and shame, attraction and repulsion, and love and resentment. These emotions often surface, at different times and with different levels of intensity, in the blatantly ethnic literature and films of Italian/American artists. (A *Semiotic of Ethnicity* 81)

The Sicilian American Guy refuses to trace his roots to post-unification Sicily, a land that was, in that precise historical moment, characterized by extreme poverty and high emigration rates. When an old man on the train asks him in Sicilian whether he is a "Sicilo-American," Guy resolutely replies, in the proper Italian learned at Princeton, "If one is born in America he is an American" (31). The little old man, though, insists: "But no, a man is a Sicilian, it does not matter where he is born. And you have the air of some of our people. You have the air of a Sicilian" (31), thus forcing Guy to rethink his assumptions on the meaning of ethnic identity and creating ambivalent feelings about it in him. When he finally arrives in Racalmorra in the still of the night, the visiting guest is confronted with the most uncomfortable aspects of his heritage:

> The road was pockmarked with manure and water that in the moonlight seemed gray. The ground felt gritty, and Guy for the first time smelled the village, a smell of human decay, long nurtured in the bowels of the villagers and now growing in their vineyards, in their stalks of wheat, and in the loins of their animals. He looked up at the stars, clean and bright in the sky, and he felt shame well up in him. Just behind them a shutter opened, a flash of white, a stream of water lanced out and hit the street with a swash, plop. (49)

Guy's unpleasant acquaintance with the sewage system of Racalmorra represents a baptism of sorts and serves to remind him of the uncomfortable truth that he should not look back to the time of Cyclops as described by Homer in order to find his roots. He, in fact, is a Sicilian because from his parents he has inherited a vernacular culture with which, eventually, he will need to come to terms in order to make sense of his American ethnic identity.

His turning point takes place in what can be considered another classic Sicilian literary *locus*, namely, the *zolfara*, or sulphur mine. Luigi Pirandello's short stories "Il fumo" and "Ciàula scopre la luna" and Sciascia's description of the life of *zolfatari* in *Le parrocchie di Regalpetra* are only some of the most accomplished literary statements on a ruthless system of exploitation, especially of young boys, or *caru-si*, who were forced to work in inhuman conditions.[8] The mines of Racalmorra are no exception in the history of mining in Sicily, as they represent a source of riches for a few like Farubi, and a source of poverty, tragedy, physical malformations, and the like for the vast majority of mine workers. Keeping with his promise that he would show Guy the "wonders" of Sicily, Father Jouffà takes him on an early morning visit to the sulphur mine. The descent into the mine shaft is a slow and painful journey into Hell. The mine has the power to turn the workers into subhuman creatures. Enveloped by sulphur dust, the miners work "naked except for a diaperlike cloth around their loins and large red handkerchiefs tied around their heads. They were singing, ending each line with 'umph' and a blow on the wall" (67). The visit profoundly affects Guy, who is led to reevaluate the meaning of his sense of belonging and community by tying it not only to the glories of Sicily's past but also to the hardships of some Sicilians' present: "Pride welled in his throat. He tried to swallow it down and he grew angry for feeling this pride, for he understood; it was a pride in belonging, being part of those who found it hard to earn a piece of bread" (70). The visit to Farubi's mine also prompts Guy to consider the role that chance has played in his life, and he starts wondering what would have happened if only his parents had decided not to leave Racalmorra and settle in the new world: "But for the accident of leaving, sheer accident, you would be naked in a sulphur mine," he tells himself (71).

Guy's descent into the mine shaft foreshadows a much more dramatically claustrophobic experience. Needing some money for his son's urgent surgery, Carlu Spina decides to kidnap the American and ask for ransom. As it turns out, Carlu, who, according to a town rumor, belonged to the mafia, had, in fact, been deported by the U.S. government because of his affiliation with the Black Hand of the Lower East Side of New York City. He is, therefore, familiar with the violent methods employed by organized crime to resolve personal issues.

Early enough in the history of Italian American literature, Ben Morreale dealt with the delicate topic of the mafia in his writings and made a point to discuss it in all of his novels. In the United States, the mafia especially became the focus of wide attention with the publication, in 1968, of Peter Maas's *The Valachi Papers*, in which the American reporter had transcribed the confessions of informer Joe Valachi, noted in America for being the first informer from the Italian American Cosa Nostra to appear before a subcommittee of inquest, presided over by Arkansas senator J. L. McClellan.[9] However, it goes without saying that the worldwide popularization of the mafia as a characteristically Sicilian social phenomenon is due to the great success, first literary, then cinematic a few years later, of *The Godfather*. In fact, since the seventies, millions of people have formed their idea of the mafia on the romanticized portrayal provided by Mario Puzo and Francis Ford Coppola, creators of the aforementioned saga. But Morreale's treatment of the phenomenon in *The Seventh Saracen* is not a romanticized tale of family, immigration, and honor, let alone a glamorization of the Italian American crime underworld, but a bitter and sad story about a father's inability to provide for his sick son and the ultimate decision to overcome that inability with the use of violence.

Later in the story, on the day of the celebrations in honor of the Black Virgin of Racalmorra, Carlu invites Guy to meet him at the local tavern to drink some wine and watch the procession pass by with the Madonna being paraded around the town. The two keep on drinking, when Guy, under the influence of alcohol, starts boasting about the greatness of America, which, he believes, "is the best place in the world" (114). Guy continues: "I feel that that land has opened up a new world . . . it has given me an education, it has taken the black shawl off my back . . . this clean suit . . ." (115). When the festival is over, the streets are empty, and Guy has drunk himself into a semi-conscious state, Carlu takes him to the old Saracen castle that dominates Racalmorra below, and there he lowers him into a well. "Make yourself courage," he says to his victim, "Those in the village won't forget an American" (124).

The search for Papa Giuliano's grandson is, however, delayed. By a strange twist of destiny, in fact, Guy's personal drama takes place at the same time that a dramatic event shakes the town of Racalmorra. As a consequence of the torrential rains that lash the town for a couple of days right after the festival, the mine floods, thus hurting the already poor economy of the town. Furthermore, just when some volunteers are getting ready to search the area for the missing American man, the poorest houses in town start collapsing due to the heavy rains. The men's attention is then diverted to the community, as they start working furiously to help the victims and the injured survivors.

Guy is, therefore, forced to spend two full days at the bottom of the well, pleading with Carlu to set him free. His wailing and crying is interrupted only once by a most interesting dialogue between the two on the issue of justice. The contrast between the victim and the victimizer is particularly significant in that it dramatizes the conflict between the Sicilian's and the Sicilian American's notions of justice. By recalling his personal experience as a Sicilian immigrant, Carlu seems to identify with all those who, at the turn of the twentieth century, arrived in the United States "with a slip of paper in [their] hand marked 'Immigrant,' and a number yoked around [their] neck" (140). However, in order to escape poverty, Carlu resorted to a notoriously Sicilian form of organized crime and joined the "men with mustaches" who run things in the Lower East Side. Ranting against the American justice system, Carlu complains to Guy: "The first thing they try to do is to make a rat out of you" (142). As a member of an organization that thrives on *omertà*, the mafia's notorious code of silence, Carlu believes that to become an informer for the police would mean not only betraying his partners in crime but ultimately sacrificing his identity at the altar of assimilation to American culture. "They wanted to make 'an upstanding American 'a me," he complains to Guy (142). In the confrontation between old world and new world views, the Princeton-educated Sicilian American makes a stand for his native country when he sarcastically asks Carlu: "So what do you want these guys to do, sit around and let you run the country?" (143). When the discussion shifts from Carlu's experience in the United States to Guy's present conditions in Sicily, the "man with mustaches" warns the "American":

> I'm on the side of the law now, Licata boy, and you're the sucker now. And if anybody breaks our law, he'll be made an example of. Have you ever seen a Sicilian example of justice, Licata boy? It's like any other justice, but when the suckers see it, they keep in line. (163)

In Carlu's representation of Sicily, the island is a self-ruling kingdom, dominated by the "men with mustaches," whose authority and idea of justice replace the law as traditionally understood. In this world, Guy is twice an outsider: because of his American birth and his education, in fact, he could never fully belong.

Guy's position as an outsider is alluded to in the novel in the various explanations provided to him by the locals. In the form of definitions, clarifications, instructions, and so forth, the tips given to Guy throughout the novel serve to inform the non-Sicilian readers as to the meaning of certain words and actions, while at the same time they remind them of Guy's foreignness to Sicilian culture. Explanations, then, fill the cultural gap between the Sicilian and the American worlds. For instance, upon his arrival in Racalmorra, Guy naively inquires about the mafia in the pharmacy of Buruanu. Among the educated *habitués* of the place, the lawyer Farauto undertakes to satisfy the American's curiosity. "The Mafia, dear sir, is a complicated affair," he announces and then continues in a tone meant to mock Guy's naiveté:

> Mafia, Mafia: an organization founded soon after the Norman invasion of Sicily, 1072 or 1090. There is a question as to the exact date. But Professor Calandruni, the great professor of history, a friend of mine, compromised and set the date at 1083, a truly great contribution to the historiography of Sicily. (73)[10]

Despite his Sicilian heritage, Guy is not able to grasp the full extent of the power exercised by the mafia and its cultural implications. He, for example, cannot understand the cultural meaning of *omertà*, succinctly condensed in the Sicilian expression: "Do not go stirring *merda* [shit] that stinks" (238). It is, therefore, only natural that once liberated, the "American" should try to bring Carlu to justice. Little by little, Guy comes to realize that his real enemy is not just Carlu Spina, the actual perpetrator of the crime, but the culture that supports, openly or quietly, the power system that Carlu represents. Father Jouffà is the spokesperson for a community of people who have not found the courage to rebel against the subversive organization led by the "men with mustaches." When Guy expresses his intention to find Carlu with the help of the police, Father Jouffà advises him otherwise:

> Listen to me, Gaetanu. They are not men that fool. Let us suppose it was Carlu. I am not saying it was, but let us suppose it was. If it was, then forget about it. It has not cost you money. You still have your skin in one piece. . . . They are desperate men. They are not joking . . . to those that inform . . . they assassinate entire families. It may take years, but they never forget. They cannot forget, or they are lost. They will kill themselves to hold onto their law. . . . Gaetanu, where there is hunger and misery, men are driven to the devil himself . . . I know. (236–237)

An American Don Quixote in Sicily, Guy engages in a solitary struggle against the windmills of the mafia.

However, in *The Seventh Saracen*, good and evil are not so purely separated. Carlu Spina's actions, in fact, are not motivated by greed, which would have made his crime an even more repulsive one. Rather, he is moved by paternal sentiments, given that he kidnaps Guy in order to provide his son with the best medical care. In a way, the victimizer is really a victim of a political/economic system that has contributed to the flourishing of an organization—the mafia—which resorts to violence as a means of solving problems. Guy, on the other hand, is not the most sympathetic character in the novel, to say the least. His stay in Sicily, in fact, is punctuated by a vaunted sense of superiority he derives from his American birth. It should not come as a surprise that one who, we are told, has "come to see in himself the American Hero, educated in a proper school, wearing proper clothes, and speaking the language properly" (33), looks down at Sicilians as inferior human beings. Often, Guy curses these "simple, coarse people" (80) who, in his opinion, are conspiring to keep him trapped on the island. While inside the well, Guy has a weird dream in which a man in black robes asks him repeatedly whether his parents are Sicilians. "I was a Sicilian," Guy answers in the dream, "but I detest them now. I spit on them. They are cowards, murderers, they even belch at the dinner table" (188). For a good portion of the novel, then, Guy is really a victimizer who, out of frustration, patronizes at best and even mistreats those he meets, including his aunts. Also, he deceives Grazia, whom he has seduced but does not want to marry because, we are told, his "plan was to marry an American girl and a protestant; for he wanted his children to have the comfort of being truly American early in life. He wanted them to be easy, natural Americans" (95). In short, Guy considers his ethnic heritage an obstacle to full participation in the American nation.

As there is not a clearly identified villain, neither is there one single hero in Morreale's *The Seventh Saracen*, but each and every character contributes to create a tale of the cultural encounter/clash of an American of Sicilian descent with his heritage. Interestingly, there is no one single character the reader might reasonably assume serves as the author's spokesperson. In other words, it is not clear whether Morreale sympathizes more with his Sicilian characters or the Sicilian American Guy. At the origin of this ambiguity, one might assume, there is the author's competence in both the American and Sicilian cultural systems as well as a willingness to delve into the possibilities offered by both cultures, and those denied by each. Guy's point of view, in fact, enables the reader to take a critical stance with respect to the mafia-ridden reality of Racalmorra. The description of the harsh conditions of life in a small mining town in Sicily, on the other hand, provides him with a better understanding of the origins of the phenomenon. In the last scene, accompanied by his aunt Pipina, Grazia, and Grazia's mother, Guy walks to the train station to take a train to Agrigento. During this short walk, he feels like everyone is staring at him, and that upsets him and reinforces his desire to break free from the island and its people:

> . . . the staring faces irritated him. The captive was being dragged in triumph through the streets by the conquerors. But there was the train; he would escape. He'd be free, away from them, and the devil take them all. He just wanted to get away now, make the break, get it over with. He looked at Grazia and quickened his step. (250)

It is not clear in the end whether Guy will ever return to Sicily to marry Grazia, and thus obtain Papa Giuliano's legacy, or if he will never come back. This open ending leaves the reader to reflect upon the feasibility of a project of grafting a Sicilian American into Sicilian soil and weighing the complexities of American ethnic identities.

Of Morreale's three novels analyzed in this chapter, the 1973 *A Few Virtuous Men* (*Li Cornuti*)[11] can be thought of as a transition of sorts from a narrative entirely set in Sicily (*The Seventh Saracen*) to one that takes place exclusively in the United States (*Monday,*

Tuesday . . . Never Come Sunday). This second novel brings back some of the characters the reader has already met in the first one, but the story revolves primarily around Father Juffa and a most interesting trip the priest takes to the United States. Whereas in *The Seventh Saracen* the focus was on a Sicilian American—Guy Licata—interacting within a Sicilian milieu, in this novel a Sicilian—Father Juffa—is shown interacting with the Sicilian American community. The two novels, read together, offer a multidimensional view of both Sicilian and Sicilian American identities and realities.

The graphemic changes in the father's name from the Jouffà of *The Seventh Saracen* to the Juffa of *A Few Virtuous Men* signify a change in the character's personality. He is still the simple priest of the church of Our Lady of the Mount, for whom priesthood is an obstacle to his full realization as a man, as he makes clear by often repeating: "If I didn't have this frock tangling my feet, I'd turn this town around and have it in my pocket" (15). But this time the emphasis is on the father's literary ambitions and his relationships with women, which take the form of a pathological devotion to his mother, Donna Rosalia. The narrator informs us that

> he had loved his mother with a filial adoration that was immense. After a meal with some good wine he found himself crying over the great sacrifices his mother had made in order to have him become a priest. It was only natural that in his *ricordi* he devoted a chapter to La Donna Rosalia, as she was known to all the village, which he began, "Mamma, Sweet and solemn returns to my lips the wonderful and adored name of Mother!!!" (27)

Father Juffa's love for women also materializes in a lustful affair with La Pippitunna. At the beginning of the novel, Father Juffa is in the process of writing his memoirs, entitled *Svolta Pericolosa*—"by which he meant 'dangerous turning' or 'life's dangerous turning point, attention!!!'" (19)—in which he intends to report the most important events in the life of a town priest. One of the first chapters is "The Temptation of Father Juffa," and it refers to the father's first encounter with the widow Grazia Pepitone, aka La Pippitunna, who, since her husband's mysterious death, has been turned by the town's mafiosi into their sexual toy. Haunted by the image of La Pippitunna's mounds of flesh pressed against him, Father Juffa makes her his housekeeper, and, eventually, his lover. Torn between filial devotion and carnal desire, the priest is ironically obsessed by the only two images from which the Catholic Church has allowed women to draw inspiration, namely, Mary and Mary Magdalene.[12]

Besides women, the other group that plays an important part in Father Juffa's life is that of the "few virtuous men" of the novel's title, as the author this time calls the "men with mustaches" who rule the town of Racalmorra. At the beginning of the novel, in fact, Father Juffa is said to be very "proud that, over the years, the men with mustaches left half a slaughtered kid on his doorstep each Christmas Eve" (8). Besides its economic value at a time in which meat was a luxury in which not many Sicilians could indulge, the gift is especially flattering for it signifies the priest's acceptance by and support from an exclusive circle of rulers.

By the time Morreale wrote his second novel, several books had already appeared that dealt with the mafia, most notably, Mario Puzo's 1969 The Godfather and Gay Talese's 1971 Honor Thy Father. In his 2006 book-length study of the figure of the gangster in Italian American literature and films and how the gangster has impacted the construction of an Italian American sense of masculinity, Gardaphé writes: "At the same time that Puzo created the Corleones and Talese was writing about the Bonnano [sic] family, Ben Morreale was bringing his own realistic version of the gangster to fiction" (From Wiseguys to Wise Men 61). Unlike Puzo and Talese, Morreale's mafioso is not a larger-than-life character who wins the sympathy of the readers. Rather, he is a wolf disguised as a lamb who plays the system to his own personal advantage. The mafioso in A Few Virtuous Men is Don Raphaeli Petrocelli, called Don Tarralla after the traditional Sicilian cookies the boss always carries in his pockets. Through Don Tarralla, Morreale lays out the workings of the mafia and shows how pervasive its power and how deleterious its effects can be on all aspects of life of a Sicilian town.

Don Tarralla's philosophy on life revolves around the word siste-mato or, as the narrator explains,

> . . . arranged, orderly, and in its place. This had become the most important thing in life to him. Everything in its place and all would be well with the world, harmonious as the blue tiles in the room behind him. Order was more important than money. He had learned that to disturb the

harmony of society, to break its laws, the order of things, is
to destroy what little beauty and meaning there is in this
life. This was very important to Tarralla . . . (31)

As it is typical of mafiosi, Don Tarralla downplays his own power and
importance within the community: "I'm a nobody in this town . . . I
know very little and can do even less" is his refrain (17). The friendship between Father Juffa and Don Tarralla grows over the years until
the moment when the priest accidentally discovers that his "virtuous"
friend might be responsible for the assassination of La Pippitunna's
husband. Right when their relationship is at its weakest, Father Juffa
gets unexpected help from Mussolini. Don Tarralla, in fact, mysteri-
ously disappears at the same time that the dictator is launching his
first serious attack on the mafia, leaving the people in Racalmorra
to wonder whether, as someone in town says, he really "was made a
saint and was sent to heaven" (57).

Several times throughout the novel the priest expresses pro-
fascist sentiments. In the years that precede World War II, the priest
conveys his enthusiasm for a historical juncture in which "Italy was
showing the world that it too had *potenza*—power. New Roman
legions were tramping again in Abyssinia. It was just the beginning
of a rebirth of the old Roman power" (42). Together with this renewed
sense of glory derived from Mussolini's military campaign in Ethiopia,
the priest also basks in the alleged safety and order of the community
at large propagandized by the regime: "Juffa felt a sense of relief and
pride in the regime of Il Duce who brought a new reality to law and
order. Now country homes were safe and disputes were settled in the
courts. One could stay in the countryside at night. If the farmers still
came in each night, it was out of habit, Juffa said" (57). What is more
important to Father Juffa, especially now that he has developed a deep
mistrust for Don Tarralla, is that Mussolini undertook to uproot the
self-styled "virile and virtuous" cancer from the island, "just as surely
as it was to bring honor, power and glory to all of Italy," and, the
narrator adds, "maybe *even* to Sicily" (my emphasis, 57). Juffa's infatu-
ation with fascism does not last long, and when the Germans make
their first appearance in town, the father puts away his fascist uniform.
Finally, three years after his disappearance, accompanied by the forces
of AMGOT, Don Tarralla makes his triumphal return home.[13] The
mafia, thus, resumes power in the town, and its relationship with
the allies is the object of the speculations of many people "who still

believe that the Americans brought Tarralla back, and a few who are still awed to think that Tarralla really brought the Americans" (68).[14]

The middle part of A Few Virtuous Men focuses on Father Juffa's preaching tour of various Sicilian American communities in the United States in order to collect money to renovate his church. By bringing into play the encounter between Sicilian and Sicilian American cultures on American soil, Morreale provides the reader with a deeper understanding of the cultural codes and dynamics that shape the Sicilian American identity of his characters, or their sicilianamericanità. Before his trip to the United States, Father Juffa shared with his townspeople the deep-seated belief that America is a land of opportunities. To the people in Racalmorra, in fact, America

> was an envelope with money, a place where half of the village had gone and sent back pictures of children grown tall, healthy and fat, with curious names such as Connie, Donny, Phil or Joe, in first communion dresses, wedding gowns, but never the notice of a funeral. (99)

Upon his arrival in Brooklyn, though, Father Juffa is confronted with the full extent of changes brought on by emigration to the core values of Sicilian culture, particularly in his host family. In the United States, in fact, Marco and Santa Di Licata's children have married "at least once" (110), one of them, Giuliano, aka Julie, has married a Jewish girl at the "City Ollu" (City Hall), while the youngest daughter, Connie—which in Sicilian sounds like cane, or "dog" to Juffa—lives all by herself in Manhattan. Commenting on the erosion of his own family, Marco Di Licata himself admits: "What family? Family. Here it's better to raise pigs. Then at the end of the year you can just slit their throats" (109).

The inner conflicts of second-generation ethnics, generated by the need to negotiate between ethnic heritage and American identity, are explored by Morreale through Connie Di Licata. By focusing on Connie, Morreale is able to show how the ethnic dilemma impinges on the life of a Sicilian American woman, especially affecting her psychological well-being. A strict Catholic by upbringing, Connie decides early on in her life to join the convent. Following some unknown events, however, she comes back home, disillusioned with the church and in need of therapy. Her psychiatrist believes that Connie's distress originates in a sexual dysfunction due to the clash in values between a "19th century Italian-Catholic ethic in 20th century multi-ethnical America" (122). Connie Di Licata initially tries to assert her own sexuality, and, eventually, in her own way, comes to terms with her bicultural identity by sleeping around with various partners. The influence of her Catholic upbringing, however, is too strong to fight, and the confusion derived from her unsuccessful therapy surfaces in the woman's nightly prayer, which parodies the "Our Father":

> Forgive yourself your frustrations, as I have forgiven mine; adjust to what your world has made of you; compensate for your hated-cherished mother-father image, envy not the penis as others fear castration, give us our daily good orgasm. In the name of Oedipus the Rex, the Libido and Phallic Symbol, Amen. (123)

According to Father Juffa, the ethnic heterogeneity of the American mosaic is the source of Connie's—and, for that matter, any other ethnic American's—psychological instability. He prompts the Di Licatas' daughter to think how the multiethnic character of America weakens one's sense of identity, "because all have to give up what took them thousands of years to become, when they come here. And to become what? You don't even know yourself," he argues (131). A core principle of Juffa's stance on the identity problem of second-generation Americans of Sicilian descent is a strong belief in the family as the only viable social institution. In his memoir, the town priest would later record his discussion with Connie by way of a learned quotation as follows: "As Cicero counseled Marcus Antonius, I spoke to her, 'I beg you, think of those from whom you have sprung, not those among whom you live" (132), thus emphasizing, to use Werner Sollors's now-popular formulation, the culture of "descent" over that of "consent."

While some second-generation Sicilian Americans struggle to make sense of their Sicilian selves, some first-generation immigrants tend to cherish their ties with Sicily and try to maintain them, especially through money. As is the case with many so-called developing countries today, remittances by migrant workers played an important role in the economy of Sicily throughout the twentieth century, affecting the island both in terms of immediate economic impact and long-term social change. In their relationship with their origins, Sicilian Americans featured as major contributors to the economy of the island and acted as catalysts for its process of modernization. Thanks to the donations of Sicilian Americans, in fact, Father Juffa can dispose of a large sum of money to renovate his church. The changes he intends to make in his house of worship are meant as a tribute to the generosity of Sicilians in the United States. For this reason, the priest envisions a series of enhancements in the fashion of the American churches he has visited there. Huge glass sliding doors to replace the front wooden portals, electric candles instead of those made of wax, a blue neon cross, and a hi-fi sound system are only the basic renovations Father Juffa has in mind for his Church of the Mount, which, eventually, will make it look like "a bit of Brooklyn-Irish-baroque transplanted to Sicily" (197). In these renovations, once again, the reader is reminded of Father Juffa's main sin: like his eponymous Sicilian hero, Juffa lacks the common sense necessary to contextualize these innovations within a completely different geographical, cultural, and economic setting. He believes that the success of his church depends on the presence of modern and flashy objects, and that by transplanting them to Sicily, he will secure his parishioners' devotion and, eventually, their generosity.

Ultimately, Morreale's *A Few Virtuous Men* ends on a pessimistic note, as readers learn that, as the result of an apoplectic stroke, Father Juffa spends most of his time in bed and eventually dies in the arms of La Pippitunna. The priest's maid, now deformed by a bad attack of the flu, starts working as a housekeeper for Carlu Spina, who, since Don Tarralla's assassination, has become the most "virtuous man" in Racalmorra. Not much later, Spina is found dead, with an axe embedded in his skull. The identity of the murderer is never explicitly revealed, but La Pippitunna is definitely the person with the strongest motive. In her article "From Saracen to Iggy," Carol Brown concludes that "the implications seem clear enough: the victim has had her thorough revenge. The 'few virtuous men' have become, one by one, *li cornuti*" of the novel's subtitle (216).

Nardu Pantaleone, a character inspired by Leonardo Sciascia,[15] is chosen by Morreale to express some final considerations that provide a glimmer of hope for the future of the island:

Pantaleone . . . grew more and more pessimistic, resigned to the fact that nothing would ever change. What he found hateful in others—a tendency to become apathetic and pessimistic—was happening to him. "This island is doomed," he found himself muttering. And yet he knew it wasn't so. It wasn't always so; it had flowered once, he told himself. After all, this is the land of Prosperina [sic] and Demeter. With some good sense and a few good men it could really be paradise, as most men wished it to be. (203)

A collective "good sense" and the work of a few non-"virtuous" and yet good men are some of the measures Pantaleone suggests to reduce pessimism and build confidence and pride in Sicilians and Sicilian Americans alike.

Later, Morreale explored both these ideas in his next novel. In his 1977 *Monday, Tuesday . . . Never Come Sunday*, the writer focused on a Sicilian immigrant couple and the struggles of the whole family to carry on their Sicilian ways in the Brooklyn neighborhood where they live. Unlike the previous two novels considered in this chapter, *Monday, Tuesday* is written in the first person from the point of view of second-generation Sicilian American Calogero Chiarocielo, aka Cholly Carcelli. The novel is a coming-of-age narrative, which presents the reader with a rather bleak but realistic account of the challenges facing the life of a young ethnic American in the 1930s. The social realism that informed both *The Seventh Saracen* and *A Few Virtuous Men* also inspires this novel, which illustrates the social problems and the hardships of everyday life of working-class people in a multiethnic section of New York. In a sense, Morreale's *Monday, Tuesday* can be considered the third part of a trilogy about Sicilians dominated by history, as it follows the life journey of a people from their birthplace, Sicily, to the place where many of them settled, America.

In this novel, the cube-like houses of Racalmorra have been replaced by tenements, and there is no *chiazza* around which the social life of the people might revolve. Most importantly, factories have taken the place of the Sicilian mines—a symptom of the industrial model of economic progress embraced by the United States, which sharply contrasts with the traditional economy of Sicily. Their differences notwithstanding, the American and the Sicilian economic systems share a model of private ownership of the means of production—the Sicilian mine like the American factory—whose goal is to increase the profits for a minority of the wealthy, irrespective of the human costs. In the United States, the class question intertwines in significant ways with the ethnic one. The status as an immigrant at the bottom of the economic and social pyramid in the United States affects Mimi's—Cholly's father—self-image to the point that the man first joins organized crime, and, eventually, overwhelmed by a sense of guilt, goes crazy. All in all, Morreale's *Monday, Tuesday* is a powerful portrait of America during the Great Depression and the effects that the economic crisis had on immigrant families, while it also sends a stronger anti-mafia message than the previous novels.

The novel opens in 1933, when, in the middle of the depression, the Civil Works Administration was established to provide temporary jobs for the unemployed. From Christie Street in Manhattan, where they live in a six-story tenement renamed by the Sicilian occupants *lu Vaticanu* (the Vatican), the Chiarocielos—Mimi, his wife Theresa, and their first-born, Cholly—gather after dinner around the kitchen table to glue rhinestones to American flags and religious pins till late at night in order to eke out a living. When Mimi gets a job through the CWA measuring the water near Coney Island, the family moves to Brooklyn. Unemployment is a constant theme in this novel, and a source of constant worry for the Chiarocielo family. In the end, it is the specter of long-term unemployment that pushes Cholly's father to resort to organized crime as a way out of poverty, and as a means of gaining respect in mainstream America. Once again, then, the "men with mustaches," this time led by *lu zi* Luigi (Uncle Luigi), pull the strings of the novel's events.

The focus on the *modus operandi* of the mafia as it bears on the question of the Sicilian diaspora in the United States is part of Morreale's interest in certain themes that, especially since the publication of Sciascia's 1961 novel *Il giorno della civetta* (*The Day of the Owl*), have increasingly become classic topoi of Sicilian literature. The unfavorable economic and social conditions faced by Mimi Chiarocielo make him succumb to the lure of mafia wealth. To this Sicilian immigrant in the United States, money represents not only the most immediate means of support but also a passport of sorts into Americanness. The degree of assimilation into mainstream America, in fact, is also measured in terms of the general standards of living that immigrants have attained. Significantly, Mimi's request for help to the mafiosi occurs right after an incident that involves a radio, a form of entertainment that was crucial in creating a sense of community, and, therefore, of belonging. When Cholly asks his father to buy a radio, Mimi interprets his son's request as a whim generated by the child's exposure to what he perceives as the generally high living standards of the country. Mimi further comments on consumerism as a phenomenon that seems to have engulfed even the children of immigrants, spoiling them to excess. The father never fails to compare his childhood in Sicily to his son's in the United States, thus underlining the gulf that separates his Sicilian world from America:

> "When I was your age I was carrying sulphur on my back," he'd say, "in the mines of Sicily, and I'd make four jumps of a dead one." (It's difficult to translate Sicilian.) He'd holler and pace up and down. "In this cursed country we have to have everything: meat every day, spaghetti before it. In the old country a piece of onion and bread in the dark, off to bed, and you used rocks for toilet paper. But we forget that here. Here they complain because we use orange wrappings." (40)

Despite his grumbling, Mimi joins his son's efforts to save enough money to buy a radio. The two eventually succeed, and the winter nights spent on the linoleum floor listening to "The Witch's Tale" strengthen the father-son bond. After two months, though, the family cannot afford making the payments anymore, and a man comes by to take the radio with him. "The next day," the narrator recalls with a powerful ellipsis, "my father didn't go to his CWA job and instead went to see *lu zi* Luigi" (41).

Mimi's new job requires some changes. Gardaphé observes that "the new association of Cholly's father with [the men with mustaches] is marked by a change in his dress" (*From Wiseguys* 64–65), a quite typical move when one becomes a gangster. The narrator, in fact, remembers his father's changes as follows:

> He got a black overcoat that looked very tight on him. Every time he wore it he seemed out of breath. He bought a white, white hat with a black band, like somebody had died. It had a very small brim, but it was high, like one of my mother's pots. On his shoes he wore spats buttoned on the side by little pearl knobs. (68)

As expected, a .45 automatic pistol completes the gangster attire. Paradoxically, right when he resorts to the old world's ways, Mimi starts feeling more American and even speaks more English than before. The power bestowed upon him by the mafia serves to improve his self-image, and the money that he makes reminds him that even an immigrant can buy "a piece of America."[16] As an immigrant in the United States, whose past as a *caruso* in the Sicilian mines still haunts him, Mimi believes that Americanness is first and foremost an economic status, which he means to achieve through his affiliation with organized crime.[17]

As a second-generation Sicilian American, Cholly, on the other hand, seems to have different ideas on the meaning of being an American:

> To be an American for me meant a lot. First, I would have a nice American name like Johnson or Scott, Carol maybe. . . . I'd live in a house on a quiet street filled with trees and brand-new Buicks, and there would be a hose to wash my old jalopy. I'd go with girls that smelled of sweet soap and clean hair and I'd only kiss them and never do anything dirty. . . . And when I grew up I would marry a pretty girl with teeth like kernels on a cob, no breasts so she couldn't be like my Aunt Santa who fed her baby at the dinner table, but she'd wear a pleated skirt and a pink sweater and brown and white shoes. . . . We'd only have two children—a girl first and then a boy. . . . And when I grew old I would smoke a pipe and say wise things to stupid young people. And I would never go to the bathroom or use toilet paper, or pick my nose, or fart or belch. And maybe I would wear spats and carry a cane with a silver handle like a real gentleman. (73–74)

The images selected by Cholly to represent the American man par excellence are clearly patterned after Anglo standards. Particularly striking in the kid's fantasy is the contrast between the refined American with no biological urges whatsoever, married to a clean, neatly dressed, flat-chested woman, and the coarse Sicilian whose foreign last name marks him as a member of a community of people with excessively physical, and, therefore, embarrassing habits. Cholly is keenly aware of the privileges of being an Anglo-American in the 1930s. "How I wished that I could be [an American] and never be Cholly Carcelli and never speak Sicilian and never be I-talian," he recalls, in a fit of nostalgia and painful memories (74).

Cholly's Sicilian American identity sets him aside not only from the (Anglo-American) dominant culture but also from the other ethnic groups with which he comes into contact in Brooklyn. Cholly's friendship with Iggy, the only child of a family of Russian Jews, is particularly significant in that it allows the reader to better understand the implications of cultural heritage through a comparison between two different ways of living one's ethnic status in the United States. A couple of years Cholly's senior, Iggy, like an older brother, represents a role model for the young Sicilian American, as a student, as a friend, and, especially, as a person. A precocious intellectual, Iggy sets out to teach Cholly the importance of a good education and free thinking. Equally important is Iggy's attempt to conscientize Cholly about working-class issues by introducing to him the concepts of "labor market," "pink slip," and "bourgeois propaganda," just to mention a few. Even a simple lesson on how to be rough on the football field turns, in Iggy's hands, into an opportunity to lecture the young Sicilian American boy on the necessity of revolution. He tells Cholly:

> Game, my aspirin! Those biscuits would break your behind if you gave them a chance! Little people have been turning the other cheek for too long. It's about time they kicked somebody in the billiards; their own are black and blue. That's the mentality they want you to have: it's only a game—so you take it easy while those biscuits take it damned seriously and you find yourself on your can, wondering what hit you! (75)

The two boys inherit two different cultural legacies from their respective parents. In this sense, the dialogue between Natasha, Iggy's mother, and Cholly's father speaks volumes about the Russian's and the Sicilian's respective historical and cultural backgrounds. Sitting on the steps of their house, Mrs. Lazarus and Mr. Chiarocielo engage in a political discussion that proceeds as follows:

> "Well, Mr. Carcello, the worker must see that the labor movement is the vanguard of the class struggle."
> "They might be okay at the beginning but as soon as they start collecting dues—they're all a bunch of rack-a-teers."

"But an organization must function."

. . .

"When I see a union boss riding around in a car, when I can't send my boy to the movies for a month, Mrs. Lazari, I feel cheated. Like if I stole from my brother. They're all a bunch of rack-a-teers." (83–84)

Drawing from her experience as a Russian Communist militant in the United States, Natasha affirms the necessity of studying dialectical materialism, knowing the processes of formation of surplus capital, and realizing the possibilities of the proletariat. As an illiterate immigrant from Sicily, Mimi, in turn, exemplifies the skepticism of many Southern Italians when he concludes the discussion as follows: "Mrs. Lazari, I'm no man of upper education, but there is one thing will help: a lot of bombs. Because, I tell you, they're all a bunch of rack-a-teers" (86). The friendship between these families of Sicilian Americans and Jewish Americans sheds some light on ethnic relations in the United States. The bond between the Lazarus and the Chiarocielo families is a remarkable literary example of interethnic collaboration and serves as a reminder of the role played by interethnic contact in the shaping of ethnic identities in the United States.

As a novel about the Sicilian ethnic experience in the United States, Morreale's *Monday, Tuesday* can be read as a cautionary tale of the plight of immigrants during the Depression. Mimi's choice to resort to the violent methods of the mafia reflects a historically justified lack of trust in the ability of the government to redress economic and social inequalities. Mimi's decision is also due, in no small part, to his status as a second-class citizen in a land where the label "immigrant" is a stigma. Unable to cope with the inner conflicts arising out of cultural cross-pressures, the Chiarocielo family degenerates into a dysfunctional state. Mimi collapses under the psychological burden of his criminal life and suffers from bouts of melancholia and persecution mania. More than in his previous two novels, Morreale makes it clear how involvement with organized crime results only in failure to thrive socially and personally. Violence takes a massive toll on the immigrant's life and his family and redemption can only come through the subsequent generations. In this sense, Morreale's novel can be read as a counternarrative to Puzo's *The Godfather*. The Corleones' saga is based on the belief that, to put it in the Don's words, "a man has only one destiny." Following this belief, Michael

Corleone, the most American among Vito's sons, turns from innocent spectator of the family business into a cold, unyielding boss.
Michael's transformation is presented to the reader/viewer in a way
that seems almost inevitable. The most Waspy of Don Vito's Sicilian
American children appears to be "destined" to follow his father's path.
His acceptance of entering the logic of violence reaches quasi-stoical
proportions. Morreale's Cholly, on the other hand, *chooses* a different
path; he chooses *not* to pursue a criminal life. A teenager at the end
of the novel, Cholly is left to recollect the pieces of his broken family as well as the shattered remains of the American dream they, like
many immigrants, had pursued. The boy is also left to make sense of
Iggy's death in Spain, where his idealist friend had gone to join the
volunteers and fight against Franco's fascist forces. The final image
of the "sidewalk of time," which is a recurring theme throughout the
novel, signals not only that time is slipping away, but especially that
Cholly seems to have lost his grip on his own life. Each tile in the
"sidewalk of time" indicates a day of the week, a season, or a month
of the year. Cholly dreams of it in the following terms:

> It was as I always knew time. But that night I saw it move
> beneath my feet, faster and faster, and I started to run. I
> ran as fast as I could, and all I could do was to stay in the
> box I knew was Friday. Then the sidewalk slid under me
> faster and faster and weeks went by, and no matter how
> fast I ran time raced under me. I opened my eyes and tried
> to think of something else. I was almost scared for I knew
> I wasn't walking forward in time anymore, but that time
> was rushing toward me and away from me, and even as fast
> as I could run I couldn't keep up with it. (168)

Cholly's nightmare reveals the trauma of a split identity and the
subconscious fear that stems from a sense of inadequacy and power-
lessness in relation to his ethnic identity crisis. Ultimately, the novel
addresses personal and social identity issues, and through the double
focus on two generations of Sicilian Americans, it offers insights in
the multifarious aspects of the ethnic dilemma.

The three novels by Ben Morreale discussed in this chapter—
*The Seventh Saracen, A Few Virtuous Men (Li Cornuti), and Monday,
Tuesday . . . Never Come Sunday*—exemplify the claims on siciliana-
mericanità that constitute the theoretical starting point of this study.

Along with Jerre Mangione, Rose Romano, and many other Sicilian American writers, Morreale has explicitly coded his ethnic literary experience by consistently focusing on the reality of Sicilians both in Sicily and in the United States. Given his familiarity with both the American and the Sicilian social and cultural systems, Morreale has been able to reproduce with equal vigor the life of a Sicilian town as well as that of a multiethnic enclave in Brooklyn. Through the use of a set of topoi and themes with which Italian literature has been concerned across the centuries, the author also has fashioned his works as part of a literary tradition that should be an essential component of the "cultural baggage" of any Italian American writer. Through his novels Morreale builds a convincing case for the reading of Italian American literature as a phenomenon that needs to be studied not only in relationship to mainstream U.S. American literature but also in relationship to Italian literature.

Morreale's attempts to present in his novels the experience of Sicilians and Sicilian Americans are only matched by Jerre Mangione's drive to delve into and understand the complex life of immigrants from the islands. These two authors together have laid down the framework for the creation of the phenomenon of Sicilian American literature, thus bridging the supposed gap between Italian and Italian American literatures.

3

"Half-and-Half"

Sicilianamericanità in Jerre Mangione's Memoirs

He who leaves a homeland,
while his heart remains there,
hopes for its return, repentant, to his body.

—Ibn Hamdīs, *Dīwān*

Few Italian American writers lend themselves better than Jerre Mangione to a critical study that links the author's self-realization as an ethnic American with the world of his or her literary imagination. In most of his works, in fact, the ethnic dimension plays a preponderant role. In his 1996 seminal study *Italian Signs, American Streets*, critic Fred Gardaphé points out that, from his early activity as a journalist and reviewer, Jerre Mangione "went on to be a spokesman for Italian and Italian American culture through his many books" (7). Besides being a prolific writer, Mangione was also a prominent critic. He is, in fact, reputed to be the author of "[o]ne of the earliest acts of indigenous Italian American criticism" with his 1935 review of Garibaldi Lapolla's *The Grand Gennaro*, which appeared in *The New Republic* (*Italian Signs* 7). For the same magazine, Mangione also reviewed, a few years later, another work of art of Italian American literature, namely, Pietro di Donato's 1939 novel *Christ in Concrete*. Also, of all the children of early twentieth-century Italian immigrant

69

parents who, during the 1930s and 1940s, wrote about their experiences, such as John Fante, Pietro di Donato, Garibaldi Lapolla, Jo Pagano, Guido D'Agostino, Mari Tomasi, and more, Mangione is the one who developed stronger literary ties with Italy, as testified by the many Italian translations of his works.[1] For all these reasons and others, the consensus in the field of Italian American critical studies is that in the late 1930s Mangione managed to open a space for Italian American writers to deal with their ethnic experiences within the American literary establishment.

Interestingly, a recurrent theme in Mangione's works is a process of ethnic identity formation that actually challenges any homogenizing definition of Italian Americanness as the author consistently and persistently portrayed himself as an American born of Sicilian descent. In an article suggestively entitled "A Double Life: The Fate of the Urban Ethnic," Mangione describes the first steps in the ethnogenesis of his Sicilian American consciousness as follows: "On the street we were Americans, though not sure what that meant; inside the home, we were Sicilians, and there was never any mistaking of what that meant" (173).[2] The question of identity in Mangione's writings involves the discursive creation of a distinct Sicilian American consciousness, or sicilianamericanità, from scratch. If, in fact, there exists a literature that is intimately tied to Sicilian American identity, its history dates back to the 1940s and precisely to the publication of Mangione's *Mount Allegro*. Although, when it first appeared in 1943, it was labeled as fiction for marketing purposes, Mangione's debut was meant as a nonfiction memoir, the autobiographical account of his youth in the multiethnic neighborhood of the same name in Rochester, New York.[3] Continuously in print since its launch, and promoted by sociologist Herbert Gans in his introduction to the 1989 edition to the rank of a "classic of American ethnic literature," *Mount Allegro* is only the first of a number of books in which Mangione undertook to explain to an American readership what it means to be a Sicilian ethnic in the United States. Thus, Mangione has earned the distinction of founding father of Sicilian American literature. What does it mean for Jerre Mangione, an American ethnic writer, to introduce himself as a "full-blooded Sicilian" (*An Ethnic* 43)? Where does he stand in relation to his heritage? How does he bridge the gap between "the Sicilian Way" and "the American Way of Life" (*An Ethnic* 176)? And, finally, how does he tackle issues of identity through literary expressions? In this chapter, I explore Jerre Mangione's sicilianamericanità as it unfolds in two of his memoirs: *Mount Allegro* and the 1978 *An Ethnic at Large*. Published exactly thirty-five years apart, the two books are complementary in that they examine two radically different and yet intimately related experiences in the author's life. While in *Mount Allegro* Mangione recounts his Sicilian education as a child, in *An Ethnic at Large* he gives an account of his American education as a young man who is desperately trying to figure out who and what he is. Taken together, these two memoirs trace the development of the author's own personal journey through ethnic consciousness and the education of American readers to the codes of sicilianamericanità.

Unlike Morreale, who undertook to *present* the reality of Sicilians and Sicilian Americans in fictional novels, Mangione relied on the more personal genre of memoir in order to, first, *understand* the meaning of ethnicity by delving into his experience as a second-generation Sicilian American, and second, *explain* it to the American public.[4] In a "Statement of Literary Purposes" written in 1972 for an unspecified "British Biographical Directory," Mangione stated:

> As a writer I am motivated by the need to understand myself and the world around me. This need was first nourished by the circumstances of being born and raised among Sicilian-born relatives in an urban American environment. That experience, which is the substance of my first book, *Mount Allegro*, accentuated for me the sharp contrast between the philosophical values of the old world and those of the new. It also succeeded in casting me in the role of the outsider who, belonging to neither world, tries to create his own world by the writing of fiction. (Qtd. in Burch 62)

To be born and raised till the age of eighteen in a household where both parents hailed from the province of Agrigento, on the southwest coast of the island, and surrounded almost exclusively by Sicilian relatives and friends, made and marked Mangione as an "outsider" to both Italy and the United States. He attempted to overcome this condition by dissecting his Sicilian American consciousness in literature before coming to terms with it. Thus, for this writer the memoir became a process of self-discovery and the most appropriate literary form to realize the full extent to which his Sicilian Americanness had affected his life and influenced his way of thinking and being. At the same time, this genre invites the reader to share and connect with the writer's experience, thus building empathy with and understanding of Mangione's ethnic community. In these two memoirs, Mangione turned his self-knowledge into literature to reveal, more clearly than in any other work, the terms of his sicilianamericanità.

In fact, questions of ethnicity and identity construction are, in different ways, addressed by Mangione in all of his four memoirs, which he claimed to think of as "a four-volume set" (Esposito 17). Besides *Mount Allegro* and *An Ethnic at Large*, the other books in question are the 1950 *Reunion in Sicily* and *A Passion for Sicilians*. *Reunion in Sicily* is a memoir/travelogue in which the author recounts the several months he spent in Sicily in 1947 on a Guggenheim Fellowship to study the effects of fascism on the life of Sicilians. Despite the negative impressions he had derived from his first trip to the island in 1936, the author went back, giving in to some sort of biological call: "I can offer no satisfactory explanation for that act. There was this much logic to it, however: Sicily was in my blood" (*Reunion* 2). After eighteen years had passed since his last visit, Mangione took a third trip to Sicily, officially for a scholarly endeavor. The author, in fact, went back to the island funded by a Fulbright grant to study the strategies of resistance enacted by Danilo Dolci. Nominated twice for the Nobel Peace Prize, activist Dolci was nicknamed the "Gandhi of Sicily" because of his choice to use nonviolent methods of resistance to mafia power—mainly hunger fasts and "strikes in reverse." The account of this experience was published in 1968 with the full title *A Passion for Sicilians: The World around Danilo Dolci.*

Besides his memoirs, Mangione's sicilianamericanità also surfaces in significant ways in his two novels, the 1948 *The Ship and the Flame*, and the 1965 *Night Search*, which, the author himself conceded, "may be more truly autobiographical than the [four] books I have written in the first person" (qtd. in Burch 63). *The Ship and the Flame* relates the vicissitudes of a number of European refugees who are trying to escape death in fascist Europe on board a Portuguese ship headed to Mexico. Among them are the Austrian radical Josef Renner, his Polish companion Tereza Lenska, and Stiano Argento, a Sicilian professor of history who is also a staunch supporter of the Movement for Sicilian Independence. When their transit visas turn out to be fraudulent, and the ship changes its course to Casablanca, the passengers seem to be doomed to either an internment camp or death. The happy ending is partially Stiano's doing, for it is he who, acting as the chairman of an action committee, convinces the U.S. immigration officers to let the passengers off of the ship in Virginia. Stiano explains to the U.S. immigration officials:

> Until my escape from Sicily, I did not attach enough importance to political thinking and action. I did not like living under a dictatorship, but I thought it would destroy itself without any help from me. In the past few months I have come to realize that dictatorship thrives on such false hope. (302)

Thus, the novel celebrates the courage to take action against injustices and the crimes of fascism.

A strong antifascist political message is also at the core of *Night Search*, in which Mangione delves into the mystery surrounding the assassination of the anarcho-syndicalist Carlo Tresca. The title refers to the actual investigation undertaken by the novel's protagonist, Michael Malory, on the assassination of his father, Paolo Polizzi—the fictional version of the real-life labor leader. Gripped by an obsession to find out whether the fascists or the Stalinists were responsible for his father's unpunished murder, after a series of vicissitudes, Michael ends up meeting with the actual assassin, a onetime friend of Polizzi. In an unexpected and rather improbable twist, readers find out that the reasons behind the assassination were exquisitely personal rather than political. Interestingly, whereas the real Carlo Tresca was an Abruzzese, in Mangione's hands he turns into a man from Monte Allegro, and therefore, from Sicily. It can be said, then, that the bulk of Mangione's literary production revolves around the necessity of exploring a hybrid identity that is contained by and different from any homogenizing notion of both Italianness and Americanness. *Mount Allegro* and *An Ethnic* are the two works most prominently concerned with questions of cultural entanglement that requires constant negotiations of dual oppositions.[5]

At the center of Mangione's 1943 *Mount Allegro* is the transference onto paper of the author/narrator's childhood memories. These are enhanced by the stories of the lively members of the Mangione-Amoroso family, who bask in retelling folktales and legends belonging to a mythical past in Sicily. Through a skillful use of humor, Mangione succeeds in conveying a colorful and affectionate portrayal of his extended family, which performs, with nonchalance, their Sicilian ways in Rochester, New York. However, their American-born children, Gerlando, the author's youthful persona, and his siblings experience a precarious balance between the culture of descent sponsored by their immigrant relatives and the mainstream one to which they are exposed at school, with its inevitable pressures for assimilation. The much-quoted incipit of *Mount Allegro*, which is worth reproducing at length, is a most successful literary attempt to explain the uncertainties engendered by a bicultural identity:

> "When I grow up I want to be an American," Giustina said. We looked at our sister; it was something none of us had ever said.
> "Me too," Maria echoed.
> "Aw, you don't even know what an American is," Joe scoffed.
> "I do so," Giustina said.
> It was more than the rest of us knew.
> "We're Americans right now," I said. "Miss Zimmerman says if you're born here you're an American."
> "Aw, she's nuts," Joe said. He had no use for most teachers. "We're Italians. If y' don't believe me ask Pop."
> But my father wasn't very helpful. "Your children will be *Americani*. But you, my son, are half-and-half. Now stop asking me questions. You should know those things from going to school. What do you learn in school, anyway?" (1)

In this excerpt of a family dialogue, Mangione skillfully dramatizes the tug of war between Italian ethnic loyalty and American citizenship. Little Gerlando's ambivalent feelings toward his "half-and-half" identity are at the core of *Mount Allegro*.

Any issue of ethnicity in Mangione's memoir is further complicated by region-based hierarchies of inequality within the Italian immigrant community, an issue which many Sicilian American writers, most notably Rose Romano, elaborated on in their writings. The life of little Gerlando seems, in fact, to proceed relatively undisturbed in his multiethnic—mainly Jewish and Polish—neighborhood as an Italian American kid, until the reality of hegemonic articulations of Italianness materializes in the words of a *paisan* schoolmate. When the boy shows his globe to Robert Di Nella, the latter points with his finger to Italy, the place from which he claims he is. Then, the narrator continues, he pointed to a tiny orange splash at the end of the Italian boot and called me a lousy *siciliano*. . . . From the way he hissed the word at me, I soon realized that while being a Sicilian was a special distinction, it probably was not one that called for cheers and congratulations. (3)

Early on, then, Gerlando is led to reflect upon his heritage because of an episode in which his Sicilian background exposes him to the scorn and contempt of other Italian American kids. However, the incident with Di Nella succeeds in sparking in the young protagonist a sudden interest in his relatives' birthplace. The now-adult narrator recalls:

I felt an urgent need to know more about Sicily, if I was going to continue taking beatings for it. I wanted to know what the difference was between Sicily and Italy, and whether Sicily was a nation or a city. From the way my relatives usually talked about it, Sicily sounded like a beautiful park, with farmland around that produced figs, oranges, pomegranates, and many other kinds of fruit that refused to grow in Rochester. The air was perfect in Sicily, neither cold nor damp as it was in Rochester most of the time. The wine tasted better, and you could pick almonds and olives off the trees. In the summer the men strummed guitars and sang in rich tenor voices, and the women went on picnics in the country. Everyone was much happier there. My aunt Giovanna claimed it was because God lived closer to Sicily than he did to America. (17–18)

However paradisiacal his relatives made the island sound, in the end they could not counterbalance the unflattering images of Sicilians in the United States. Little by little, Gerlando grows to feel that *siciliano* rankles as much as an insult, especially when accompanied by words such as "blackmailer" and "murderer" (4).

In *Mount Allegro*, Gerlando was first confronted with this ethnic stigma when his father forbade him and his brother to join the Boy Scouts, an episode that the narrator recalls as follows:

Even before [Robert Di Nella] came along, my father had indicated that there might be some doubt about the good standing of Sicilians, by being on the defensive about them and by forbidding Joe and me to carry knives because of the unpleasant association they had in the public mind with Sicilians. (7)

Like many other Sicilian American writers, Mangione was keenly aware of the stereotypical connections between Sicily and organized crime in the United States. Forced on the defensive by a series of prevailing cultural prejudices against his group, Mangione undertook to explain Sicilian culture to outsiders in part to correct the negative impact that the mafia has on the image of Sicily and its people. The mafia weighs on the psychology of many Sicilian Americans as an almost inescapable collective sense of shame, and it causes an array of ambiguities and conflicted feelings toward ethnic belonging in many writers. If on the one hand, these writers are drawn to the past of Sicily, to its variegated history, charming stories, and legends, on the other, they are especially haunted by the pervasiveness of the mafia, in reality and social perceptions alike. Rather than exploring the intensity and meaning of this collective feeling, or addressing the impact that the mafia has had on every aspect of the lives of Sicilians in Italy and in the United States like Morreale did in his novels, Mangione decided to downplay it in his first memoir. The humorous tone of the beginning of the chapter entitled "Uncle Nino and the Underworld" functions as evidence that the stigma of the mafia drove the author to counterbalance the negative image of Sicilians in the United States:

In the sphere of crime, my relatives were a distinct disappointment. From the newspapers one gathered that Sicilians in general had a passion for murder and blackmail, but my relatives did little to uphold that reputation. Considering their large numbers—there were several hundred in Rochester alone—the crimes they committed were few and hardly the kind to enhance my prestige with my playmates. Except for mundane misdemeanors like playing the numbers and occasionally bootlegging, they led such respectable lives that they might as well have been Polish, Irish, German, or even Northern Italian, for all the glory I got out of them. (181)

As a Sicilian American writer, Mangione felt the pressure of a certain social ideology and the responsibility to protect his group from the infamy of the mafia. After all, the author confessed that, by writing *Mount Allegro*, he hoped that "[a]t last, the Sicilian immigrants, the most maligned of the Italian Americans, would be presented as [he] knew them to be, not as the criminals projected by the American press" (*An Ethnic* 243).[6] In many respects, Sicilian American writers like Jerre Mangione are victims of the collective sense of shame they inherit as a historical and cultural legacy. Their eagerness to explain aims to inform, charm, and eventually de-opinionate the non-Sicilian public.

Determined to pursue and address more positive aspects of his ethnic legacy, Mangione turned to the rich oral literary tradition of the island, which proved to be an inestimable source of inspiration for some other Sicilian American writers, too, most notably Gioia Timpanelli, as I will show later. The Sicilian oral tradition in *Mount Allegro* is readily evident in the numerous stories told by the members of the Amoroso family, which are set in a mythical or historical past in Sicily. Remembering in 1984 the important role that the constant exposure to storytelling had on him and other second-generation Italian American writers who entered the American literary scene in the 1930s and 1940s, Mangione wrote: "The art of storytelling was virtually ingrained in [us]. . . . I attribute my own love of narrative to those childhood evenings when I would listen to my relatives spinning their marvelous tales" ("Remembrances and Impressions" 52). These "marvelous tales," memories, and legends provide the American-born writer with a sense of Sicilian peoplehood that transcends temporal as well as spatial connections. In terms of literary strategies, nothing epitomizes better sicilianamericanità in literature than the combination in *Mount Allegro* of folk stories drawn from Sicily embedded in an American prose narrative. As Gardaphé notes, "In America, Italian oral culture collided with the literary traditions of Anglo-Saxon culture. . . . Creating texts through narrative contributed to the re-creation of selves forged out of the elements of Italian and American cultures" (*Italian Signs* 24–25). In fact, by transferring into written form fragments of Sicilian wisdom, Mangione is breaking with a tradition of oral performances. On the other hand, the presence of myths and legends originally meant for oral transmission in a memoir challenges the literary conventions of a culture for which education is wedded to the written word. In other words, by attempting to translate Sicilian oral storytelling to the American printed page, Mangione gave form to his sicilianamericanità in the realm of literature.

Critic Justin Vitiello speculated on the possibilities and limits of the written sign to reproduce in an adequate way the oral storytelling performance. In his 1993 article "Sicilian Folk Narrative versus Sicilian-American Literature," Vitiello compared a corpus of oral histories collected in Trappeto, Sicily, in 1988—which he considered "genuine" Sicilian storytelling—to *Mount Allegro*. Ultimately, Vitiello dismissed Mangione's attempt to compromise between the old world epistemology and the new world literary tradition as an aberration. However, comparing the oral histories told to Vitiello by a number of elderly nonliterate Sicilian informants to a memoir written by an educated, American-born young man of Sicilian descent poses some obvious methodological difficulties. While the Trappetese informants, Vitiello argued, belonged to a preindustrial society characterized by a "mytho-poetic" vision of life and stories, the American-born Mangione was also, and preeminently so, a product of a modern and industrial culture. Moreover, even though the Sicilian cosmology informs the stories featured in *Mount Allegro* at their inner core, the memoir is ultimately a memoir, and as such it cannot ignore a set of previous literary precedents and paradigms. Critic William Boelhower's warning that "the student of American culture must not forget that immigrant autobiography is preeminently a model fighting for status in American literary history" seems rather apropos here (*Immigrant Autobiography* 31). In other words, although drawing freely from the Sicilian storytelling tradition, as a memoir, *Mount Allegro* must accommodate itself to Western aesthetic conventions. The interweaving of Sicilian storytelling and Western written literacy epitomizes the implications of ethnic identities and ultimately brings into form a new concept of literary category that defies any preconstituted genre, which is key to sicilianamericanità in literature.

Boelhower offers a very insightful reading of Mangione's treatment of the storytelling tradition in a chapter of his 1982 book *Immigrant Autobiography*. According to the critic, by turning himself, for a good portion of the book, into a mere transcriber of his family's stories, Mangione is subverting any traditional notion of authorship as the celebration of exquisitely individual creativity. Also, the inclusion of folktales, which, by definition, are communal, transforms the personal memoir into something that encompasses the ancestral as well as the mythical dimensions of the life of the Sicilian people. The personal life of the ethnic writer is enriched by cultural narratives of Sicilian identity and self-awareness, which help the creation of what Boelhower calls a "transindividual self" (192). Finally, *Mount Allegro* manages to transcend the individual boundaries of a bildungsroman and becomes a kind of "group-biography" that can be read as "radical substitute for the traditional type of solitary self common to the American autobiographical tradition" (185). For all of these reasons, Boelhower concludes, Mangione's 1943 book is "by far the most critical as well as the most positive [immigrant autobiography] in that it completely substitutes the American Self, its habitat, values, and behavioral codes with a new concept of the self and a new sustaining world view" (181).

Most of the folktales in *Mount Allegro* amount to parables with didactic purposes, and they dispense lessons based on peasant moral values. Among the most memorable characters are the Saccas, who, according to Uncle Luigi's story, would celebrate the Sicilian Feast of the Dead by laying out a sumptuous banquet for close relatives who had died, leaving tons of food to rot for days. Also, Aunt Giovanna reports the miserable fate of Angelina Tosta, who, because of her stormy sentimental life, earned the title of *strafalaria*, an epithet "more powerful than 'hussy' or 'slut'" (152), which was accorded by Gerlando's Sicilian relatives to "any woman who either flaunted her sex brazenly or was suspected of misbehavior with men" (152), and almost all American women. *Compare* Calogero's story teaches about the dangers of giving in to the temptations of the flesh. Because of his weakness for women, in fact, the man comes close to losing the most important thing in the life of a "respectable" Sicilian: his family. Carmelo Primavera, on the other hand, exemplifies the Sicilian young man of honor who does not hesitate to kill a man who jokingly calls him his brother-in-law, an expression that may cast doubt on Carmelo's sister's virginity. Transferring these stories onto paper may prove a difficult task, especially since the written transcription of folktales lacks the precious array of paralinguistic features that are essential to storytelling. Mangione himself seemed to be perfectly aware of this risk when, before reporting a story originally told by his Uncle Nino—which features an improbable, and yet successful, wedding between a rich and older Baron Albertini and the virtuous young daughter of a poor weaver—he put in his narrator's mouth a disclaimer of sorts: "It would be futile to try to tell it as my Uncle

Nino did but here, at least, is the gist of it—without the benefit of his tantalizing pauses, his eyebrows, and his magnificent leer" (*Mount Allegro* 141–142). By overcoming the problems posed by the translation of oral performance into written narrative, Mangione succeeded to create a hybrid culture out of two. *Mount Allegro* is the product of intercultural synergies, which bring forth the need for a constant negotiation between two different, and at times conflicting, selves.

The young Gerlando's ethnic journey takes place in various stages meant to illustrate the collective consciousness of Sicilians as it surfaces in their rituals, beliefs, and cultural norms. Following a progression from the individual, through the family, to the community, each chapter in the memoir also presents an instance in the narrator's education in the Sicilian cultural codes, as well as in his process toward an accomplished sense of Sicilian Americanness. Gerlando can count on a rather large number of relatives, friends, neighbors, and *compari* who gather on a regular basis to help him build his "half-and-half" identity. "My relatives were constantly seeking each other out to celebrate the existence of one another," the narrator recalls (24). These reunions are an essential medium for community building. It is at these gatherings that Gerlando learns the ropes of Sicilian "cultural grammar."[7]

At the same time, the education of the American reader to the Sicilian cultural codes takes place in *Mount Allegro* following Gerlando's vicissitudes. A quick look at the titles of the chapters—among which, "Family Party," "God and the Sicilian," "Evil Eye," and "Sicilian Virgin"—reveal the desire to probe into and expose non-Italian American readers to an array of Sicilian values, norms, habits, and behavioral patterns. Being persuaded that "[b]eing a Sicilian in the United States has never been a picnic" ("On Being a Sicilian American" 40), Mangione took it upon himself to relate and comment upon the experience of Sicilian immigrants in Rochester in the 1920s.

In the memoir, the "picnic" metaphor takes on a real and visual dimension in the description of the actual outdoor meals the Amorosos would enjoy every once in a while in public parks. In the eyes of little Gerlando, these occasions would reveal, in all its painful details, the gulf between the American family and the Sicilian one. Not surprisingly, food is one of the first elements that identifies the ethnic family vis-à-vis the American one. The narrator recalls that "[s]paghetti, chicken, and wine were consumed with pagan abandonment" by his relatives, while the American family would be "quietly munching neatly cut sandwiches that came out of neatly packed baskets—and drinking, not wine of course, but iced tea with trim slices of lemon stuck into the brims of their glasses to make them look pretty" (222). Other "disturbing contrasts" include the level of noise produced by the Amorosos compared to the "subdued, well-mannered Americans" (222) and, also, the clothes sported by the two parties, with Sicilian women being awkwardly overdressed in comparison to their American counterparts who wore "crisp and oh-so-neat dresses" (222) especially designed for such an occasion. Little Gerlando is particularly disturbed by the nonchalance with which the women in his clan expose their breasts to feed their babies in public. The breasts of American women, the young boy ponders, would never be as large as Sicilian breasts. "I was also confident," the narrator continues, "that the breasts of American mothers were purely ornamental and never used for the messy business of feeding hungry brats" (223). In instances like this one, the author's Sicilian heritage conflicts with the American environment, and when the gulf between the two halves of his Self reveals its depth, sicilianamericanità asserts itself most dramatically.

However, these side-by-side comparisons serve a double purpose in this memoir: on the one hand, they show the learning path through which Gerlando Amoroso had to navigate as a young ethnic American; on the other hand, they illustrate the cultural and social dynamics of the Sicilian community in the United States. In this sense, works of ethnic literature like *Mount Allegro* can be read not only as "handbooks of socialization into the codes of Americanness" (*Beyond Ethnicity* 7), as Werner Sollors recommends doing, but also as manuals of (correct) procedures to interpret an ethnic culture. By portraying himself as a spokesperson of sorts for his group, the writer ends up performing the role of a "diplomat"[8] who conducts negotiations between his ethnic milieu and mainstream American culture in order to reduce preexisting hostilities and make a case for a more comprehensive version of American nationhood.[9] Thus, Mangione works in the tradition of what critic Daniel Aaron has called the "local colorist" ("Hyphenate Writer" 214). In Aaron's 1964 article "The Hyphenate Writer and American Letters," the local colorist occupies the first stage of the "process by which the 'minority' writer has passed from . . . 'hyphenation' to 'de-hyphenation'" (214). According to the critic, in writing about the members of his hyphenated group, the purpose of this self-appointed spokesperson is that of correcting distorted images in order to overcome damaging stereotypes of the group, which may persist in mainstream America. Aaron adds:

> It was as if he were saying to his suspicious and opinionated audience: "Look, we have customs and manners that may seem bizarre and uncouth, but we are respectable people nevertheless and our presence adds flavor and variety to American life. Let me convince you that our oddities—no matter how quaint and amusing you find them—do not disqualify us from membership in the national family." (214)

In other words, Mangione resorts to explanation as a most effective literary mode of operation in order to convince mainstream America of the worthiness of inclusion of his ethnic group in a more comprehensive version of American nationhood.

In *Mount Allegro*, Mangione also focuses on Sicilian unique religious attitudes to tap into the educational potential of ethnic literature. In fact, a great deal of attention in the memoir is paid to the Sicilians' religious views as they set them aside not only from non-Catholics but also from the more orthodox Catholic Irish in the United States. In his 1974 social commentary *Blood of My Blood*, Richard Gambino commented profusely on the distinctiveness of the religious attitudes of Italian Americans, which are "rooted in a fantastic amalgam of pagan customs, magical beliefs, Mohammedan practices, Christian doctrines, and, most of all, *contadino* pragmatism" (194). Among the magical beliefs, some of the most interesting items the Southern Italian cultural encyclopedia offers are the *malocchio*—or evil eye—and the *fattura*. The bearers of *malocchio* are *jettatori*, people believed to have supernatural evil powers with which they cast malefic spells on unsuspecting victims through a simple gaze. One of the most famous literary treatments of this belief is Sicilian writer-playwright Luigi Pirandello's 1915 short story "La patente," translated in the United States as "The License," or "The Jinx." Accused of being a *jettatore*, the protagonist, Rosario Chiàrchiaro, loses his job and finds himself penniless with a family to support when the idea comes to him that he could turn this unfortunate situation to his best advantage. Not only does he accept his role as *jettatore* in town, but he wants it sanctioned by a "license" released by the authorities, through which he could officially turn his stigma into a profitable business. In Rochester's *Mount Allegro*, Mangione's narrator claims that *jettatori* are easy to spot. Because they are creatures of the devil, these ominous figures have distinct features that give them a demonic look: "Persons who had the *mal'occhio* . . . usually had a cadaverous and olive-skinned face, and their eyebrows came together in an unbroken line" (102). The fear of catching the evil eye gives way to a whole range of preemptive strategies and apotropaic rituals of which the narrator provides a sample:

> The best way of protecting yourself from the Devil was to carry a pointed amulet, preferably a horn, so that you could grasp it when someone with the evil eye looked at you. If you did not have the amulet, then the next best thing you could do was to form your hand in the shape of two horns. Making the sign of the cross would give you the same protection, but the trouble with that was that it was too obvious. It might offend the person with the *mal'occhio*. (101–102)

Malocchio, however, is nothing compared to the more catastrophic spell called *fattura*. The latter, in fact, "presupposed the services of a witch with a professional knowledge of black magic" (104). When Gerlando's cousin Rosina shows signs of insanity, her relatives, being unfamiliar with the etiology of the psychosis, claim she must be the victim of a *fattura*. A middle-aged spinster is believed to be the one who commissioned the spell to a licensed witch, because "this jaded virgin had become . . . envious of Rosina's beauty and her three young sons" (105). Traditional medicine appears to be an insufficient and ultimately ineffective method to cure the sick woman. Gerlando's relatives believe the *fattura* must be healed by a different kind of professional. Unfortunately, though, the self-styled Devil-fighter Cristo—who, the narrator points out, unlike Christ, demanded a fee for his services—turns out to be a charlatan, and Rosina is eventually confined to a psychiatric ward. This story is much more than an episode in the narrator's life. By letting his American readers in on the subjective religious experiences of Sicilians in the United States, Mangione is, in fact, attempting to disarm their skepticism and fear of nontraditional spirituality, and, eventually, to charm them with the creativity, humor, and wit of his ethnic community.

Sicilians' attitudes toward religion are a reflection of the island's troubled history and many conquests. In fact, magical reasoning is not the only remnant of the pagan culture of Greek and Roman antiquity that has managed to blend harmoniously with the most orthodox aspects of Catholicism. In *Blood of My Blood*, Gambino notes that

> [w]ith the coming of Christianity, many of the pagan customs were joined to those of the new religion. . . . The old pagan polytheism became Christianized as a whole panoply of saints was pressed into service to fulfill the functions of the gods they supplanted. As was true of the ancient gods, each saint was seen as having domain over a specific area of life and often to be in competition or rivalry not only with other saints but with Satan and other demons, with witches, and even on occasion with God himself. Thus the worship and appeasement of saints became a complicated affair. (196)

Among the major deities of the Catholic Pantheon is Saint Joseph, who is one of the most revered saints in Sicily, whom Sicilians honor on his day with the Saint Joseph's table. According to the legend, the origins of the *festa* can be traced back to the Middle Ages when a severe drought hit the west of the island, threatening the life of the inhabitants of the area. When the hopeless farmers turned to Saint Joseph for help, their prayers were heard, and miraculously it started raining. Acres of crops and thousands of lives were saved, and as a form of thanksgiving, people decided to honor Saint Joseph every March 19th with huge banquets to which everyone was invited. With time, however, this tradition took a more individualistic approach, and the table became a way to thank Saint Joseph for fulfilling personal requests.[10] In *Mount Allegro*, in fact, Gerlando's aunt Sarina asks Saint Joseph's intervention to cure her sick husband. The saint does not let her down, and the man recovers from his illness. In order to keep her part of the covenant, a couple of days before the saint's feast, Sarina walks around the neighborhood begging for alms to fund her table. The fundraising campaign proves successful, and, as the narrator recalls, Aunt Sarina's Saint Joseph's table "stretched from one end of her living-room to the kitchen, and was piled high with a dazzling variety of meats, fruits, and pastries" (90). By recounting these colorful stories, Mangione is fulfilling the autobiographical mode of the memoir, which allows him to recover, and, eventually, make sense of his most poignant and formative experiences as a young Sicilian American. But the writer's avowed intent in writing this book is also that of instructing the non–Italian American reader on the roots and dimensions of Sicilian traditions that are most at odds with the dominant culture. The "diplomat" thus promotes a better understanding of the Sicilian people that leads to a better appreciation of the diversity brought to the United States by this foreign group.

However, in an effort to portray a most positive image of Sicilians in the United States, Mangione ended up providing an edulcorated version of his neighborhood and people. In his review of the memoir, Paul McBride rightfully noted: "Not everyone swam in the melting pot; many drowned. Jerre Mangione's masterful *Mount Allegro* exalts those who swam rather than mourning those who drowned" (112). McBride was especially unconvinced by the unidimensional aspect of Mangione's characters. This book "creates postcard photographs rather than Picasso paintings" (112), he objected.[11] In an attempt to convey a positive image of Sicilian immigrants, in fact, Mangione chose not to explore the darkest sides of Sicilian culture, nor did he hint at the most horrific encounters between ethnic and mainstream cultures. In order to counter the traditional depictions of ethnic ghettoes as receptacles of crime, misery, and immorality, in his memoir he conveyed an image of his multiethnic neighborhood as a sort of cocoon of comfort. The author himself had reservations about his autobiographical omissions and voiced them in a Finale added to the 1981 edition of the memoir. The following passage that he wrote about his father Gaspare Mangione/Peppino Amoroso helps readers to understand his mechanisms of self-censorship:

> The father presented in *Mount Allegro* is not nearly as complex as he actually was. For all of his vitality, he suffered from periods of black despair that tortured our childhood with the fear of losing him. . . . we could not help but recall the fate of his own father who, on a Christmas Eve, had drowned himself in the Mediterranean, leaving behind a family of several young children of which he was the youngest. (297)

Selective memory, but also humor, contribute to making this reading experience a comfortable and safe one, so to speak, for Italian Americans and non–Italian Americans alike.

Critic John Lowe analyzed humor as a major literary mode in Mangione's *Mount Allegro*. In his essay "Humor and Identity in Ethnic Autobiography," Lowe focused on Mangione's memoir and Zora Neale Hurston's *Dust Tracks* to show how these two ethnic writers used humor as a *captatio benevolentiae* in order to reverse the negative stereotypes that mainstream America holds of their respective groups. Humor, Lowe notes, is one of the discursive engines that can facilitate the performance of ethnic autobiographies. The life stories of ethnic authors, the critic continues,

> become mechanisms for bringing opposites together, fixing in words a mirror whereby opposites look at one another, understand each other, and thereby come to a firmer understanding of their own self. The vehicle for much of this process, the circumambient ether of the experiments, is laughter, chief agent of the carnivalizing mode. (97)

By capitalizing on humor, Mangione manages to construct his own difficult position as a Sicilian American, while at the same time he corrects stereotypical cultural representations.

Lowe further notes that "[b]oth [Hurston's and Mangione's] books are conservative in a way. . . . Both writers demonstrate in some detail their wide experiences outside the group and display their hard-won credentials in various mainstream hierarchies" (96). As a matter of fact, Mangione never made a secret of the fact that, as a young man, he resented his Sicilian upbringing and thought it necessary to break free from his family, neighborhood, and city in order to become American.[12] As a second-generation ethnic, what he feared most was the strong influence of immigrant parents from whom, he argued, the American-born child inherits "a ghetto psychology which, incorporating the darkest fears and suspicions of his immigrant forebears, made him resistant to social change" ("On Being a Sicilian American" 49). The "ghetto psychology" discussed and feared by Mangione reflects the findings of sociologist Herbert Gans's 1962 *The Urban Villagers*, a study conducted between 1957 and 1958 in a predominantly second-generation Italian American low-rent neighborhood in Boston. In Gans's examination, the values, processes of socialization, and structure of the peer group of the Italian Americans under observation reflected the patterns inherited by their immigrant parents. This legacy affected the relationship of these American-born adults with the outside world by turning them into the "urban villagers" of the book's title. Gans, however, was more prone to argue that what Mangione defined as a "ghetto psychology" was less a cause of the ethnic heritage of the Italian Americans than a working-class style. Whatever its nature, early on, Mangione felt the need to avoid this legacy by escaping from Mount Allegro. In retrospect, the author also realized that he needed to bracket his experience as a Sicilian son before being able to report it in such a complacent way in his first memoir. In a 1983 interview, he concluded: "If I had never left Rochester, I would never have been able to write about them as I have" (Mulas 75). *Mount Allegro* was written half during a residence fellowship at the Victorian manor house of Yaddo and partly in a barn on Kenneth Burke's farm in New Jersey. By then, Mangione had already made the leap from "urban villager" to "urban ethnic."

Although it was the last of the four memoirist books to appear in 1978, it is to *An Ethnic at Large* that one must refer in order to trace the transition from "urban villager" to "urban ethnic," as well as to get a deeper understanding of the elaboration of a Sicilian American consciousness in Jerre Mangione's works. The author considered *An Ethnic* as a "companion volume" to *Mount Allegro* and thought they should be read together (*Mount Allegro* 300). *An Ethnic* is, in fact, a sequel of sorts to the first memoir, picking up chronologically where the former left off. In one of the last chapters of *Mount Allegro*, the narrator recalls:

> At eighteen, I left my Sicilian relatives. Living among them, I had the sense that though I was born in America, I was not really an American. I decided to become a part of the outer world; perhaps in that way I could rid myself of the feeling that I was more Sicilian than American. (225)

In *An Ethnic*, Mangione tells the story of the second part of his education as a Sicilian American, which is the one that took place in mainstream American culture. A quick look at the titles of the chapters that make up this memoir will immediately reveal the difference between it and *Mount Allegro*. "Manhattan Miasma," "Into the New Deal," "Washington at War," "The Philadelphia Front," and "White House Weekend" are only some of the chapters that represent some of the stages of the author's process of becoming educated in the codes of Americanness. The only chapter that looks back to Mangione's past in Rochester is the opening one, tellingly entitled "Growing Up Sicilian." While this cue ties the writer's 1978 memoir to his debut book, most importantly, it signifies a transition from an exquisitely ethnic to an almost exclusively American life. The growth of a sense of Americanness here appears to be inversely proportional to the author's independence from the Sicilian community-oriented model. In literary language, this autonomy translates into a memoir that is, this time, compliant with Western literary traditions. The "transindividual subject" that, as Boelhower argued, characterized *Mount Allegro* is only a vague memory. *An Ethnic* focuses on the "I" as an individual, a change in style that reflects the author's transition from an ethnic, peasant, small-town scene to the intellectual milieu of New York. If from his birth to age eighteen Mangione had especially developed his Sicilian self, so to speak, it took him exactly the same amount of time to balance it with an equal amount of Americanness. Between his 1943 and 1978 memoirs, we can reconstruct the years that coalesced into the gradual unfurling of Mangione's sicilianamericanità.

Unlike *Mount Allegro*, where no exact time frame is provided to the reader,[13] *An Ethnic* is set in a precise temporal dimension. It, in fact, encloses the author's life from when, at the age of eighteen, he "arrived in the winter of 1928 [at] Syracuse University" (35), till his thirty-fifth birthday, which "came about a month before Franklin D. Roosevelt suddenly died of a cerebral hemorrhage, and six months before World War II ended with Hiroshima" (367). This event, the writer adds, "marked the end of my apprenticeship as an American" (367). In this memoir, the personal and the historical interweave to portray the emergence of Mangione's Sicilian American Self in the context of the "miasmal Depression that was devastating the country" (57). The bulk of *An Ethnic* is the story of the author's life as a student at Syracuse University first and as a job seeker during the Depression era later. The reader learns about his many sentimental and, occasionally, sexual exploits, his more or less famous friendships, and follows his ascending professional career. In his initial efforts to eke out a living anywhere for the sake of not going back to Rochester, the author tracks his own peregrinations to Manhattan, Washington, and Philadelphia. Starting out as a member of the editorial staff of *Time*, Mangione also worked as an assistant bookkeeper in a garage, an assistant librarian, a book editor for the McBride publishing firm, and as the national coordinating editor of the WPA Federal Writers' Project.[14] At the end of the memoir—which coincides with the eve of Pearl Harbor—Mangione was working as director of the public relations program of the INS. Ironically enough, he, as an Italian American, was put in charge of publicizing the Alien Registration Act, which required German, Italian, and Japanese nationals to register as "enemy aliens."[15]

From *An Ethnic*, the reader gathers that the years spent away from Rochester and his relatives were, paradoxically, those in which Mangione learned more about his Sicilian heritage. The contact with mainstream America provided him with a looking glass through which he could calculate the influence his Sicilian upbringing had on him. At times, this confrontation engendered in him a sense of inadequacy. In one instance, he elaborates on the envy he felt toward the guests at a house party thrown by artist Peggy Cowley. Mangione felt that these people, who were unencumbered by an immigrant family, moved around with a higher degree of self-assurance:

> They were also fortunate to have had parents whose roots were deeply embedded in American soil and who spoke the native language. They had no identity problems, none of the conflicts that gnawed at the psyche of every son and daughter of immigrant parents to whom English was a foreign tongue. (133)

However, the fact that, in some ways, his ethnic identity represented a social handicap of sorts did not immediately translate into a rejection of his heritage *in toto*. Rather, Mangione's "apprenticeship as an American" turned out in the end to be a period of learning more about his Sicilian roots. At Syracuse University, as feature editor of the college's newspaper, *The Daily Orange*, Mangione took to interviewing prominent writers who came to lecture at the school. On one of these missions, the author met British novelist John Cowper Powys. Mangione recalls that

> on learning I was full-blooded Sicilian with parents from the ancient province of Agrigento, he chided me for not using my baptismal name of Gerlando, then discoursed eloquently about the glories of Sicilian civilization which, I learned for the first time, antedated that of Rome by two thousand years. (43)

Having experienced firsthand the folk aspects and traditional values of the Sicilian culture, the author was then informed of a different aspect of his Sicilian American identity, one that engendered in him a sense of pride rather than inadequacy.

Upon learning from the British writer of the "glories of Sicilian civilization," Mangione took an interest in the island and explained it as follows: "Yet for all my faith in the American Way of Life and the Lucky Break, the Sicilian Way began to obsess me as it never had before. Sicily became an irresistible magnet which I needed to explore and fathom" (176). The exploration was first a scholarly endeavor, carried on through travel and history books. In 1936, in an attempt to get closer to his relatives' reality, ascertain his own identity, and ultimately make cognitive sense of his status as a U.S. ethnic with a strong allegiance to the island, Mangione took his first trip to Sicily. Reported both in the two final chapters of *Mount Allegro*—entitled "Welcome to Girgenti" and "Blighted Land"—and in *An Ethnic*, the author's first encounter with the island and its inhabitants was a crucial moment in the articulation of his sicilianamericanità.

In many ways, Mangione undertook his first trip to Sicily not only for personal but also for political reasons. Although he never was a member of the Communist Party, Mangione was a fierce antifascist.[16] In New York, he had attended several meetings of a leftist group, the John Reed Club, and wrote under pseudonyms for several left-winged newspapers, among which the organ of the group, *The Partisan Review*, and the *New Masses*.[17] In the city, Mangione had also befriended Carlo Tresca, labor agitator, editor, and publisher of *Il Martello*. All throughout the 1930s, the anarchist Tresca had conducted a systematic campaign against Mussolini, a courageous mission that eventually resulted in his assassination. Mangione painfully recalls that day as follows: "On the morning of the party when I dashed to a newsstand to read what the critics had to say about my book, I was confronted by the front-page headlines of his murder" (*An Ethnic* 306).[18] Tresca, in fact, was gunned down in the streets of New York the day before he was supposed to attend a party to celebrate the publication of *Mount Allegro*.

The friendship with such a notoriously staunch enemy of Mussolini was one of the factors that compromised the happy outcome of Mangione's first trip to fascist Italy in 1936. In constant fear of being conscripted as an American of Italian descent, and also of being recognized as the author of venomous articles against the dictatorship, let alone as a friend of Tresca, Mangione developed "a sense of caution that sometimes veered on paranoia" (194). The writer officially undertook the trip as a correspondent for *Travel* magazine, with an ingratiating letter addressed to the minister of propaganda, duly signed with fascist greetings. Nevertheless, all during his stay in Italy, his mail from the United States was constantly checked, his movements closely monitored, and he was even interrogated a couple of times at police headquarters. Much to his own dismay, Mangione realized that most of the people around him, his relatives included, to different degrees, supported the regime. When they did not adamantly refuse to talk politics as a potentially dangerous pastime, they just uncritically repeated or, sometimes, enthusiastically embraced the propaganda messages with which they were bombarded. Significantly, the only person in fascist Agrigento who had managed to escape the brainwashing was an "ex-American." According to this man, his experience in the United States—from where he had been deported to Italy for some mysterious crime—had endowed him with a critical perspective on fascism that was lacking in those who had never crossed the ocean. "'This town stinks, the whole country stinks. If you ask me, their system of government stinks. But none of these guys know it. They been here all their lives; that's all they know, they don't know no better,'" the returned immigrant tells the author (184). While confessing that he has been cooking up a scheme to illegally reenter the United States, the man adds, "I'd rather be dying in Brooklyn than living in this friggin' country" (184). In this atmosphere, Mangione's resentment toward the regime grew to the point that, in a moment of exasperation, on top of Giotto's tower in Florence, he could not resist the temptation of adding to the work of some graffiti writers by writing "the words 'Abbasso Mussolini' (Down with Mussolini) across the torso of a female saint with a broken nose" (200).[19]

Despite all the problems caused by Mussolini's regime, Mangione's trip to Sicily helped him to better understand the feeling he had started developing in New York, which was "a root feeling, a connection with a substantial past that made the uncertain present more bearable" (175). The author's connection to Sicily starts delineating itself in terms of a symbiotic yet conflicting relationship as the boat approaches the shores of the island. Overhearing some of the crewmembers talking to each other in the Sicilian dialect, the author feels "overwhelmed with the emotion of being *a full-blooded Sicilian in direct touch with his life source*" (180, emphasis added). As soon as he steps off the boat in Palermo, though, his enthusiasm wanes. For the first time in his life, in fact, Mangione has the chance to evaluate the impact of nostalgia on his relatives' memories of Sicily. Poverty and the stark barrenness of the (is)landscape strike him as incongruous with the picture provided to him in Rochester. "The mythologists who placed the gates of Hades in Sicily were certainly more reliable than the memories of my Rochester relatives," he concludes (181).[20]

This first trip to Sicily also enabled Mangione to evaluate the impact of Americanness on his immigrant relatives. As for gregariousness, warmth, and conviviality, the author noted that his Sicilian relatives were certainly comparable to those living in Rochester, as a number of more or less close relatives vied to offer hospitality to the newly arrived guest. Most of the differences between the indigenous Sicilians and the immigrant ones were, according to him, accounted for by political and economic considerations, which made the "Rochester relatives . . . a more contented lot than their Sicilian counterparts" (188). However, deep down, the author concludes, there is not much difference between Sicilians and first-generation Sicilian Americans, and he adds: "The champions of the American melting-pot theory were wrong. Despite three decades of American residence, my Rochester relatives remained Sicilian to the core" (187). Challenging the long-held notion of the Anglo-Saxon character of America, Mangione understands ethnicity as a foundational aspect of American identity. In lieu of an old articulation of a monolithic and homogenous American identity, as pushed forth by the early twentieth-century supporters of the melting pot theory, Mangione was acknowledging that his specific group was among the most resistant to complete assimilation, thus proving that identities cannot be reduced to a single dimension of experience, but they are shaped as much as they are inherited.

Back in the states, Mangione continues his education in mainstream America. The end of the writer's "apprenticeship as an American" is recounted in one of the last chapters, entitled "White House Weekend." In it, the author recalls a 1944 three-day weekend spent at the Roosevelts' residence. The personal encounter with the presidential couple may very well represent the acme of the author's process of Americanization. In "A Not-So-Final Note," Mangione recaps his process of construction of a "half-and-half" identity as follows:

> I resolved [my impressions of identity] by becoming an ethnic at large, with one foot in my Sicilian heritage, the

other in the American mainstream. By this cultural gym-
nastic stance I could derive strength from my past and a
feeling of hope for my present. (369)

After eighteen years spent in a Sicilian milieu, and just as many
struggling to become part of the American mainstream, Mangione
had somehow managed to figure out just who and what he was.

Jerre Mangione is arguably the most prominent of the authors
on this side of the Atlantic whose works, although subsumed under
the broader context of American literature, have focused especially
on his ethnic experience as a Sicilian American. Betraying the principle of what has come to be known as "Hansen's Law," according
to which the son wishes to forget the legacy of his immigrant parents,[21] Mangione delved deeply into his heritage, in both his life and
works. From an interplay of first- and secondhand experiences with
Sicilianness, the author derived the sense and meaning of sicilianamericanità. For Mangione, to present himself in various occasions as
a "full-blooded Sicilian" meant to acknowledge the import that the
culture of descent had on him. His self-identification is a reflection
of both his group's efforts toward cultural preservation and a response
to what he perceived as discriminatory attitudes in both dominant
Italian and American culture. In order to correct some of the most
unfavorable prejudices, and especially the ones that originate from the
mafia, Mangione undertook to explain many aspects of the Sicilian
culture to his non-Sicilian readers. However, the question of identity
in his writings points to a complex process of representation and
self-representation, for, as an outsider to both mainstream American
and mainstream Italian cultures, Mangione elaborated on the complexities of his "half-and-half" identity. The necessity to overcome
the dual oppositions inherent in his bicultural identity led sometimes
to negotiations that, in the realm of literature, took different forms,
among which the translation of Sicilian oral storytelling tradition into
stories written on paper, for instance. Overall, the need to understand
himself led Mangione to an autobiographical exploration that was
as literary as it was ethnographic. During a conversation that took
place on his third visit to Sicily in 1965, Mangione reflected on the
fact that Sicilian culture is disappearing in the United States. "In a
couple of generations," Mangione prophesized, "there won't be any
trace of it, except for a few Sicilian names that Americans have
trouble spelling" (A Passion 102). When his non-Sicilian interlocutor

asks him whether he thinks that it is a desirable thing for Sicilians "to become like everyone else, like the Italians who live in an industrialized society" (102), the two are interrupted, and the discussion is never again resumed. Whether the prophecy will be fulfilled or not is perhaps too early to say. What Mangione has left is a space in the American literary panorama for Sicilian American authors to capitalize not only on their ethnic Italian but also on their distinctly Sicilian American voice.

"The Scum of the Scum of the Scum"

Rose Romano's Search for Sisterhood

The Negro is not the man farthest down. The condition of the coloured farmer in the most backward parts of the Southern States in America, even where he has the least education and the least encouragement, is incomparably better than the condition and opportunities of the agricultural population in Sicily.

—Booker T. Washington, *The Man Farthest Down: A Record of Observation and Study in Europe*

The discourses on ethnic identification and belonging in Ben Morreale's novels and Jerre Mangione's memoirs serve the dual purpose of problematizing any hegemonic notion of Americanness measured against Anglo-Saxon standards and challenging any monolithic configuration of Italianness. In her poetry, Rose Romano undertakes to preserve the same spirit of ethnic islandness that pervades much of the writing by Sicilian American authors. However, any exploration of sicilianamericanità becomes an even more intriguing task when issues of identity overlap with contestations of traditional gender roles, heterosexual scripts, as well as racial categorizations. In the "post–Civil Rights" and "post-feminist" early 1990s, poet and editor Romano used her queer Sicilian American woman identity to question the nationalist homophobia of American culture at large, the patriarchal and sexist Italian American way of life, and even the discriminatory practices of the lesbian publishing community toward her "race." Unlike Mangione, who considered it his responsibility as a Sicilian American to mediate between his parents and relatives' culture and American society at large, in Romano's hands, the self-ascription to the Sicilian ethnic subgroup created a discourse of sub-alternity in the United States. In the process, Romano adopted a rebellious attitude and crafted a poetic persona so idiosyncratic that she gained a reputation as the *enfant terrible* of Italian American literature. In her 2002 study of Italian American women writers, *Writing with an Accent*, critic Edvige Giunta defined Romano as "[o]ne of the most polemical figures on the Italian American literary scene in the early 1990s" (23), while Helen Barolini compared her to a "stand-up comedian" who "stresses a blue-collar past and present, writes fast and smart, and presents herself defiantly vaunting all her differences" (*The Dream Book* 48). These differences, as I will show, allegedly stem from a combination of her ethnic status in the United States, her Sicilian heritage, and her sexual orientation. Through her poetry, Romano has declared: "I'm a Sicilian-Italian-American Lesbian, / the scum of the scum of the scum, / forgotten by those who scream / in protest because they are / forgotten, / and I am neither seen nor heard" ("The Fly," *Vendetta* 40), thus portraying herself as an outsider to the Italian American community, mainstream America, and the heterosexual world. In this chapter, I explore Romano's two poetry collections, *Vendetta* (1990) and *The Wop Factor* (1994), to show how she used her Sicilian Americanness to set up a powerful critique of multiple systems of domination in tones so controversial that she ultimately turned a poetic possibility into a polemic reality. By bringing to the fore a sexualized and racialized subjecthood, Romano became the defiant troublemaker who takes an openly oppositional stance toward any form of authority or preconstituted roles.

Further, Romano's work needs to be inscribed in the complex historical and cultural climate of her time, when sexuality and sexual preferences were being acknowledged as legitimate sites of political struggle. In the early eighties, issues of gender and sexual preference intersected with the ethnic revival, and the unexpressed and repressed desires of queer women of color in the United States finally took shape with the explicit goal of overturning the historically subservient position of women in general, and multicultural lesbians in particu-lar. Chicana poet-writer-theorist Gloria Anzaldúa quickly became a spokesperson for all lesbian women-of-color. Soon after the publication in 1987 of her groundbreaking *Borderlands/La Frontera*, the metaphor of the border and the concept of *mestizaje* became widespread topoi in the articulation of theories and works of scholars in several disciplines. This self-described "dyke" was, until her untimely death in 2004, one of the leading figures of third-world feminism and lesbian theory. Anzaldúa's work, along with the works of Cherríe Moraga and Ana Castillo, to mention just two, served as a springboard for many other lesbian ethnic writers and theorists, including the Sicilian American Romano. Thanks to her poetic and publishing endeavors, Romano soon became a central figure in the newly developing field of Italian American feminist and lesbian writing, so much so that in his 1996 *Dagoes Read* Fred Gardaphé praised her as "the avant-garde of an Italian/American cultural consciousness that is ready to explode" (196). Refusing to be overwritten by heterosexist narratives, she openly embraced her ethnicity and queerness in her poetry, thus enriching the Italian American literary tradition in the same way Audre Lorde, Gloria Anzaldúa, Cherríe Moraga, Paula Gunn Allen, and others enriched the traditions of their respective ethnic groups.

Romano's ethnic quest and her notion of sicilianamericanità are informed by many factors and personal considerations. First of all, the poet argues that the adjective Italian, which is appropriately used to categorize people from the mainland, is a misleading label when applied to Sicilians. Sicily was an important overseas possession for many colonizing countries and empires. Because of Sicily's particular history of conquests and cross-cultural contacts, Romano argues that culturally—and, as I discuss later, even racially—Sicilians are markedly different from Italians from the mainland. The contestatory potential of Sicilian Americanness as a discourse in Romano's works is easy to discern when one introduces the element of choice in the poet's process of self-ascription. In fact, Romano is the daughter of an interregional couple. According to the family history, her grandparents on her father's side "were Neapolitan / nobility, owned property on the bay, named [her] / father Victor, after the king—they knew him / personally" ("Just Two More," *Vendetta* 10). Ironizing on the self-aggrandizing family mythology, the poet wonders why no adequate explanation has ever been provided to her as to the reasons that pushed this allegedly rich couple to leave their fortunes and titles—count and countess—behind in Naples to become in the United States just "two more / wops" (10). Her mother, on the other hand, was born into a family of Sicilian peasants. When the woman died prematurely, the eight-year-old Romano was left in the care of her paternal grandmother, a fact that caused a weakening of the ties with the Sicilian side of her family. In a recollection of her childhood, the poet brings out memories of how region-based hierarchies of inequality within the Italian immigrant community affected her upbringing:

> I grew up
> in a Neapolitan family,
> always silently
> defending Sicilians. . . .
> If I misbehaved
> or did something
> stupid, it was because
> I'm Sicilian.
> I don't remember
> ever doing anything
> that got me called
> Italian. I grew up
> thinking Naples
> is in Northern Italy. ("Mutt Bitch," *Vendetta* 37)

The poem suggests that a pecking order is in place within the Italian American community, which relegates Sicilians to the lowest echelon of the social ladder. In Romano's hands, this social formation serves the purpose of creating a discourse of ultimate subalternity. By portraying herself as a Sicilian American, in fact, the poet can claim a subaltern status both vis-à-vis mainstream American culture as an ethnic citizen and in relation to the Italian community as the Southerner par excellence.

Romano's poetic speculations echo the observations of Luciano Iorizzo and Salvatore Mondello in an early study of Italian immigration in the United States. In their 1971 *The Italian Americans*, calling attention to the question of interregional relations, the two scholars noted:

> Italians have had a class system which placed the northerner over the southerner and gave preeminence to the Tuscan while relegating the Sicilian to the lowest ranks.

> Neapolitans who scorned the condescending attitudes and
> actions directed against them by their northern brethren
> were just as quick in denigrating their countrymen farther
> south. Even in America, the Sicilians were ostracized by
> other Italians, who believed them to be of non-Italian and
> even savage origins. (4)

Following the unification of Italy, in fact, hierarchical distinctions
were established so that meridionali were relegated to second-class
citizenship. The industrial North had control over not only the
means of production but also of the political apparatus, while the
Mezzogiorno, with a conservative agricultural economy, hardly partici-
pated in the hegemonic projects of newborn Italy. Southern Italian
masses experienced various degrees of difficulty in participating in
the nation's economic and political life. As an island at the southernmost extreme of Italy, Sicily occupied a peripheral position in the
newborn country, and its people were looked down upon by those
both socially and geographically further up. These ranking dynamics
contributed to Romano's choice to capitalize on her Sicilian heritage
in order to portray herself as the most vulnerable Italian American
subject. In her poetry, then, sicilianamericanità reflects not only an
actual ethnic filiation, but most importantly, it signifies a conscious
act of self-politicization. Just like mestizaje is more than a biological
category, for it is the notion around which Anzaldúa constructed her
conscientized Mexican identity, in Romano's poetry, sicilianamericanità is an identity statement that bespeaks a position of subalternity.
    Romano's goal in asserting her identity in the context of a dis-
cussion about discrimination was to challenge any overly simplistic
notion of ethnicity and the history of the struggles of American ethnics. Unlike Mangione, who gave a rather edulcorated image of the
ethnic encounter between Americans and Sicilians with the goal of
eliciting sympathetic acceptance in the former and collaboration in
the latter, Romano invites everyone to remember even the most painful occurrences in the history of Sicilian immigration in the United
States. Among them, the most infamous one remains the New Orleans
lynching, which Richard Gambino, borrowing from some documents
of the time, defined in his 1977 monographic study Vendetta as "the
slaughter of eleven men by what the grand jury called 'several thousand of the first, best and even most law abiding of the citizens' of
New Orleans on March 14, 1891" (ix). Recognized as the largest

lynching in American history, according to Gambino's research, it
involved some estimated twelve to twenty thousand people against
eleven Sicilians, who were held responsible for the death of New
Orleans police superintendent David C. Hennessy. One of the youngest police chiefs in the country, Hennessy was thirty-two years old
when he was shot to death. Asked by his friend/colleague O'Connor
right before dying who had "given it to him," Hennessy reportedly
whispered "the Dagoes."

While "dago" is an ethnic slur for Italian Americans in general,
Sicilians had since 1880 arrived en masse in Louisiana to replace
black labor in the sugar and cotton plantations. In her essay "Walking
the Color Line: Italian Immigrants in Rural Louisiana 1880–1910,"
Vincenza Scarpaci calculated that "nine out of every ten immigrants
during this period were Sicilian and originated in a cluster of towns
in the central and western provinces" (68). Therefore, Hennessy was
thought to be a victim of the Sicilian vendetta. Following the murder,
many Italians were arrested, some of them with the most improbable excuses. Nineteen Italian Americans were accused of Hennessy's
murder. When six out of nineteen of the accused were acquitted, a
mass meeting was called in town "to take steps to remedy the failure of justice in the Hennessy case. Come prepared for action," the
newspaper of New Orleans warned its citizens (*Vendetta* 77). What
followed is reconstructed by Romano in her poem "Dago Street" with
an abundance of details and angry emphasis:

> Six Italians were shot,
> Their bodies ripped apart, by sixty
> men, white and black alike. In
> the pile of bodies, Monasterio's hand
> twitched. Someone came close, aimed,
> and shot away the top of
> Monasterio's head. Someone
> laughed. One Italian was shot
> in the head. One was hit in his
> right eye by a shotgun blast, half
> his head blown away. One was
> shot in the head, his right hand
> blown away when he raised it
> to defend himself, the top of his
> head gone; he waited nine hours

to die. Two Italians were shot.
Only half dead, they were brought
outside, tossed overhead by the
crowd to the other end of the
street, and were hanged, and were shot,
and were left hanging to be viewed. (*The Wop Factor* 21)

Romano does not sacrifice descriptive accuracy at the altar of
poetic prudery and the assault is recounted in all its cruelty. The prosy
nature of the poem signals the poet's intention to convey a clear message and to deprive it of any metric sophistication that could alter
its immediacy. To Romano, the act of remembering such instances
of discrimination in the history of Italian immigration in the United
States is not a pointless poetic exercise. Rather, to overlook, or, worse
still, forget such an atrocious episode as the New Orleans lynching is
equal to the reperpetration of the crime.

However, although Romano's poetry contributes to the discursive creation of a distinct Sicilian American consciousness, or
sicilianamericanità, it also challenges it at its very core. In fact, as
a Sicilian American, the poet is particularly aware of the culturally
disruptive potential of her lesbian identity, insofar as it threatens the
all-too-important social institution of the family. In his 1912 study *Il
popolo siciliano, la famiglia e la casa*,[1] scholar of folklore Giuseppe Pitrè
described the role of *la famiglia* in Sicilian culture and the place that
women occupy within it as follows:

> Sicilians have a very strong sense of the family. Within
> it, the father exercises the absolute government, and his
> power is undiscussed; the mother governs the house, by
> serving its interests and commanding the children through
> the authority bestowed on her by her husband, whom she
> loves and respects even when he does not deserve it. (29)[2]

The woman, Pitrè continued, "sacrifices herself fully [to her husband],
both her life and her services, which no one can match, as much as
nothing can compare to her love for her children: *a mother's love, and
a wife's service*" (29).[3] A woman's self-actualization was thus supposed
to be attained within the boundaries of the family, exhausted in the
two roles of wife and mother. Romano draws from her personal experience as a "Sicilian-Italian-American Lesbian" to denounce the stifling

expectations of the family, which force homosexuals to disguise their sexual identity in order to fulfill traditional gender roles.

Interestingly, though, Romano's Sapphic poems are rarely explicitly sexual. Hardly ever does she explore the various aspects of lesbian physical love, a fact that might suggest that, despite her outspokenness and the provocative imagery and language of her poetry, sexual taboos might still be an issue Romano did not manage to resolve in the literary realm. In "Over the Edge," a poem included in *Vendetta*, the poet shyly crafts her lesbian poetics by focusing on the emotional and sexual turmoil she experienced when her lover's breasts accidentally emerged from her blouse during a serious conversation. But the most explicit stanza on the theme of lesbian eroticism in Romano's poetic production is one that graphically celebrates the abundance of flesh and culinary appetite in connection with lesbian eroticism as follows: "Sweet creases where her bellies meet, / run my tongue along them. / Caressing, moist, her bellies suck my / tongue and I am dizzy" (*Vendetta*, "And She Laughs" 20). As the poem proceeds, though, the focus shifts away from the initial emphasis on Sapphic erotica to focus on the lover's relationship with food. This reticence again suggests that while issues of ethnic identity and gender are relatively easier to deal with in poetry, the dominant heteropatriarchal order is much more problematic and difficult to oppose in verse.

In fact, while Romano's poetry celebrates pride in her lesbian identity, it especially explores its challenges. Be she a lesbian from Bensonhurst, shouting profanities to a bunch of men hitting on her in the streets; or a femme from the Lower East Side, strolling along Second Avenue; or a butch from the Village, who thinks about the traditional Italian Sunday dinner she is about to have, where she will carry "to the head of the table / not only the endurance of the Grandmother / but also the will of the Grandfather"; Romano proudly proclaims that "there is nothing in this world as wonderful / as an Italian American Lesbian" in a poem by the same title (*The Wop Factor* 55). Her poetic imagination also brings forth imagery of utopian lesbian communities, such as the one described in "To Show Respect." In this poem, a group of Italian American lesbians enjoys a most complete Italian American menu. Sipping "deep red wine / made in the cellar," Romano's women start their meal with *antipasti* ("black olives / stuffed green olives, marinated olives, / salami, provolone, mozzarella dipped in / bread crumbs and fried, mushrooms dipped in / breadcrumbs and fried, scungilli dipped in / bread crumbs and fried") and go on to enjoy several *primi piatti* ("Escarole soup, / spaghetti, ravioli, lasagna, linguine, baked / ziti, stuffed shells, like vulvas, oozing / ricotta"), before moving on to *secondi piatti* ("Meatballs, / sausage, veal, lamb"), traditional Italian *dolci* (*cannoli*), and, finally, "espresso in tiny cups" (*Vendetta* 22–24). To be sure, food is a traditional topos in Italian American writings, but "Romano's tavola," Giunta observes, "is undeniably not a traditional one, for gay and lesbian Italian American have not quite negotiated their seat at the Italian American table" (*Writing with an Accent* 106). Therefore, Romano's poetic project focuses particularly on the difficulties engendered by her sexuality and the institutional and cultural homophobia that pressures lesbians to perform a heterosexual act to avoid ostracism and discrimination. In "Coming Out Unnoticed," for example, Romano recalls a meeting she once had with a best friend from her teenage years. Acknowledging that, as a girl, she felt an early attraction to her friend, she painfully remembers how difficult it was to claim a lesbian identity even back at a time when "[t]he only thing better than / a large number of lovers was / a great variety of lovers" (*Vendetta* 18). When she finally concedes to her friend that she has had it with men, the poet still prefers to "come out unnoticed," by letting her friend take the statement "as one of those jokes / that introduces the long / tender moaning of straight women / complaining about their own / true loves" (15), thus complying with dominant cultural demands on women and self-sabotaging her empowerment as a feminist and a lesbian. In her 1994 polemical essay "Where Is Nella Sorellanza When You Really Need Her?" the poet confesses she came out of the closet at the age of thirty (148). Before that time, though, she too had been a victim of—to use Adrienne Rich's famous formulation—the "compulsory heterosexuality" of her community, as proved by her own marriage. Romano's first collection of poems, *Vendetta*, is also dedicated to her daughter, with a bittersweet explanation that leaves no room for doubt as to the poet's degree of awareness of the familial expectations of Italian American culture: "to Megan, my daughter, for proving I can do what's necessary."

By finally coming out, Romano was not only coming to terms with her own personal sexual identity, but she was also entering the dialogue of ethnic lesbians who adamantly refused to be placed at the bottom of the social hierarchy by a heteronormative culture. In her introduction to the 1996 collection of essays by Italian American lesbians and gays, *Fuori*, critic Mary Jo Bona notes how, for many,

> coming out as gay or lesbian is a process of discovery and
> recovery, not only of their sexual selves, but of their rela-
> tionship to more than one family: to the Italian/American
> family reconstituted; and to a community of gays and
> lesbians, to which there are varying degrees of loyalty and
> connection. ("Gorgeous Identities" 4–5)

However, Romano's relationship with the multicultural lesbian community was fraught with difficulties and conflicting feelings. The
disagreements between them especially revolved around the concept
of race, and, consequently, of racial hierarchies, a discussion that
Romano used to compare her oppression and experience to other
multiethnic and multiracial lesbians.

According to the poet, in fact, Sicilians are a racially defined
group as they do not belong to the Aryan stock of Northern Italians.
Claiming to fit uncomfortably into the generally accepted "white"
versus "of color" racial bipolarization in the United States, Romano
attempts to add one more nuance to the palette, namely, "olive."
Always in her poetry as well as in her polemical essays, Romano
speaks of/from her olive lesbian identity, so much so that, borrowing the definition from Noel Ignatiev and John Garvey, Gardaphé
defines her—along with several other Italian American writers—as
a "race traitor" for being "militant in her attempt to avoid being
white" (Leaving Little Italy 133). What this olive-ness means exactly,
the poet tried to explain in "Permission–Two Friends" in the collection Vendetta. The poem is an attempt to resignify dominant modes
of understanding racial categories in the form of a dialogue between
the poet, who defends her racialized identity and a friend who challenges it:

> you can't say
> Italians are people
> of color. I never
> said that. I said
> Southern Italians
> and Sicilians
> are Olive,
> neither white
> nor of color. But,
> she explained,

you can't say
Italy is a third
world country.
I never said that.
I said Southern Italy and Sicily are as
poor as some third world countries. She said,
well, that's true. But you can't say it. (33)

In Romano's poetry, olive-ness becomes one of the defining aspects of her Sicilian American identity. On the basis of this racialized and sexualized sicilianamericanità, the poet attempted to build allegiances and solidarities inside and outside her ethnic community.

To be sure, Romano is not the only Sicilian American writer to claim a racialized identity. Maria Famà, for example, echoes Romano's theme in a poem tellingly entitled "I Am Not White." Originated from an apparently real event in the poet's life, the poem speaks proudly of a hybrid identity: "The dentist says my teeth tell of inva-sions / mixed blood / the tale of a proud, mongrel people / I am Sicilian / I am not white / I will not check the box for white / on any form" (*Mystics in the Family* 14). In "Hail Mary," Rosette Capotorto joins the discussion by pointing to the power that painful memories of a racialized identity can have to cure the historical amnesia of racist Italian Americans:

My mother is black I say and the
room goes silent. A simple way
to halt racist talk
My mother is black.
Dark hair, dark skin, long legs. Terrono
Sicilian is Black is African.
Africani/Siciliani they chant
under my window.
The Black Madonna del Tindari
Lives around the corner.
Sicilians have a lot of explaining to do. (Painter and
    Capotorto, "Italiani/Africani 250–251)

Also, in her reflection "Black Madonna," Ronnie Mae Painter opens up a more complex discussion on racial issues, which is informed by her biracial identity.[4] As the daughter of an African

American father and a Sicilian mother, Painter shows the arbitrariness of any definition of race by focusing on the crucial role played by perspectives:

> My mother is white but only to me.
> She's Italian American not black like me
> My black friends say she's white
> So what else could she be
> Other white folks say hell no
> You're Italian American from Sicily
> So we all look in the mirror
> My brothers and sisters to see
> If we're really black or really white
> Or from Sicily? (250)

The questions formulated by Painter at the end of her poem call attention to the arbitrariness of racial designations and demarcations. The lines between U.S. and Italian history are blurred and overlap in matters of social inequalities and discrimination.

In certain respects, with regard to some discourses circulating first in Italy and then in the United States, Romano's discussion on racial identity is not entirely farfetched. The racialization of Southern Italians, in fact, is rooted in the nefarious doctrines of racial superiority disseminated in Italy by the School of Positivist Criminology of Cesare Lombroso, Alfredo Niceforo, Giuseppe Sergi, Enrico Ferri, and others. At the end of the nineteenth and beginning of the twentieth centuries, these sociologists and criminologists claimed that anthropological differences between the "Germanic" Northern Italians and the "African" Southerners accounted for the superior civilization of the former and the barbarity of the latter. In the United States, where racial distinctions were much sharper than in Italy, the discourses on the genetic inferiority of Southern Italians found a fertile environment and provided a rationale for discrimination of newly arrived immigrants. Among the early ethnic slurs hurled at Italians that Richard Gambino surveys in his 1974 *Blood of My Blood*, "black guinea" and "black dago" speak volumes about the early racialization of Italian immigrants in the United States (98–99). Among them, Sicilians especially felt the sting of racial prejudice. In her 1994 essay "Sorelle delle Ombre," Roseanne Quinn discusses issues of racism and homophobia in contemporary Italian American women's literature, and she recalls:

> I was taught that Sicilians were not really Italian because they gave *malocchio*, they were in the Mafia, they weren't white like we were. . . . I did not understand why my family called our Sicilian neighbors 'Black Italians' until I understood that they were saying essentially the same things about African Americans. (237)

Most likely because of the island's geographical propinquity as well as its historical ties with Africa, Sicilians, arguably more than any other Italian regional group, were often racially associated with their African neighbors.[5]

However, at the time when Romano was bringing forth her discourse on olive-ness, Italian Americans as an ethnic group had already benefited from the realignment of racial divisions in the United States and made the figurative leap into "whiteness." Therefore, the poet's endorsement of a discourse of perpetual olive-ness hardly seems like a viable political program for the Italian American community at large. The racial ambiguity of the Italian American past, though, is particularly significant as it reveals in all its strength the bigotry of designated racial identities. Particularly apropos in this sense are historian Rudolph Vecoli's observations. Addressing an Italian American audience in 1994, Vecoli pointed out: "Our experience has taught us the fallacy of the very idea of race and the mischief of racial labels. . . . For these reasons, we, Italian Americans, have something important to contribute to the national dialogue" ("Are Italian Americans Just White Folks?" 17). Seen from this perspective, Romano's politics of identity has the merit of pointing to the shifting meanings of race in different historical contexts and therefore exposing the socially constructed nature of race-based categories.[6]

Romano approached the multicultural lesbian community to resignify the term "of color" so as to encompass the experience of a self-styled olive Sicilian-Italian-American lesbian. In fact, her poetry initially appeared in important publications of the time, such as the now-defunct Iowa-based quarterly journal *Common Lives/Lesbian Lives*, Buffalo's semiannual *Earth's Daughters*, *SageWoman*, and the *South Coast Poetry Journal*, among others. However, she soon discovered the bitter taste of rejection when editors explained to her that the comparison between Italian Americans and people of color was not appropriate. "I have been censored in the lesbian press and ostracized in the lesbian community because I call myself Olive," she lamented in a talk she gave at the 1989 American Italian Historical Association conference ("Coming Out Olive" 161). Romano questioned the coalitional politics of the multicultural lesbian community, where identity was assessed through the place occupied in what she calls the "hierarchy of pain" (161). According to this categorization, the poet continues, "[a]s the skin colour of members of other races and ethnicities becomes lighter and lighter, those races and ethnicities are considered to have suffered less and less. Therefore, the lighter one's skin, the less respect one is entitled to" (161). Romano goes on to explain that "far more important than literary merit to a lesbian editor is the extent to which a lesbian writer has suffered from oppression. . . . It's racist for lesbian literary journals to give space to light-skinned women when they might have given space to dark-skinned women" (165). In the racial classification adopted by the lesbian publishing community, Romano was assigned a position of privilege for being white. She was, therefore, expected to sit elbow to elbow with the white oppressors, with whom she supposedly shared the burden of historical, cultural, and social responsibilities. In other words, the equal opportunities advocated by her fellow *sisters* or *hermanas* did not, in fact, apply to her, an olive woman, looking for *sorelle*.

The paradox within the lesbian community was too self-evident to Romano to go unnoticed: a movement of ideological opposition, which supported the positions of a wide array of ethnic minorities, stubbornly persisted in an attitude that tended to silence her, a Sicilian American woman—or olive—and asked her to disregard part of her heritage. Unable and unwilling to carry a WASP past on her shoulders, the poet promoted the recovery of a legacy she felt like she was expected to negate:

> They tell her the past
> is passed, why think of
> pain all the time, didn't
> the immigrants come to
> America to get away
> from the pain. They tell her
> to forget the pain of

prejudice, forget the pain
of lynchings, forget the
pain of denial and of being
denied respect. ("Wop Talk," *The Wop Factor* 41)

In Romano's poetry, cultural and ethnic pride are juxtaposed to the homogenizing expectations of those who remind her how easy it is for Italian Americans to pass and also to the chameleonic attitude of those Italian Americans she calls "wuppies," who "drop the vowels from / their names. They've / lightened up their heritage / and them-selves. They / cook pasta by American / recipes, laugh at wop / jokes, and never complain" ("Wop Talk," *The Wop Factor* 43–44). To claim one's whiteness in light of the recent achievements in social mobility of Italian Americans, in Romano's view, means to sweep under the carpet a not-too-distant past of discrimination and injustices. "In this time of lesbian feminist multiculturalism," the poet bitterly concludes, "some of us are more multi than others" ("The Drop of a Hat," *The Wop Factor* 10).

Unabashed by the ostracism she experienced within the multi-cultural lesbian publishing community, and in order to turn the col-lective literary efforts of Italian American women into a legitimate site of struggle, in 1988 Romano founded her own literary journal, *la bella figura*, and malafemmina press, which produced a series of chap-books of poetry, including her own two volumes, namely, *Vendetta* and *The Wop Factor*. The latter title is especially striking as it includes a derogatory slur commonly used against Southern Italians. The use of self-disparaging definitions and ethnic slurs—among which "the scum of the scum of the scum," "mutt bitch," "wop," and "dyke"—is one of the strategies adopted by Romano to reclaim historically harmful hate speech, deprive it of its disparaging potential, and eventually appropri-ate it as an expression of pride. In her poem "Wop Factor," Romano wittily explains that while pondering how to improve her self-pub-lishing operations, she eventually resolved that what was needed was an increased literary density, which would make her journal heavy enough to produce a metaphorical "WOP" sound when tossed on the table. "So I've been thinking about that / a lot," she writes,

and I think maybe
la bella figura
should be enhanced

> by the wop factor—
> we want that extra weight—
> prose of substance,
> good and heavy poetry
> and when you slap us down
> we make noise. ("The Wop Factor" 24)

About the wop factor, Mary Jo Bona aptly points out, "The importance, then, of 'wop talk,' is to make it clear that Italian Americans do, indeed, have a culture, one that must and will be talked about" ("Learning to Speak Doubly" 166). Bona also underscores Romano's role in creating and securing a deeper degree of collaboration among Italian American women writers. Romano's message, Bona argues, is clear: "whether we are Italians, Sicilians, or lesbians (or all three designations, which the poet would claim), we cannot afford to be silent, thereby implicitly allowing others—the old culture and the new—to interpret and define our behavior" (*By the Breath* 168). Acknowledging the fact that "[i]t's not easy being an angry poet / when you come from a culture / whose most profound statement of anger / is silence" ("Mutt Bitch," *Vendetta* 37), Romano understood that only by speaking up and writing down their stories can Italian American women become effective agents of resistance and change. If praxis had to be developed, the voices of Italian American women needed to be structured around a new philosophy of *sorellanza*—or "sisterhood"—through the creation of common forums of discussion. Even though both the journal and the press were short lived, thanks to these publishing platforms, Romano helped to build a sense of community, artistic support, and identity necessary to turn the collective literary efforts of Italian American women into a legitimate site of struggle.

In the Italian American literary panorama, feminist-lesbian-editor-writer-poet Rose Romano is one of the descendants of Sicilian immigrants who have especially informed their works with a sense of sicilianamericanità, or Sicilian Americanness. At the core of sicilianamericanità as it surfaces in Romano's confessional poetry is a process of identity construction built upon essentialist grounds that pushes her to rewrite the position of Sicilians in both the Italian and the U.S. contexts in exceptionalist terms. Romano's sicilianamericanità has a subversive potential that serves to denaturalize dominant constructions of national identity, traditional gender roles, and sexed poetic expressions. Romano's legacy goes beyond the immediate horizon of the Italian American community as her experience as a Sicilian American lesbian exposes heterocentric biases, the socially constructed nature of notions of ethnicity and race, and the arbitrariness of hierarchies of oppression in any shape or form. Through the trope of "the scum of the scum of the scum," Romano questioned all kinds of mutually exclusive categories of identification, because dualisms and dichotomies such as (hetero) men versus (hetero) women, Italian versus American, and "of color" versus white do not take into account the complexities of a multifaceted identity such as that of a Sicilian American lesbian. Even if her participation in the multicultural lesbian writing scene of the late 1980s and 1990s was short lived and, at the end, restricted in scope, the seminal work of this self-styled "Sicilian-Italian-American lesbian" poet has served, and will continue to serve, the purpose of encouraging the efforts of women writers to challenge existing discourses and assert their own particular diversity and distinctiveness.

Once upon a Place

Gioia Timpanelli and the
Sicilian Storytelling Tradition

No man is an Iland, intire of itselfe;
every man is a peece of the Continent,
a part of the maine.

— John Donne, "Meditation XVII"

Arrigordatinni la nanna,
ca poi quannu si' bedda granni,
sti cunti li cunti tu.

— Elisabetta Sanfratello quoted in Giuseppe Pitrè's
1875 *Fiabe, novelle e racconti popolari*, vol. 1

The process of preservation and reelaboration of a distinctly Sicilian
ethnic heritage that characterizes the writings of Jerre Mangione,
Ben Morreale, and Rose Romano also informs the works of Gioia
Timpanelli. Like Romano and several other Sicilian American wom-
en writers, principles of feminism influence Timpanelli's discourse on
sicilianamericanità. However, unlike Romano, who shows a more
reactive than proactive approach toward traditional gender roles,
Timpanelli's strategy to resist and subvert the predominant male-oriented culture involves a unique recovery of traditional Sicilian and
Western oral tales with a modern American feminist twist. In the

1930s, Mangione had already underscored the importance of these "marvelous tales" ("Remembrances and Impressions" 52), stories, and legends to provide the American-born children with a sense of Sicilian peoplehood. Timpanelli extends these claims by initiating a textual recovery of ancient Sicilian storytelling with influences that reach well beyond the island's shores and the American borders. In this chapter, I focus on Timpanelli's written work by analyzing her 1998 *Sometimes the Soul: Two Novellas of Sicily*. This book is a perfect example of how some seemingly provincial tales of insular Sicilian life bear the hallmark of timeless and spaceless pieces and help to build bridges between people, cultures, and literatures across generations.

Hailed by some as the dean of storytelling in the United States, the Sicilian American Timpanelli was part of a multifarious group that included authors, folklorists, mythologists, performers, and poets who, during the late 1960s and 1970s, initiated the revival of story-telling in the wake of a renewed interest in the folk arts.[1] Therefore, Timpanelli's work is mostly oral, in the form of performances in parks and cemeteries, appearances on public television, storytelling work-shops and seminars all around the world, broadcasts, and poetry and dramatic readings. As a storytelling practitioner, in 1987 Timpanelli received the prestigious Women's National Book Association Award in recognition of her indefatigable work in popularizing the oral tradi-tion. But despite her success, not much has been written about this author, especially outside the field of Italian American studies. In fact, the art of storytelling in general has received scant attention in schol-arly discussions. During a 2004 Storytelling, Self, Society conference held in Boca Raton, Florida, Jo Radner observed that "unlike drama, music, film, or dance, storytelling has not yet developed either a criti-cal vocabulary or a secure footing in academic scholarship" (Radner et al., "Visions for Storytelling Studies" 8). Many of the papers pre-sented at that conference explored the relationship, or lack thereof, between the art of storytelling and its scholarly criticism and academic study. However, many Italian American critics regard Timpanelli as an influential Italian American woman author who has successfully managed to raise the oral tradition to literary status. For instance, in her 2002 critical study *Writing with an Accent*, Edvige Giunta writes:

> Gioia Timpanelli's invaluable work on folk tales, particularly
> on those from Sicily and Southern Italy, which she revital-
> izes in her spellbinding storytelling, constitutes yet another

facet of a large project of cultural excavation, affirmation, and reinvention of cultural origins and identity undertaken by Italian American women authors. (31)

Timpanelli's sicilianamericanità attempts to capture the core of universality in wildly different cultural experiences, and the revitalization of old Sicilian folktales is what makes her work especially important for a study of the construction of a Sicilian ethnic discourse in the United States.

As much as the oral medium is Timpanelli's preferred means of communication, it did not take this natural-born storyteller long to translate these stories into written words.[2] Timpanelli recalled in a 2011 interview with Lisa Grove for the *California Journal of Poetics* that

> the transition to fiction came during a similar moment of realization after years of storytelling. While translating a folk tale from Sicilian into English, the sentence which begins *Sometimes the Soul* just came to me. I wrote it down, and I knew it was not a translation, but rather I had written the beginning of a piece of fiction. I began to write fiction spontaneously, and I have never stopped.[3]

In fact, Timpanelli's first attempt to publish stories from the oral tradition was the 1984 *Tales from the Roof of the World: Folktales of Tibet*, a short book that targeted young readers with its four tales about faith and superstition, which she "retold" in written form. The beautiful illustrations by Elizabeth Kelly Lockwood that accompany the book complement the exotic Tibetan setting. Everything conjures up a quasi-magical atmosphere for young American readers to enjoy, and the supernatural element is introduced in the form of, among others, a magic necklace and a speaking horse. All in all, though, the oral antecedent overburdens this collection. In a review of the book, Dorothea Hayward Scott pointed out that "all of the stories are unusual enough to hold attention but some more critical readers may find the endings of the first two stories somewhat inconsequential" (124). In another review published anonymously in the *Bulletin of the Center for Children's Books*, the author of the review lamented that the four folktales are "rather lengthy and sometimes rambling" (17). The stories per se are more or less original—in fact, the first two had already been translated into English from Tibetan—and the retelling is not always compelling, but this book represents Timpanelli's first real attempt at establishing a connection between the spoken word and the written one.

Not long after her first written storytelling experiment, Timpanelli turned to her own personal treasure trove of stories for inspiration, and her interest in Sicilian *cunti*, or stories, brought her to study the tradition in a more formal way. In the introduction to his 1956 *Fiabe italiane*, Italo Calvino pointed out: "It is generally accepted that Italian tales from the oral tradition were recorded in literary works long before those from any other country" (*Italian Folktales* xv). In fact, Italy's written folk tradition includes works such as the 1555 Decameron-inspired *Le piacevoli notti* (*The Facetious Nights of Straparola*) by Giovanni Francesco Straparola, a collection of seventy-five folk and fairy tales, and Giambattista Basile's *Lo cunto de li cunti* (*The Tale of Tales*), aka *Pentamerone*, which appeared posthumously between 1634 and 1636. These publications preceded the works of most other famous European folktale collectors, such as the French Charles Perrault and the German Brothers Grimm. As for Sicily, Calvino himself singled out the island, along with Tuscany, for its "choicest selection, both in terms of quantity and quality" (xxvi). In 1870, Swiss folklorist Laura von Gonzenbach published *Sicilianische Märchen*, the first collection of the precious array of oral stories from Sicily, translated by the author from Sicilian into literary German. However, the most systematic collection of the many folktales of the island in its dialect(s) is folklorist Giuseppe Pitrè's 1875 *Fiabe, novelle e racconti popolari* (*Sicilian Fables, Stories and Popular Tales*), a collection of Sicilian *cunti* that make up four out of the twenty-five volumes of the *Biblioteca delle tradizioni popolari siciliane* (*The Library of Sicilian Folk Traditions*).[4] In this monumental research project, compiled between 1871 and 1913, the Palermo-born physician with a passion for lore, with the help of some friends, collected traditional oral pieces from the voice of the people of forty-six different towns in Sicily. The result is a work that rivals that of the Brothers Grimm in importance by gathering all aspects of the traditions and customs of the Sicilian people and by transcribing its large body of vernacular stories, tales, prayers, legends, nursery rhymes, and proverbs, which were meant to educate, inform, and entertain the subaltern classes.

Timpanelli's scholarly research drew from these antecedents, but it also intersected and overlapped with her personal life. The writer explained:

Storytelling is a varied form. In Sicily, for example, there were two kinds of oral tellers: the *novellatore/novellatrice* and the *cantastorie*. A *novellatrice* like my great-grandmother told stories at home or close to home. I think of these as hearth tellers. It was they who told the old folk or fairy-tales. The *cantastorie* used more obvious forms of poetry and appeared in large gatherings to recite the communal or social history of Sicily. The *cantastorie* told the larger epics from the Middle Ages, the Knights of Roland. ("Visions for Storytelling Studies" 15).

In an environment in which formal education and book learning were privileges bestowed upon a few, *novellatori* and *cantastorie* were keepers of the Sicilian collective memory and, therefore, helped shape the Sicilian character. Thanks to her grandmother, a hearth teller, the American-born Timpanelli was trained in the Sicilian language and acquainted with a large body of traditional oral narratives from the island. Through these stories, Timpanelli came to know the place where she can trace both her origins and inspiration. Finally, fourteen years after the Tibetan experiment, in 1998, Timpanelli published *Sometimes the Soul: Two Novellas of Sicily*.

The book is introduced by a reflection on life that is placed before the first of the two novellas, A *Knot of Tears*, and gives meaning to the book's title:

Sometimes the soul is tested. The body feels sore, the mouth dumb, the big red hands hang useless on their arms. Time passes. Surely, the soul will have its way. It lolls. Time passes. And the soul waits. Nothing happens. . . . Then, one day, it gets up and stretches. Today is not like yesterday. The soul notes the difference. . . . Finally, now, the soul lifts its arms and with its graceful hands brings down the fertile rain. (13–14)

The lethargy of the soul and its subsequent awakening fore-shadow the stirring up of Costanza, the protagonist of the book's first novella, after a long period of emotional slumber. The awakening of the soul in the introductory pages is perfectly rendered by the soul's stretching and, especially, by the metaphor of the "fertile rain" (14). The theme of rebirth is again announced with a black and white reproduction of Botticelli's *Primavera*, one of the allegories of fertility par excellence in the pictorial world. A *Knot of Tears* reinforces the importance of storytelling as an art that regenerates itself and, also, as an empowering resource that can educate and liberate women by making them mindful of their history, conditions, and traditions. Going against the common representation of Sicily as a conservative and backward-looking society, in Timpanelli's first novella the island is the backdrop for a feminist lesson in transnational female self-empowerment, a message that speaks volumes of the variety of experiences that characterize sicilianamericanità.

A *Knot of Tears* takes place in Palermo, most likely at the beginning of the twentieth century within a week in June, between a Sunday and the following Saturday. In this story-within-a-story, a parrot entertains the lady of the house by telling her stories with the ulterior goal of keeping her from getting out and meeting another man. A reader familiar with Sicilian folklore will immediately note the resemblance to the second story Giuseppe Pitrè included in his collection *Fiabe, novelle e racconti popolari*, namely, "Lu pappagaddu chi cunta tri cunti," or "The Parrot with Three Tales to Tell." Pitrè himself recognized in his tale the matrix of a much earlier collection originally written in Sanskrit, the *Śuka Saptati*, or *The Seventy Tales of a Parrot*. He also acknowledged that many variants of the three stories might be found, both as a whole and separately, with more or less important differences that have crept in through the normal process of oral retelling (*Fiabe, novelle* I:13). The basic storyline in all major versions is the same and is listed under tale-type number 1422 of the Aarne-Thompson-Uther classification, "Parrot Reports Wife's Adultery" (Zipes and Russo 807).[5] The typical device of this folktale, the *mise en abyme*, is amplified in the novella: through an unknown narrator, the author Timpanelli is telling a tale that contains three tales told by a parrot, which had already been written by Pitrè who, in turn, heard the story from quilt-maker by profession and storyteller by passion Agatuzza Messia, who heard it from someone else, and so on. A comparison between Pitrè's *cuntu* and Timpanelli's novella shows how, from the mouth of a Sicilian *novellatrice* to the pen of a Sicilian American author, these stories have made the leap from the island to the United States, and they have become part of the American literary scene bearing the hallmark of sicilianamericanità.

In both the Sicilian and the Sicilian American versions, a lady, the *Signura*, is locked in a house. However, in Pitrè's tale, the woman's husband locks her in upon her suggestion while he is out of town.

"Gather all the provisions I might need, and lock me inside. Have all the doors and windows nailed, except for one window high up, and then put a basket there with a wheel and pulley for me. Once you do all this, you can leave without worrying" (Zipes and Russo 37), she suggests in an effort to reassure her husband of her faithfulness and love. Since her first appearance, Timpanelli's Costanza, on the other hand, strikes the reader as a different and more modern kind of woman. Costanza is not married and has chosen to live in voluntary seclusion for reasons that are not explicitly stated. However, the seeds of change are within her as the reader learns that she "is an egg resting patiently, a snail waiting for water, a safe cocoon" (28). In other words, Costanza's soul is ready to awaken.

In both stories, a *cammarera*, or faithful maid, accompanies the woman. While Pitrè's servant has no name, Timpanelli's Agata is a fully developed character, who even shows signs of feminist consciousness when she confesses that she "enjoyed being a spinster, not compromising her sovereignty in her own home" (27). Agata is also a very sympathetic character whose joy of life, wisdom, and matter-of-factness easily invite identification. For instance, regarding Costanza's state of self-seclusion, Agata wonders:

> And the *Signura*, poor creature, what good could come from never seeing people? Never going out for a little walk, a *passeggiata*? The poor thing had turned their lives inside out by this strange behavior. Whatever this game was, it had gone too far. What benefit could come from being without good company? (26)

As a non-protagonist main character, Agata assists Costanza during this important week, at the end of which the lady will eventually be ready to "begin a new journey" (91).

In both Pitrè's and Timpanelli's versions, what sounds like a panic attack will set off a chain of events that will forever change the lady's life. Costanza, in fact, suddenly feels what the narrator defines as "an overwhelming oppression and an unfamiliar knot of tears welled up in her chest" (*Sometimes the Soul* 18). This "knot of tears," which gives the novella its title, turns out to be what Costanza needed to awake from her emotional slumber:

> It was as though she was waiting for some whisper from God. She had waited and waited, and then without warning

> it had finally come but it was not as soft as a whisper. It
> was from the painful knot of tears, the *gruppu di chiantu*,
> that this entire part of her life would find its meaning. (29)

The symptoms of suffocation bring the servant to open a high window
so that the lady can breathe more easily. And that is when, from the
corso below the window, two men, a gentleman and a lawyer, catch
sight of the lady; they both fall in love with her, and they bet on
who can get to talk to her first.

What happens next is a crucial moment in the tale. Here, Pitrè's
version and Timpanelli's diverge. In fact, according to the *cuntu* that
the seventy-something-year-old Agatuzza Messia from Palermo, the
most talented of Pitrè's storytellers, gave the physician, the lawyer
proceeds to sell his soul to the *virsèriu*, or the devil, who turns him
into a parrot. The lawyer-turned-bird flies into the house through the
window and, once inside, keeps the lady away from his rival by telling
her stories. In Timpanelli's novella, on the other hand, the "beautiful
bright green parrot" (21) that flies through the open window into
Costanza's house is a real bird belonging to a storyteller in flesh and
bones: the Sicilian sailor Edmundo Patanè. When the bird flies in,
Costanza and Agata enjoy the diversion and plan to keep it in the
house. Lady Costanza suggests they put him in a beautiful cage: "Find
the cage, Agata, that great big one. Be sure it's the large silver one,"
she tells her maid. The pragmatic Agata retorts: "Oh, yes, yes, the
silver one, but to tell you the truth, *Signura*, cages are cages. . . . Ask
those who are caught and put in them whether they see gold, silver,
bamboo, or walls" (23–24). Outside the house, the lawyer strikes a
deal with Edmundo: he will pay the sailor to get Costanza out of
the house with the excuse of claiming his parrot. Meanwhile, the
gentleman has made his own arrangements with an actress, whom
he hires to entice Lady Costanza out of the house under the pretext
of taking her to church.

However, both men's plans fail. When Edmundo the sailor,
working on behalf of the lawyer, shows up at the door to claim the
parrot, Costanza invites him in for coffee. The two and Agata sit
down to sip their coffee and talk, and a bond starts to form: "It was
all so familiar somehow, like a family's Sunday together. . . . And
because of this feeling, it was agreed that Edmundo would stay and
help them put away the provisions in the storerooms" (46). As for
the gentleman's plan, when the actress shows up at the door, the par-

rot starts plucking his own feathers and requests a story. The urge to listen to a story is too hard to resist, and Costanza apologizes to the auntie/actress and shows her out. Edmundo arrives and volunteers to tell "an old folktale he had heard from his great-grandmother" (54), just like Timpanelli herself had heard the tale.

The Sicilian formula "*Si cunta e si ricunta*," or "it is told and retold" (24), which is used by Edmundo at the beginning of every story reminds the readers that what they are about to read is *not* the creative written act of an individual but part of a collective oral Sicilian inheritance. Timpanelli is thus abjuring the role of the "author" in the modern traditional sense to assume that of one of the countless and anonymous *novellatrici* who were once the listeners and later became the tellers. In fact, the traditional Sicilian folktale as heard and transcribed in dialect by the folklorist Pitrè and its Sicilian American version written in English by Timpanelli converge again, more faithfully than ever, in the recounting of the three tales of the parrot. Except for a few adjustments to facilitate the comprehension of the American public, Timpanelli's version of all three *cunti* is a translation of Pitrè's from Sicilian into English.

This novella can be divided in two parts, of which one is a frame that contains the parrot's tales and the other one consists of the tales themselves. A lot can be said about the parallelisms between the inner stories—the parrot's tales—and the frame that contains them, and, in the end, the three *cunti* have a strong impact on Costanza's decision to end her seclusion. However, the novella's Boccaccio-esque *cornice*, or the framing part that is original to the author, offers a most intriguing view of the interplay of yesterday and today, of Americanness and Sicilianness. In fact, as a social document, Timpanelli's *cornice* reflects and portrays a culture and a worldview that are very different from the end-of-the-nineteenth-century Sicilian environment in which Pitrè's storyteller Agatuzza Messia lived. Costanza's costumes and thoughts are more in line with those of a liberated and educated twentieth-century American woman. As it turns out, the two apparently conflicting models work quite well in concert to create a unique framework for the Sicilian ethnic experience(s) in the United States.

A deeper look at Costanza's life and behavior helps the reader realize how different things were once upon a time and once upon a place. In fact, in Palermo in the late 1800s, it might have been not only admissible but even laudable for a woman to suggest that her husband lock her up while he is away for work, which is what the "good wife" does in the Sicilian version of the folktale collected by Pitrè. Timpanelli's Costanza, on the other hand, is a modern heroine with feminist leanings. Costanza is not married and does not live with her parents, as was customary for single women back then, and to a lesser extent even today, in Sicily. Intrigued by the stranger who knocks at her door to get his parrot back and startled by his beauty,[6] she invites the young handsome sailor in, first for coffee, and then for the night "without much ado" (48), which is a liberty that was certainly uncommon for a Sicilian woman at the beginning of that century—or even the current one, for that matter, because, as the narrator explains, "strangers do not easily go in and out of Sicilian homes" (44). Costanza does not go to church and prefers to listen to the tales of a parrot in her house than those of a priest in the House of the Lord, which is something that makes her a somewhat bad Catholic too. Finally, just like a modern-day blogger, Costanza sits every night to write her personal reflections in her diary. The reader learns that Costanza is actually a writer, maybe even a regular con- tributor to journals, and that her voluntary seclusion might be due to a "political intrigue" to escape some controversy she created with the "fiery articles" she published in a journal, as Edmundo suggests (92). For this modern and liberated Sicilian woman, writing is the means to resist and subvert any attempts at silencing women and imposing a male-oriented perspective onto their experience. Timpanelli's pro- cess of recovery of traditional Sicilian oral tales turns into a feminist rewriting of the stories from the point of view of a modern ethnic American woman writer.

The act of writing itself is Costanza's means of asserting her iden- tity as a woman author as well as her own freedom and independence. Every night, Costanza retires in her study to enjoy some quiet respite from the hustle and bustle of life. Timpanelli writes, "It was here, in this room, that she breathed normally again" (27), as it is in her small and dark study, by reading and writing, that she can be herself. In her diary, Costanza records her own personal thoughts and daily life, but she also engages in critical considerations of several topics, including the art of storytelling. In one such entry, Costanza writes:

> I take consolation tonight in remembering. Although I know
> we humans at times have short, selective memories, our
> internal gods do not. They forget nothing. While we are
> asleep or awake, these little gods chatter intimate stories

to anyone who will listen, and we get away with nothing, neither in exile nor in isolation. (51)

The act of remembering allows for a whole culture to be passed down in the form of stories from one generation to the next and across the oceans.

On the topic of storytelling, Costanza also writes: "Writing and telling—they don't compare easily. Birds and stones" (63). The first obvious difference between the two is that storytelling is a communal art while writing is primarily a solitary experience. Practitioners of storytelling capitalize on their listeners' responses, which are vital to the performance. In some ways and to different degrees, tellers and listeners both perform during a storytelling event. What is sacrificed in the transposition of oral narratives onto paper is the most characteristic quality of storytelling itself: the interaction with the audience. Another difference between writing and telling is that, as has already been mentioned when talking about Mangione's *Mount Allegro* in chapter 3, as much as the word is, obviously, the founding tool of both art forms, nonverbal language accompanies the oral performance. Pitrè himself in his Prefazione to his *Fiabe, novelle e racconti popolari siciliani*, reminded his readers that without Agatuzza Messia's mimics, the narration is severely weakened:

> Those who read only find the naked and cold word; but Messia's narration relies less on the word than the rapid movements of the eyes, the flailing of the arms, the use of the whole person, who gets up, walks around the room, bends down and then straightens up, modulating her voice to sound calm first and then excited, fearful, sweet, squeaky, imitating the voice of the characters and the actions they are performing. Non-verbal cues, especially in Messia's case, are very important and you can rest assured that without them narration loses half its strength and efficacy. (21–22)[7]

It is nearly impossible to transfer onto paper the looks, gestures, and facial expressions—in short, the physicality of a performance. For all these reasons and more, Costanza concludes, comparing writing and telling is akin to comparing apples and oranges.

However, it is also true that the two forms in which Timpanelli engages, the oral and the written, have fed off each other for centuries.

Myths, fables, tales, and stories obviously preceded the written word, but writing has preserved spoken texts and, thus, helped their circulation. Orally grounded texts have seen the light in published form, and books have worked side by side with memory as agents of cultural transmission. In its peregrinations in time and place, the tale of "Lu pappagaddu chi cunta tri cunti" reached the ears and eyes of Gioia Timpanelli and became a Sicilian American novella. Ultimately, this is a story about the power of stories and their meaning, but the stories are especially important in terms of their implications for a woman who is open to heeding the lessons of the past to answer the questions of the present.

A final comparison between the endings of Pitrè's *cuntu* and Timpanelli's novella reveals how, with time and distance, Sicilianness can turn into Sicilian Americanness. In fact, Pitrè's lawyer-turned-parrot successfully keeps the lady in the house with his three stories. Yet when the lady's husband returned from his trip, "the parrot seized him by the throat, strangled him, and flew away" (Zipes and Russo 47). Changing back into his human form, the lawyer asks for the widowed lady's hand and manages to marry her. In the end, the stories have only served the man's purpose, and the lady remains the victim of his ruse and, more generally, of a patriarchal order personified by a despotic first husband and a devilish second one. In Timpanelli's story, on the other hand, the parrot's ancient tales influence Costanza's behavior. To Edmundo she reveals: "Being with you and your quiet ways and your good stories has changed something for me. Your old story touched me, Edmundo" (96). After listening to the three tales, Costanza is a stronger woman and learns to leave all fears and anxieties behind to experience freedom and happiness. It is only appropriate that the epilogue of the story take place on the day of the celebrations for Saint Rosalie, the patron saint of Palermo. The day has a certain resonance with the story for a couple of reasons. First, it is the most important day for the city of Palermo, where the novella is set. Also, it is easy to see certain parallelisms between the life of Costanza and that of the saint, especially in that both women lived by choice as hermits.[8] But the parrot's *cunti* have empowered Costanza, who finally resolves to take control of her life by leaving her isolation and going back to Catania. Thanks to Saint Rosalie's protection, she also manages to escape the lawyer's last desperate attempt to kidnap her. Costanza finally reasserts her independence when, at the very end, Edmundo the sailor confesses his love for her and she politely turns him down. To the captain of the ship that will take her to Catania, Costanza reveals her plans to join her folklorist friends and "launch a Sicilian folklore journal based on the work of Vico and Giuseppe Pitrè" (97). The importance of storytelling is, then, reflected in the woman's courageous choice to finally break out of the cocoon to fulfill a life dedicated to the oral art. Timpanelli's Costanza shows that, in the end, a woman can choose her own destiny, and she chooses free-dom over marriage and literature over illiteracy. This woman belongs to two worlds: one that is now and here and another one that is very distant, both in time and place. The past and the present, Sicily and the United States, all converge in Timpanelli's A Knot of Tears to create a model of sicilianamericanità for other Sicilian American women writers to emulate.

Like A Knot of Tears, the second novella in Sometimes the Soul, namely, Rusina, Not Quite in Love, testifies to the interplay of oral-ity and textuality, and old world and new world forces, while at the same time it draws inspiration from different sources in terms of time, place, language, and medium. In fact, this novella shows no greater deference to the Sicilian oral narratives than to world-renowned fairy-tales as Rusina's story is influenced by the famous tale of "Beauty and the Beast."[9] The main plot of the story is categorized in the Aarne-Thompson-Uther folklore classification system as a subtype of the "search for a lost husband" (ATU–425C), and it is one that stands out for the quality, quantity, and variety of adaptations. Its printed history dates back to the publication of Gabrielle-Suzanne de Villeneuve's original "La belle et la bête," a long narrative embedded in her 1740 novel La jeune américaine et les contes marins. The fairytale was later republished, in a much-abridged version, as a didactic children's story by Jeanne-Marie Leprince de Beaumont in her 1757 Le magasin des enfants. This is a collection of fairytales that the governess writer put together with the goal of providing her young and marriageable female pupils with lessons on appropriate feminine behavior, especial-ly in terms of courtship rules, marriage, and everything that follows. Beaumont's rewriting outweighed the fame of the original story, and it is at the basis of countless variants and modern interpretations in the form of short stories, novels, and even feature films, among which are Jean Cocteau's 1946 La belle et la bête and Disney's Beauty and the Beast (1991). In Timpanelli's version, the far-off country is Sicily and Belle/Beauty is Rusina, a lovely eighteen-year-old girl who ends up living with a feral creature to settle her father's debt. But Rusina is a much more empowered woman than her French counterpart, and her experience in the beast's villa eventually reinforces her feminism even further and gives her a whole new appreciation of her native island and, therefore, her roots. Thus, once again, Timpanelli is able to recover her Sicilian American heritage and share it in the form of a feminist and modern tale in ancient dress.

Like Beauty, Rusina is the youngest daughter of a merchant who dotes on her more than her sisters. Because of her looks, beautiful Rusina's vain and jealous sisters verbally and emotionally abuse her. To add injury to insult, because of her beauty and other qualities such as humility and industriousness, Rusina is the one whom the beast selects to settle her father's debt. Due to an unexpected financial downturn, in fact, Rusina's father owes an enormous amount of money to the mysterious Master Gardener of a Dante-esque *Selva Oscura*, who lives in a beautiful and old villa in the middle of a dense wood. At the beginning of the novella, the reader follows Rusina's father on his journey to the master's remote villa to arrange a debt settlement. The two men sit down to enjoy a meal, and, during the course of the conversation, the father extols Rusina's virtues to the beastly Master Gardener. Finally, the latter makes a proposition: he will cancel the debt if the debtor's daughter will join him, and his old uncle and aunt, at the villa.

A lot has been written on the deal between the merchant and the beast, and how Beauty is treated like an object to be traded. In her article "Desire and Desirability in Villeneuve and Leprince de Beaumont's 'Beauty and the Beast,'" Tatiana Korneeva writes:

> The commercial nature of the marriage transaction is underlined throughout "Beauty and the Beast" tales. Indeed, it does not seem to be a mere coincidence that Beauty's father is a merchant, and in several instances the Beast in Villeneuve's version specifically refers to his power to "trade" his daughter. The hero thus reduces Beauty's role to that of object of his desire in the negotiation, ultimately qualifying the female body as merchandise in the marriage economy. (239)

And so it happens that beautiful Rusina, just like the French Beauty, becomes a commodity object for the two most important men in her life: her father and her future husband.

However, Rusina is an assertive and independent woman who refuses to be an object of pity. In fact, at the end of her father's account of the encounter with the Master Gardener, she announces, "That is where my father's story ends and where mine begins" (118), thus showing a desire and the ability to author her own life. The act of textual self-empowerment results in a first-person style narration, in which Rusina tells her own story rather than being a passive puppet in a governess's pedagogical narrative. For instance, on the topic of the deal between her father and the Master Gardener, the young girl addresses what she calls the "moralists" thus:

> I ask you not to judge my father too quickly. My great-grandmother and grandfather inherited debt as did my mother and father and on and on, for what child does not inherit parents' debts? Debts from character and disposition. Debts from unlived life, sickness, unremembered dreams, poor work, hungry stomachs, stingy imagination, or little love. It is a rare and blessed child who comes into this world without debt. (118)

An outspoken realist, Rusina is not the object of the agreement between two (male) parties. As much as it hurts her to leave her father behind, she actually looks forward to breaking away from her abusive sisters. Also, Rusina always was one to appreciate the thrill of adventure. Among the insults that her sisters hurl at her, one in particular seems to fit her like a glove: "There was one word, *vagabonda*, in which I reveled. I knew from an early age that my path would not be fixed, and on my walks I called myself *vagabonda*" (125–126), she writes, thus revealing that despite her understandable fears, deep down in her heart, she welcomes the terms of the deal between her father and the beastly Master Gardener, and she will make the most out of her time at the villa.

The three people Rusina joins in her new adventure are known in town for being quite decent, but rather eccentric. However, Rusina adds, "since we are an island of eccentrics, no one pays serious attention to the term" (121). The young girl enjoys the company of Zia Graziella and Ziu Luiginu, an elderly brother and sister who spend their time arguing over philosophical questions and remembering the days of their youth. As for the other protagonist of the novella, unlike Beaumont's Beast, who wants to kill Beauty's father for stealing a rose from his garden and accepts that his daughter comes to die in his place, Timpanelli's Master Gardener is from the beginning a distant but goodhearted man, whose only monsterlike qualities reside in his looks. When, upon his return to the house, Rusina's father tells his three daughters of the strange encounter with the beastly man, he describes him as a bizarre Earth creature, who "spoke in our tongue so beautifully that then I knew for certain that he was from the Island, from these very mountains of the interior, from the *umbilicus*" (114).[10] The master is a gardener who is very familiar with all the fauna and flora native to Sicily, all the trees, plants, flowers, bulbs, and herbs. He even bears a resemblance to the island to which he belongs and to which he tends, and Rusina's father continues to describe him as follows:

> He was a mountain of a man, Mongibello itself, and when he turned his face toward me I shuddered, for he was so ugly I could not look at him directly . . . he was beastly, with small unblinking eyes that mercifully never looked at me. He had a full beard and hair over his brow. . . . His grizzly red-brown hair was unkempt; his chest was huge but his shoulders small and narrow. His gardener's hands hung down like a great beast's paws. (113–114)

Timpanelli's Sicilian American version of the hideous beast is described as Mount Etna, also known as *Mungibeddu* in Sicilian, the volcano at the feet of the city of Catania, on the east coast of the island. Just like the still-active volcano, the man "looked powerful, sorrowful, and even angry" (114).

Despite his scary appearance, the Master Gardener does everything in his power to make Rusina happy and to ensure that all her needs are met. Rusina also enjoys a high degree of independence from stifling gender roles in a place where she can roam around freely and is surrounded by "tapestries covering two walls, scenes where only women were the hunters and both men and women tended the land" (112). Timpanelli's Beauty is not a hyperfeminized Disney princess in a castle, and even her fantasies of dressing in men's clothes are indulged when she notes: "Coming home one afternoon from a long climb, I spied a pair of trousers drying over a laurel bush and thought how useful they'd be. The next morning hanging in the armoire were two pairs of pants, two shirts, and a green jacket" (130). The aunt and the uncle also provide Rusina with precious learning opportunities. In fact, at one point, the two elderly residents offer the young girl a sum of money for her work at the villa. When the girl protests on the account that she is there to pay off her father's debt, Zia Graziella retorts: "No, dear girl, this money is for your work and independence. Unless they are in a place where talent, heart, and intelligence (both practical and theoretical!) are measures of strength and authority, women need money to keep themselves in this new world" (162). The villa turns out to be an ideal place for Rusina to develop and refine her feminist consciousness.

During her time at the Master Gardener's place, Rusina can also indulge her intellectual curiosity and love of books. Even in the nineteenth-century version of the tale, Beaumont's Beauty is well read and educated, an unusual trait for a young girl in her times. A great deal of emphasis is given by Beaumont on the fact that the father "spared no expense in educating his children, and he hired all kinds of tutors for their benefit" (Zipes, "Beauty and the Beast" 805). When she arrives at the Beast's castle, Beauty is delighted to have a room for herself, "but what struck her most of all was a large library, a harpsichord, and numerous books of music" (810). The girl's love of books is especially emphasized in Disney's 1991 movie, where she is shown in the first scene strolling around town with her nose in a book. Belle is actually mocked by the community and reprimanded by her suitor Gaston for being an avid reader. In the movie, in an effort to please her and conquer her heart, the Beast even surprises her with a huge library complete with floor-to-ceiling bookshelves. However, in her feminist reading of the movie entitled "Romancing the Plot: The Real Beast of Disney's *Beauty and the Beast*," Jane Cummins points out that "Belle's desires, her interest in exploration and education, have no meaning except in terms of how they can be manipulated into a romance to benefit the Beast and the bewitched servants" (24). Unlike some critics, who see in Belle a strong female protagonist and, as such, a new kind of Disney heroine because of her reading habits, Cummins concludes that

> Belle's propensity of reading ultimately has little weight in her development as an intelligent woman. . . . Belle is only once shown reading, for a very little time (exactly fourteen seconds) after she is given the library. We do not know what she is reading or what she thinks about it. (25)

Unlike Beaumont and screenwriter Linda Woolverton, Timpanelli is very specific about what kind of books Rusina is encouraged to read in her lovely bedroom in a Sicilian villa. In fact, Rusina's library is made up of the tales that Sicilian doctor and writer Giovanni Meli collected between 1810 and 1814, of several books of medieval Sicilian poetry, and "a beautiful set of encyclopedias with hand-colored illustrations" (130). Also, the inclusion of Ovid's *Metamorphoses* among the books in Rusina's library should not come as a surprise in a novella that culminates with a spiritual and moral transformation. Surprisingly, though, a much more modern book appears next to Ovid's classic work of mythology, namely, a poetry collection by Sicilian poet Vincenzo Aurelio Guarnaccia.[11] In 1927, together with Ignazio Buttitta and Giuseppe Ganci Battaglia, Guarnaccia founded *La trazzera*, a Palermo-based monthly literary journal in dialect, which was suppressed by Mussolini only two years after its first issue. Next to these books, Rusina also finds "an old edition of Christine de Pizan's *The City of Ladies*" (130). Finished in the early 1400s in France, the book was written as a response to the misogynist and male-dominated medieval literary tradition in France. In her article "Women Warriors: A Special Case from the Fifteenth Century: *The City of Ladies*," Laura Rinaldi Dufresne defines Christine de Pizan's book as a "feminine utopia," where "the stories of women contributing to history through traditional and non-traditional means, including the 'masculine' arena of combat, are told" (112). According to the scholar, de Pizan's main goal in writing her book was to ensure that a history of women is "remembered and told to gain power and respect for past, present, and future generations of women" ("Women Warriors" 113). Thanks to all these various readings, Rusina is presented with invaluable lessons on the history of women's struggles and accomplishments as well as on the history, culture, and literature of her native island.

Timpanelli's sicilianamericanità reveals itself in the successful attempt to draw from her own Sicilian origins and American life to endow Rusina with an old soul and a modern feminist consciousness. Rusina is, at the same time, a Sicilian maid in the days of yore and the heroine of a twenty-first-century story. Like Beauty in Beaumont's tale, she is an unusually independent young woman; but unlike the French merchant's daughter, Rusina is able and encouraged to express herself in more fundamental ways for a modern girl. Significantly, unlike Beauty who is well read but never writes, Rusina brings to the villa "four empty notebooks" (129), where she jots down the conversations between Zia Graziella and Ziu Luiginu, and where she also draws objects that she cannot describe. Little by little, she starts keeping a "proper journal, at first to continue to write down my 'lessons' so that I could learn from them and then to record my new life faithfully" (139). Like Costanza in *A Knot of Tears*, Rusina establishes a writing routine in the villa that helps her make sense of her life and gain control of her own story.

Rusina's narration of her life in the Master Gardener's place is interspersed with journal entries. In one of them, the young girl writes her thoughts after an encounter with the beastly man, whose real name is Sebastian:

> His eyes are so terrible that I think if I were a child I would run from him. They are either absent, innocent, or piercing. His clothes are worse than ever and his appearance so unkempt. Yet when he speaks of flowers and walks in the field I am amazed by him. (173)

Sebastian's life is motivated by a great appreciation for nature, and, especially, for the Sicilian native flora and fauna. The man is eager to share his love of rural life in Sicily with Rusina, who turns out to be an ideal student of lessons regarding insects and larvae, as well as hyacinths and bulbs. Sebastian also encourages Rusina's learning and self-expression through drawing, which, along with her diary, becomes a way for the girl to attune her soul to her surroundings. To inspire her further, the monstrous man gives Rusina a "marvelous album with insect metamorphoses (1683–1713), an album of original drawings by the great artist Maria Sibylla Merian. . . . This artist had recorded flowers and plants and natural life, the most vivid of insects and their metamorphoses, painted on small watercolor paper," and Rusina reflected, "from that day on, I studied it and the flora around the villa" (143). The purpose of the album is twofold: first, it reinforces Rusina's feminism by providing the example of a successful woman artist; and second, it encourages the girl to learn about the natural history of Sicily and, by extension, about her roots. Sebastian thus becomes the young girl's mentor in the development of a Sicilian feminist consciousness.

As a further expression of the Master Gardener's role in Rusina's journey of self-discovery, Sebastian gives her a book of hours that belonged to his mother. During the Middle Ages, the book of hours was a widely available prayer book, usually decorated with illustrations and miniatures, which accompanied devotional practices among laics. In her article "'For the Use of Women': Women and Book of Hours," Virginia Reinburg focuses on the importance and meaning of the diffusion of books of hours among women of higher and lower social status. Reinburg notes how even if both women and men could obviously use them, these prayer books were in most cases designed for female devotees. Richer women would commission their own books of hours from gifted artists, and some of them were personalized with the lady's name or portrait. The books of hours were also common wedding gifts. Reinburg writes:

> Books of hours were precious possessions. They were valued not only for the prayers and images enclosed in their covers, but also because they testified to and even embodied their owners' lives and relationships. Women considered their books of hours intimate possessions, objects to be passed down as a precious legacy to daughters, goddaughters, and dearest friends. Patterns of gift giving and inheritance show this. . . . Men gave books to the women in their lives, usually their wives and daughters. (237)

In Timpanelli's novella, the book of hours that Sebastian gives to Rusina has the priceless value of a wedding promise and, particularly, of an heirloom passed down from one woman to another through a man. Sebastian's mother's legacy, though, is not a traditional one as evidenced by the book's illustrations. Rusina writes:

> Having the Book of Hours, made centuries before, in my hands was like holding both history and eternity. The meditations were in a tongue that I could not read, but the illuminations were of the fauna and flora of the land surrounding the villa. I marveled at how familiar they were to me. (144)

Once again, the emphasis is on Sicily's natural history and ecology, its animal and plant life. Rusina's moral journey through life can be accomplished only through worship of her island.

Later, Rusina starts devoting more and more time to the sharpening of her drawing skills. This leads her to pay close attention to the land surrounding the villa and to the effects that the learning process have on her as a budding artist and, especially, as a person. Transformed by this learning experience, Rusina finally comes to her senses and realizes that the *laidu*, or ugly, is her Prince Charming in a Sicilian farmer's garb, and she eventually agrees to marry him. Unlike Costanza, Rusina's happiness-ever-after will coincide with marriage, but not before her full metamorphosis. In a significant reversal of roles compared to the fairytale of "Beauty and the Beast" as we know it, Rusina is the one who undergoes a transformation in Timpanelli's novella. Sebastian changes in the sense that, thanks to Rusina, he learns to appreciate more the company of humans rather than spending his whole time tending to his garden. But other than that, he remains the same throughout the novella. Unlike Beaumont's tale, where Belle has a civilizing influence on the Beast, in Timpanelli's story, Sebastian is the one who imparts lessons to Rusina. When, finally, the young girl confesses her love to the Master Gardener, the scene does not mark the culmination of the hideous man's transformation into a prince as in Beaumont's version.[12] Rather, that is the moment when Rusina's gradual transformation into a strong and conscious Sicilian feminist is fully realized. Rusina writes:

> Sebastian filled always with spirit now changed in form *to me*, and this man, this Master Gardener, was looking at me with his beautiful soft eyes with as much love as I have ever seen. And I knew him and he was beautiful *to me* as my own life. (183, my emphases)

Sebastian changes in Rusina's eyes, which means that what really changes is not him but the way she sees him. Unlike Beaumont's Beast, Sebastian was never a prince who needed a woman to love and marry him in order to break the evil spell cast by a malevolent witch. He is and remains a gardener inside and outside, in his heart and in his clothes. Rusina, on the other hand, has grown into a strong and conscientized young woman. In the end, Timpanelli's *Rusina, Not Quite in Love* is a feminist tale in which the Sicilian heroine learns that, just like the native flora and fauna, she is also the fruit of an island that she needs to appreciate and respect. Sebastian is the spokesperson of Timpanelli's discourse on sicilianamericanità. Despite his half-human-half-animal form, in fact, the Master Gardener is able to teach Rusina an invaluable lesson on the importance of studying one's roots and connecting with them. Similarly, thanks to her half-oral-half-written tales, Timpanelli teaches her readers an appreciation of one's ethnic cultural heritage and the significance of recovering and reclaiming cultural origins.[13]

As a very skilled performer, Gioia Timpanelli has presented to the English-speaking public a large body of oral literature in its traditional spoken form. As a writer, she has helped to preserve and circulate such stories. As a Sicilian American artist, she has acted as a tradition bearer by facilitating the transmission from one literary form to another, one language to another, one culture to another, and from the archaic to the modern. She has thus made available to Sicilian Americans, and more generally, Italian Americans, a part of their heritage that, formerly, only their memories could hold. More specifically, she has built connections in the community based on the recognition of their common oral and vernacular literature. Timpanelli's work, both in the oral and written forms, draws from Sicilian sources. However, she incorporates a system of values and themes that are essentially American and function in the society out of which her works spring and which they address. Timpanelli's sicilianamericanità manifests itself in a preoccupation with keeping a collective and social memory intact that would otherwise be threatened by assimilation to mainstream America. Her twenty-first-century voice echoes a most archaic form of communication with a modern twist. After all, as Timpanelli herself pointed out, "although these old spoken stories come from the language, the culture, the place that held them, they travel, slowly or swiftly, finally belonging to everybody who has an ear for the words and a heart for the story" ("Stories and Storytelling" 131). Through this fertile act of pollination, Timpanelli gives new life to old Sicilian folktales and Western fairy tales.

Finally, an important lesson in storytelling comes in the form of a dream that Costanza records in a notebook one night, after the parrot's first *cuntu* in *A Knot of Tears*. It is the story of a woman who suffers from panic attacks. One morning, during her sleep, she "sees" a stone hearth at the center of a kitchen. At its center, there is a mound of ashes from a fire that once was and is not anymore. But buried underneath the ashes, she could also see *"a glowing piece of burning coal which never went out, and suddenly she felt an overwhelming elation as though she had been shown something"* (63, emphasis in the text). Costanza continues to write that *"that night after dinner,"* the woman went *"to her own study, sat down, and changed her life"* (64). The piece of coal burning underneath the ashes can be read as a metaphor for storytelling. No stories, no matter how old, are burned by the flame of time and reduced to cold ashes. Inside of them, there is always a glowing burning coal ready to start the fire again. This is what Timpanelli has done with the spoken traditions. This oral body of literature is now preserved in writing in a different cultural, social, historical, and linguistic context. Maybe it will take years or decades, maybe more; maybe the writer's name will not be remembered or associated with the stories told; but one or more themes, motifs, or keywords from these Sicilian American tales will be reactivated in some other form of literature, either oral or written, in the United States, or maybe somewhere else, "for the stories are in specific languages and yet in all languages; in specific places yet many places; they are like the small bag of magical food that is given and when taken by the heart is never used up" (*Tales from the Roof* x). By bringing the Sicilian storytelling tradition to the United States, Timpanelli has placed them within a much wider context, which transcends time and place; and, she has turned herself into a bridge that the stories have crossed to get away from the island, see the world, and keep living.

Conclusion

Italy without Sicily forms no image at all in the soul; only here
is the key to everything.

—Johann Wolfgang von Goethe, *Italian Journey*

It is probably Goethe's fault, and of his journey to Sicily: only
here, he wrote, is the key to everything. However, he doesn't
count: he found too many keys in too many places.

—Andrea Camilleri, in Salvatore Ferlita and Paolo Nifosì,
La Sicilia di Andrea Camilleri: Tra Vigata e Montelusa

In this study, I have sought to show how a distinct sense of Sicilian
American identity, or sicilianamericanità, has seeped into Italian
American literature. My goal was to initiate a discussion about the
ways this literary discourse in the United States parallels the coding
of a Sicilian literary identity in the works of Giovanni Verga, Luigi
Pirandello, Maria Messina, Giuseppe Tomasi di Lampedusa, Vitaliano
Brancati, and, more recently, Leonardo Sciascia, Vincenzo Consolo,
Dacia Maraini, and Andrea Camilleri, just to mention the most widely
known Sicilian writers. In fact, for the geographical, socioeconomic,
and cultural reasons explored throughout this book, some Sicilian
American authors also have shaped their identity in relation to the
island. While attempting to redefine the concept of Americanness
and expand the canon of American literature so that it embraces
articulations of ethnic identities, several Sicilian American writers
have emphasized the role of islandness as an identity shaper. In these
authors' works, this marked propensity to identify as Sicilians takes
the form of a constant preoccupation with the compelling questions of

a hybrid consciousness: sicilianamericanità. Hence, my investigation has provided an opportunity to examine this specific process of identity construction and to evaluate its reflections on Italian American literature. The American authors of Sicilian descent considered in this study, namely, Jerre Mangione, Rose Romano, Ben Morreale, and Gioia Timpanelli, have, in different ways and through different genres, turned their works into literary manifestations of their ethnogenesis. As ethnic works, all of their memoirs, poems, novels, and novellas deal with the interplay of ethnic heritage and national status, and they explore the possibilities offered by Italy and the Unites States as well as those denied by each or both.

However, the works presented in this book are only a few reflections of the prismatic phenomenon of sicilianamericanità as it surfaces in Italian American literature. The reinvestment of the Sicilian cultural heritage in the works of other Sicilian American writers takes the most disparate forms as it intertwines with the authors' all-too-personal aesthetic choices and ways of dealing with issues of regionalism, gender, class, sexual preference, political affiliation, religious sentiments, among others. Further studies might investigate the immigrant's transformation from Sicilian to Sicilian American by focusing, for instance, on poet Vincenzo Ancona's poetry. Ancona drew inspiration from Sicilian oral traditions, folklore, and humor for his poems, which were collected in the 1990 book *Malidittu la Lingua/Damned Language*, published in Sicilian with English translations. The paucity of his published production is consistent with the performed nature of his art. Ancona, in fact, imported to the United States the tradition of the *poeta contadino*—"poet-farmer," or "illiterate poet"—who was able to improvise verses and complex rhymes in his local dialect. In his poems, Ancona kneads together traditional Sicilian folk culture with tales of personal dislocation to create a unique poetic account of a first-generation Sicilian immigrant in the United States.

Like Ancona, third-generation Sicilian American Tony Ardizzone also weaves, in an original fashion, Sicilian folkloric tales with a recollection of immigration stories in his remarkable 1999 novel *In the Garden of Papa Santuzzu*. In an early review of the book, Gardaphé writes:

> Ardizzone . . . has been dipping into his Sicilian American background here and there throughout his earlier work. . . . In this latest book, he embraces Sicilian culture

and doesn't let go until he wrings out a masterpiece composed of different points-of-view. (*The Art of Reading* 17)

Ardizzone plays with sicilianamericanità through a literary trip back
in time and place to Sicily in the early 1900s. That is the origin of
a series of tales of immigration, displacement, and adjustment to the
New World through which the Sicilian American characters as well
as the author are able to inscribe their presence onto the American
palimpsest.

Some Sicilian American writers have felt the urgency to recon-
nect with their roots through literature and, also, in an actual, physical
way. Born in Brooklyn in 1924 to a Sicilian family, third-generation
Nat Scammacca settled in Trapani, in the northwest of Sicily, in
1965. Soon after, he cofounded the Antigruppo Siciliano, a grassroots
and populist antiestablishment cultural and literary movement that
emphasized the importance of socially committed poetry to educate
and inspire the masses, promote democracy and participation, and,
eventually, reverse the status quo. A poet, essayist, novelist, memoirist, and leader, Scammacca played a crucial role in the history and
development of the poetic movement. Besides his extensive personal
publishing records, this Sicilian American author contributed his pen
and voice by writing and performing poetry in the streets and piazzas
of Sicily and organizing populist poetry events and recitals; he edited
the *terza pagina*, the cultural page of the weekly newspaper *Trapani
Nuova*—the official organ of the movement—for almost twenty-five
years, from 1967 to 1991, and helped with various anthologies, like
the 1971 *Un tulipano rosso*, *Antigruppo '73*, and *Antigruppo 1975*;
finally, he was also cofounder of other journals and literary reviews,
such as *Anti*, *Antigruppo Palermo*, *Impegno '70*, *Impegno '80*, and more.
Scammacca always showed a keen awareness of his ethnicity, and a
quick look at the titles of some of his publications reveals how much
his status as an ethnic influenced his thoughts, and, ultimately, his
literary production: *Bye bye America*, *Ricordi di un wop* (1972), *Due
mondi* (1979), and *Sikano l'amerikano!* (1989) are just some of the
prose works in which Scammacca probed into his upbringing as an
American in a Sicilian environment, his life in Sicily, and ultimately,
his sicilianamericanità.

The questions and issues raised by women writers like Rose
Romano and Gioia Timpanelli echo the sentiments of several other
Sicilian American women writers who have denounced the patriarchal

and sexist practices within the Italian American family and community in their works. For instance, in her 1988 novel *The Right Thing to Do*, Josephine Gattuso Hendin fictionalizes interregional, gender, and assimilation conflicts in the lives of a Sicilian man, his Neapolitan wife, and their rebellious American-born daughter. Also, the emotional problems faced by a dysfunctional Sicilian American family inform Rachel Guido deVries's 1986 novel *Tender Warriors*. The DeMarco siblings try to overcome their respective social "handicaps"—Rose is a lesbian, Lorraine an ex-junkie, while Sonny suffers from epileptic seizures—for the sake of recovering the sacredness of family unity. Together with Romano and deVries, Dodici Azpadu contributed to the discussion about gender and sexual identity with her 1983 novel *Saturday Night in the Prime of Life*. The protagonist, Neddie Zingaro, is a Sicilian American woman who is estranged from her family, and particularly from her mother, because of her sexual identity. Interestingly, Azpadu, too, like Romano, portrays her Sicilian American characters as racially defined. What especially connects Neddie to her mother, Concetta, in fact, is that they are both characterized by a markedly olive complexion. Despite their many connections though, the mother cannot accept Neddie's lesbian identity, and in one last desperate attempt to save their relationship, she breaks with her daughter for good. Azpadu investigated again the strained relationship between a lesbian woman and her Sicilian family in her novel *Living Room* (2010), where Carmen Khalise heads back to New York to attend her mother's funeral and ends up participating in the final days of her ex-girlfriend's battle against cancer. The aforementioned Sicilian American women writers negotiate a feminist subjecthood within and against the boundaries of both the greater Italian and American national identities. Through their feminist and lesbian counternarratives, these writers are able to subvert a centuries-old passivity and acceptance of the normative role of women in traditional Sicilian culture and thus rewrite the larger social and sexual narratives of Italian American identity.

Although a sense of sicilianamericanità is not a clearly distinctive trait in their works, other American authors of Sicilian descent, such as Sandra Mortola Gilbert, Rita Ciresi, Edvige Giunta, Mary Cappello, Carol Maso, Theresa Maggio, Domenica Ruta, Kym Ragusa, Renée Manfredi, Diana Cavallo, Karen Tintori, Anthony Valerio, Diane di Prima, Maria Famà, Grace Cavalieri, Phyllis Capello, Lewis Turco, Emanuel di Pasquale, Antonino Provenzano, and others have occasionally dealt with their Sicilian American identity. Sicilianamericanità also informs the quest of feminist scholar Lucia Chiavola Birnbaum, who digs into the realms of spirituality to unearth and bring forth the existence of the African dark foremothers of Sicilian and all Southern Italian women, namely, the black Madonnas of the title of her 1993 study. All the authors I have discussed in depth or simply mentioned in this study are truly representative of sicilianamericanità because each explores the conflicts due to the continuous negotiations between traditional Sicilian and modern American ways. Overall, their writing makes quite a substantial body of work within the more encompassing field of Italian American literature.

As scholars who continue to develop and study the literature of Italian America, we should expand the scope of our investigations to include new and previously unexplored directions and alternative approaches. The same holds true for the field of Italian studies. In fact, as I hope to have shown in this book, Italian American literature is a phenomenon that relates not only to U.S. national literature but also to Italian literature. Further studies might be able to identify a parallel treatment of certain themes in both traditions and thus ascertain the power of the forces of descent on U.S. ethnic literature, while others might point to how certain themes are treated in ways that disclose the authors' closer identification with their national identity rather than their ethnic heritage. The lack of or insistence on certain themes and topoi and the use of certain stylistic devices and literary strategies might be significant signs of convergence or divergence of the two literary traditions as well as perhaps revealing symptoms of the dominant ideologies in each culture. In any case, critical investigations that take into account both Italian and Italian American literatures could bring scholars and readers only to a better understanding of both, and the abandonment of disciplinary loyalties could open a venue for intriguing dialogues between the two fields. Seen from this perspective, Italian American literature as a whole would be twice a literature of belonging: if on the one hand, in fact, it naturally belongs to the greater domain of U.S. American literature, on the other, it should rightfully aspire to be included in a systematic way in the curricula of Italian studies in North America and in Italy to develop a more comprehensive understanding of what it means to be Italian.

Notes

Introduction

1. The earliest statement about the literary achievements of Italians in the United States appeared in 1949, with the posthumous publication of Olga Peragallo's notes for her dissertation *Italian American Authors and Their Contribution to American Literature*. It took exactly twenty-five years before another attempt to promote the cause of Italian American writers went to press; in 1974, Rose Basile Green published *The Italian-American Novel: A Document of the Interaction of Two Cultures*. Without underestimating the pioneering roles played by Peragallo and Green, whose works, however potentially groundbreaking, were still at an embryonic stage, another Italian American woman's work, that is, Helen Barolini's 1985 anthology *The Dream Book*, and Fred Gardaphé's 1996 book-length study *Italian Signs, American Streets* are the beginnings of a consistent critical effort in the field of American literature written by authors of Italian descent.

2. "Alcuni temi sulla questione meridionale" is an incomplete writing that would be better described as a series of scattered thoughts around the "southern question" that Gramsci articulated in 1926. The text was published for the first time in its incomplete form in 1930 in the communist journal *Stato Operaio*, published in Paris under the supervision of Palmiro Togliatti.

3. Of particular interest for this study is Franco Cassano's *Il pensiero meridiano* (1996), a manifesto of sorts of Global Souths, in which the Italian sociologist-turned-politician attempted to restore some balance between the North and the South. In Cassano's own words, "Southern thought basically means this: Give back to the South its ancient dignity as the subject of thought; interrupt the long sequence whereby it has been thought by others" (1–2). Cassano's cult book has only recently been made available to the English-speaking world in a translation by Norma Bouchard and Valerio Ferme.

4. The punch line of the sentence is the verbal pun that plays on the Italian adjective for "Southerner." Loosely translated, Prampolini's expression would sound more or less like this: "Italy is divided between Northerners and Filthy-Ones."

5. For a good selection of the most influential theories of anthropological criminology on the inferiority of Southerners vis-à-vis Northerners, see Vito Teti's 1993 anthology *La razza maledetta: Origini del pregiudizio antimeridionale*.

6. "Enorme eccitabilità del proprio *io*" (all translations, unless otherwise noted, are my own).

7. "Nei mediterranei bruni l'irrequietezza e la eccitabilità dell'*io* generano: l'*inattenzione* . . . ; la *debolezza della volontà* . . . ; l'*eccesso delle emozioni banali* . . . ; l'*impulsività* . . . ; l'*eccesso della immaginazione* . . . ; la *mancanza del senso pratico della vita* . . ."

8. "*L'intelligenza pronta e rapida.*"

9. Among those who most vehemently criticized the school of Social Positivism, Napoleone Colajanni's 1906 work *Latini e anglosassoni* deserves special mention. Rather than improbable genetic reasons, Colajanni looked at political economy in order to explain the poverty of the South. See Teti's *La razza maledetta*.

10. Some scholars, most notably, Alison Goeller in her 2003 article "Persephone Goes Home: Italian American Women in Italy," and Edvige Giunta in her 2004 "Persephone's Daughters," have discussed the centrality of the myth of Demeter and Persephone's abduction by Hades in some works by Italian and Italian American women writers. Giunta shows how the story of Persephone's forced journey to the Underworld "is perhaps the myth that resonates most powerfully for women of Southern Italian ancestry" (768). The Greek myth has, in fact, seeped into the literature of several Sicilian and also non–Sicilian American writers and artists, such as Susan Caperna Lloyd, Lucia Perillo, Diane di Prima, Chickie Farella, Phyllis Capello, Joanna Herman, Rita Signorelli-Pappas, Robin Pastorio-Newman, sculptor Nancy Azara, and filmmaker Mariarosy Calleri. The quantity, quality, and variety of Italian American works influenced by this Greek Sicilian myth testify to the impact of some aspects of *Siciliana* on Italian American culture at large.

11. Mangione, as I show in chapter 3, devoted most of his literary production to Sicilian and Sicilian American themes. Regional identity also features prominently in John Fante's works. John was the son of Nicola Fante, a bricklayer who had emigrated from the rocky mountains of Abruzzo to pursue the American dream in Colorado. The Abruzzese immigrant was fictionalized under several names in many of Fante's short stories and novels, most notably in the 1938 *Wait Until Spring, Bandini!*, always keeping his birthplace intact. Another Abruzzese by descent, Pietro di Donato, was very conscious about regional differences within the Italian communities in the United States. The writer's 1939 *Christ in Concrete* is an example in which the novel's finest portraits of Italian American characters emphasize regional identities in many ways.

12. D'Agostino's later novels also always present the Italian American theme, but there is no special emphasis on Sicily and its people and culture.

13. Ancona's and Provenzano's works have appeared for the most part through Legas Publishing, an independent multilingual publishing company, thanks to the efforts of Gaetano Cipolla, an active supporter of all things Sicilian in the United States. Cipolla himself is the author of several Sicilian-inspired booklets and studies, among which is the 2005 *Siciliana: Studies on the Sicilian Ethos*, and he is also the translator of many Sicilian writers. Cipolla is also the president of Arba Sicula, a New York–based organization that promotes, through various programs and events, the Sicilian culture and language in the United States; and, finally, he is editor of a bilingual journal on Sicilian literature and folklore by the same name.

14. Tommaso Bordonaro's 1991 *La spartenza: La storia di tutta la mia vita da quando io rigordo ch'ero un bambino*, which quickly became a literary case in Italy, deserves special mention. The book is the account of the life of the author himself, who immigrated to the United States at the age of thirty-eight in 1947. As the work of a man with limited formal education, *La spartenza* lacks any traditional literary quality and is written in a mixture of Sicilian-ized and Americanized Italian. However, the memoir was the first of its kind to be published in Italy that showed the complexities of an immigrant's life from the point of view of one of the millions of people who suffered the *spartenza*—dis-parture—from their homeland during the twentieth century. Because of this, Bordonaro's book was awarded the Pieve Santo Stefano literary prize. The jury was composed, among others, of Natalia Ginzburg, who also wrote the introduction to the 1991 edition published by the prestigious Einaudi. *La spartenza* is currently available only in its original language.

15. "Si sa che la Sicilia è plurale, che il Regno delle Due Sicilie avrebbe dovuto chiamarsi delle Dieci, delle Cento Sicilie. Crocevia e ombelico ambiguo del mondo, amalgama di razze e vicende diverse, la Sicilia non ha mai smesso di essere un grande ossimoro geografico e antropologico di lutto e luce, di lava e miele."

Chapter 1. Of Sicily and Its Ripples:
Sicilianamericanità and Sicilian American Literature

1. "Cinquant'anni di vita unitaria sono stati in gran parte dedicati dai nostri uomini politici a creare l'apparenza di una uniformità *italiana*: le regioni avrebbero dovuto sparire nella nazione, i dialetti nella lingua letteraria. La Sicilia è la regione che ha più *attivamente* resistito a questa manomissione della storia e della libertà. La Sicilia ha dimostrato in numerose occasioni di vivere una vita a carattere nazionale proprio, più che regionale . . . La verità è che la Sicilia conserva una sua indipendenza spirituale."

2. The Italian state has recognized some of these claims. After World War II, the newborn republic had to grant a "special statute" to five out of twenty regions in acknowledgment of their particular social, cultural, and

economic contexts and to quell any secessionist aspirations. Sicily was the first region to obtain a certain level of autonomy in May of 1946, followed by Sardinia, Valle D'Aosta, Trentino-Alto Adige, and Friuli-Venezia Giulia.

3. The term "islandness," Baldacchino further explains, "is preferred to the more commonly used term of *insularity*. The latter has unwittingly come along with a semantic baggage of separation and backwardness" ("The Coming of Age of Island Studies" 272).

4. "Soffre, la Sicilia, di un eccesso di identità, né so se sia un bene o sia un male."

5. "Non è una segregazione solo geografica, ma se ne porta dietro altre: della provincia, della famiglia, della stanza, del proprio cuore. Da qui il nostro orgoglio, la diffidenza, il pudore; e il senso di essere diversi."

6. There are, of course, exceptions to the rule, the most notable one being England, which, until the mid-twentieth century, held under its rule the largest number of overseas possessions in history.

7. Less than two miles divide Sicily from mainland Italy, and therefore, from Europe, while the northeasternmost point of Africa is about one hundred miles away from Sicily's southwest coast.

8. From 1943 until 1946, the traditional autonomist aspirations in Sicily found a spokesperson in Andrea Finocchiaro Aprile, leader of the MIS (Movement for the Independence of Sicily), a movement that advocated the separation of the island from Italy and the constitution of an autonomous republican government. This is how Finocchiaro-Aprile justified his separatist thesis in 1944: "Noi vogliamo che la nostra Isola faccia da sè, noi vogliamo che dal nuovo assetto internazionale la Sicilia esca come Stato sovrano e indipendente. L'unità italiana è stata deleteria per noi. Noi nulla avemmo dall'unità che non fossero l'abbandono, lo sfruttamento e il disprezzo. Quando si ripete che la Sicilia non fu considerata che come una colonia, si dice meno della verità. . . . Vi fu un momento che Addis Abeba ebbe più cure e più interessamento da parte del governo italiano di quello che non avevano mai avuto nessuna delle nostre città e nessuno dei nostri territori: fummo insomma anche meno di una colonia" (qtd. in Petraccone 236–237).

Finocchiaro-Aprile's nationalistic project survives today in the anachronistic and provincial claims of some right-winged movements in Sicily.

9. In their essay on "Island Governance," Warrington and Milne identify seven patterns of governance that become "the *leitmotif* of an island territory's history, and a metaphor embodying critical political, sociological and economic phenomena" (398). The two scholars identify Sicily, along with Haiti, as an "archetypal fief" (398). They explain: "as the polar opposite of the civilization, a fief experiences to an extreme degree the peripherality, vulnerability and dependence commonly attributed to islands, compounded by neglect, repression and exploitation at the hands of a rapacious 'imperial' power or by the design of its own elites" (402).

10. "Si può dunque dire che l'insicurezza è la componente primaria della storia siciliana; e condiziona il comportamento, il modo di essere, la visione della vita—paura, apprensione, diffidenza, chiuse passioni, incapacità di stabilire rapporti al di fuori degli affetti, violenza, pessimismo, fatalismo— della collettività e dei singoli."

11. "Una tendenza all'isolamento, alla separazione, degli individui, dei gruppi, delle comunità—e dell'intera regione. E ad un certo punto l'insicurezza, la paura, si rovesciano nell'illusione che una siffatta insularità, con tutti i condizionamenti, le remore e le regole che ne discendono, costituisca privilegio e forza là dove negli effetti, nella esperienza, è condizione di vulnerabilità e debolezza: e ne sorge una specie di alienazione, di follia, che sul piano della psicologia e del costume produce atteggiamenti di presunzione, di fierezza, di arroganza."

12. The Antigruppo Siciliano was a grassroots and populist antiestablishment cultural and literary movement that operated in Sicily between the late 1960s and the early 1990s and emphasized the importance of socially committed poetry to educate and inspire the masses. A Sicilian American poet, Nat Scammacca, was one of the founding leaders of the movement.

13. On a linguistic note, the expression was a rather felicitous choice since in Italian it rhymes with *solitudine*—or solitude—which hints at the isolation of the island.

14. "Alla difficoltà di esserlo, siciliano, si somma sovente una certa insofferenza a sentirselo ribadire così spesso."

15. "Basta la sicilitudine e tutto si spiega: per le più stridenti contraddizioni, per gli scempi plateali, ma anche per i delitti più banali, arriva sempre l'autoassolutoria analisi 'sicilianologica,' con immancabile corredo di citazione colta."

16. "Uno stereotipo falsamente etnografico," "enorme incrostazione 'culturale,' astorica e auto-assolutoria."

17. "Una selezione della memoria e della storia collettiva, omettendo tutto quello che non corrisponde ai paradigmi della presunta sicilitudine e aggiornando, reiterandoli, i soliti *topoi* sull'ontologia dei siciliani."

18. In Canto VIII of his *Paradiso*, Dante Alighieri remembers the Vespers and attributes them to the king's bad treatment of Sicily when he says: "[I]ll government, which always burdens the / hearts of the subjected peoples, . . . moved / Palermo to shout: 'Die, die!'" (*Paradiso* 171).

19. Today, the memory of the Vespers among Sicilians is still associated with the "chickpeas" story. According to this legend, in order to identify French soldiers who were trying to pass for Sicilians to save their own lives during the uprising, the locals would ask them to pronounce the word *cìciri*—Sicilian for chickpeas, a particularly difficult word for French speakers to pronounce. In her poem "Chickpeas," Maria Famà remembers the importance of this story for her heritage: "This is how we pass down our history

/ my father holds up a handful of roasted chickpeas / makes us repeat the word after him / "ciceri" "ciceri" "ciceri" / we are children anxious to leave the table / play laugh shout in English/ in Philadelphia USA / where our family set down roots / fragile and tough as chickpea plants" (*Mystics in the Family* 31).

20. "Immobilismo, fatalismo, paura del futuro sarebbero caratteri difficilmente attribuibili all'identità dei siciliani se si considerasse che, quantomeno nel corso del primo secolo di unità nazionale, le sue classi subalterne sono state assai vivaci, progressive, conflittuali e combattive."

21. "Non sono più gli operai e gli artigiani, bensì i contadini l'elemento trainante del processo formativo dell'organizzazione. Il centro di gravità si sposta dalla città alla campagna."

22. "La proclamazione della dottrina della lotta di classe passava dalle parole ai fatti, e le campagne si rivelavano effettivamente terreno adatto alla penetrazione del messaggio socialista."

23. "Organizzazioni popolari, di ispirazione socialista, sorte in contrasto e come contestazione del potere constituito."

24. The literature of many islands the world over is similarly affected by islandness. The works of the 1926 Nobel Prize–winner Grazia Deledda and Marcello Fois, just to mention a couple of Sardinian-born writers well known internationally, reflect a particular attachment to their island and its Weltanschauung, and so does the literature of world islands as diverse as Ireland; Malta; the Caribbean islands of Jamaica, Trinidad, Dominica, Barbados, Puerto Rico, Cuba, Haiti, and Guadeloupe; New Zealand; Hawaii; Samoa; Fiji; Tasmania; Newfoundland; Prince Edward Island; and more, many of which have been analyzed through an island focus. To understand the interest that scholars have recently taken in islands as shapers of literary discourses, I suggest reading critical texts such as Brinklow, Ledwell, and Ledwell's edited volume *Message in a Bottle: The Literature of Small Islands*, which collects a selection of papers presented at an international conference held in 1998 on Prince Edward Island, and Dorothy Lane's *The Island as Site of Resistance* (1995).

25. *Gallismo* comes from the Italian word for rooster, or *gallo*, a most powerful symbol of sexual prowess and masculinity for rural communities. However, in Brancati's works, the Sicilian *dongiovannis* are more verbally hypersexual than actual womanizers, and their "conquests" are imaginary and rarely translate into reality. In his 1973 *Il borghese e l'immensità*, a collection of thoughts written between 1930 and 1954, Brancati writes: "I piaceri del gallismo non consiston tanto nell'usare questa forza gagliarda, quanto nel credere di possederla e nel confondere a tal punto le carte dei ricordi, spesso poveri e meschini, da combinare a se stessi uno strano passato pieno di successi con le donne" (148).

26. Since the appearance in 1994 of *La forma dell'acqua* (*The Shape of Water*), which marked the beginning of the Montalbano series as well as the

very successful TV adaptation of Montalbano's adventures produced by RAI, Camilleri has become an icon of pop literature in Italy and abroad, thanks to the many translations into German, French, Spanish, Portuguese, Greek, Japanese, Dutch, Swedish, and English. The bulk of the stories take place in Vigàta, an imaginary Sicilian town modeled on Camilleri's hometown, Porto Empedocle, where Salvo Montalbano, a Sicilian detective in the local police force, is busy solving the crimes of local mafia dons, the misdeeds of lawyers and priests, homicides, kidnappings, and whatever other cases death, vendettas, money, mafia, politics, hatred, and family can generate. Sicily features prominently and everything—from food to friendship, prostitution and religion—has a unique Sicilian accent.

27. As a reference, I will point to a few works, starting with the section devoted to Sicilian literature in the pioneering history of Italian literature subdivided by regions that Walter Binni coedited with critic Natalino Sapegno in 1968, *Storia letteraria delle regioni d'Italia*. A good history of twentieth-century Sicilian literature is Giorgio Santangelo's *Letteratura in Sicilia da Federico II a Pirandello*. Besides Sciascia and Guglielmino's *Narratori di Sicilia*, other valuable anthologies are *Novecento siciliano*, edited by Gaetano Caponeto et al.; *Cento Sicilie: Testimonianze per un ritratto*, edited by Gesualdo Bufalino and Nunzio Zago; and *Narratori siciliani del secondo dopoguerra*, edited by Sarah Zappulla Muscarà, among others.

28. Geographer Russell King points out that "the build-up of island populations has limits set within a particular economic and technological system. When this limit is reached, one of three outcomes occurs: malnutrition or starvation results; help has to be sought from outside, for example, in the form of food shipments or welfare payments; or, most likely, emigration takes place. . . . Emigration may become institutionalized as part of island society, and necessary for its stable survival" (23).

29. "Chi scompiglio chi ci è tra li paisi / Tra li famigli e tra tutti li casi / Di po' chi l'america s'intisi, / Pi la partenza ogniuno fa li basi / Cu si pripara mutanni e cammisi / Cu n'avi grana s'inpigna li casi / Afflittu cu la famiglia s'allicenza / E poi pi l'america partenza."

30. "Quel suo carattere di permanenza, essendo tutta o quasi tutta transoceanica, o come quella sua straordinaria capacità di rapidissima crescita, per cui nel volger di pochissimi anni erano partiti dall'isola più di un milione di uomini, costituiti per lo più da giovani nel pieno vigore fisico e morale."

31. "Da Palmieri a Quasimodo ogni siciliano che fugge dalla Sicilia sarà nella condizione dell'esule, di colui cioè che *non può tornare*. E in alcuni questa condizione si fa dolente memoria, nostalgia, mito; in altri la volontà di dimenticare, insofferenza, rancore." Interestingly, the 1967 edition of the aforementioned anthology featured, among others, Sicilian American writer Jerre Mangione. Born in Rochester, New York, Mangione is the only "narrator of Sicily" in the anthology who was not born on the island and whose piece—part of his 1943 memoir *Mount Allegro*—is originally in a language

other than Italian, and, therefore, appears in translation. Unfortunately, Mangione was removed from the second edition of the same anthology, published in 1991; this editorial choice was made by Salvatore Guglielmiño, who decided to eliminate Mangione as well as some other narrators of Sicily featured in the first edition in order to make space for Sciascia (who had meanwhile passed away), Elio Vittorini, Vitaliano Brancati, and others who had been left out in 1967. However, this later deletion does not alter Sciascia's initial choice. By including this American-born writer of Sicilian descent in his *Narratori di Sicilia*, Sciascia was validating the existence of sicilianamericanità in Italian American literature.

32. Scammacca was the organizer of the first international conference on Homer's *Odyssey* in Trapani in 1990. Interestingly, he also supported Samuel Butler's thesis on the Sicilian origins of the *Odyssey*, and together with his wife Nina in 1986 he translated a text by L.G. Pocock on the topic, namely, the 1957 *The Sicilian Origin of the Odyssey*.

33. "In cifre assolute e percentuali l'emigrazione incise dunque soprattutto sulle regioni che erano più ricche di analfabeti e, quindi, di dialettofoni."

34. Scholar of folklore Giuseppe Pitrè, who undertook to record all aspects pertaining to the life of the Sicilian people in the monumental *Biblioteca delle tradizioni popolari siciliane* (1871–1913), noted that originally the terms *mafiusu* and its female form *mafiusa/mafiusedda* had also a positive connotation, meaning beautiful and proud, courageous. In the Sicilian dialect, the terms are still sometimes used in this sense.

35. "Le famiglie di mafia, come quelle naturali, si dividono e si ricongiungono nell'intreccio di relazioni che attraversa nei due sensi l'oceano."

36. An interesting deconstructive reading of the figure of the gangster in the United States comes from critic Fred Gardaphé. In his "A Class Act," Gardaphé suggests that "the gangster has become a necessary figure in U.S. culture" (52), and that the North American obsession for all things mafia should be read in the light of the "moral fanaticism of Anglo-American based culture" (56). According to the critic, in the realm of representations in the media, "[t]he mafia myth has . . . served an important function in American society in both defining what is American and what is acceptable behavior in American society" (57), for "[a]s American man strived toward his notion of pure good, he had to be able to measure his progress by personifying evil in others" (56).

Chapter 2. From Sulphur Mines to Tenements: Sicilianamericanità in Ben Morreale's Novels

1. "Tutti amiamo il luogo in cui siamo nati, e siamo portati ad esaltarlo. Ma Racalmuto è davvero un paese straordinario." In his 1974 study *Blood of My Blood: The Dilemma of the Italian-Americans*, Richard Gambino

explains the meaning of the Italian word *campanilismo* by rightfully linking it to the issue of regionalism in Italy: "The extraordinary regionalism of Italy, strong to this day, was particularly characteristic of the Mezzogiorno. Not only each region, but each town considers itself a self-contained, unique culture, its people feeling no kinship with those even a few miles away. The attitude is labeled *campanilismo*, from the Italian word for 'bell' (*campana*), meaning that whatever "national" affinity the people feel is limited to those who live within hearing range of their village's church bell. Italian Americans retain the habit of friendly banter and rivalry between those derived from different regions. Sicilians and Neapolitans maintain that Calabrians have *testedure*, 'hard heads,' meaning that they are stubborn. Sicilians are called schemers by others, and Neapolitans rascals, etc." (65).

2. *Le parrocchie di Regalpetra* was translated in English and published by Orion Press in 1969 with the title *Salt in the Wound*.

3. At the age of twelve, the writer went to Sicily for the second time and, in his parents' intention, for good. This stay, however, only lasted two years, because when Morreale's father found out that he was about to be drafted in the Italian Army, the family went back to New York and settled there permanently (*Sicily, the Hallowed Land* 10–11).

4. Dino Cinel questions the usefulness of such a book. While he is ready to admit that a book like this is sorely needed, especially among the young Italian Americans, on other hand he notes that "such narratives are usually passionate, but they should also strive for objectivity. . . . In ethnic studies we have not found the way to write histories that are both popular and scientifically accurate. Perhaps this is a reflection of our larger inability to find a resolution between ethnic and national identities. This book is a further reminder of an agenda that we, both as scholars and citizens, cannot escape for much longer" (1311).

5. In *Le parrocchie di Regalpetra*, Sciascia chronicles the social and political forces that affect the life of this little town. Sciascia informs that the golden age of mining in Racalmuto was the nineteenth century, when the town counted no less than five or six mines on its territory. However, by the early 1950s, around the time that both Sciascia and Morreale were writing, only one was still open, the *zolfara* Gibellina.

6. In her 1991 study *Giufà il furbo, lo sciocco, il saggio*, Francesca Corrao shows that even before Pitrè, Giufà had appeared in a few Sicilian anecdotes as recounted by Agatino Longo in 1845, and, in 1871, by Laura Von Gonzenbach (23).

7. Father Juffa is also the protagonist of Morreale's 1973 novel *A Few Virtuous Men*. As we shall see later, one of the three parts of the novel tells of the Sicilian priest's trip to the United States and Canada.

8. The *caruso*—Sicilian for "young boy"—is one of the most tragic figures of the history of mine labor in Sicily. The young son of a poor family, the *caruso* was literally sold by his parents to the mine owner for little

money. His job usually consisted in transporting the extracted material inside big baskets that rested on his back and that usually turned him, with time, into a hunchback. Before Pirandello, Giovanni Verga had already dealt with the figure of the *caruso* in a short story entitled "Rosso Malpelo," included in his 1880 collection *Vita dei campi.*

9. Joe Valachi was a member of Vito Genovese's Family. In 1962 Valachi learned that Genovese had ordered his death. Convicted with a life sentence for the murder of a prisoner and afraid of Genovese's threat, Valachi decided to make his story public.

10. It must be noted here that the name of the "great professor of history" adds to the general mocking tone, given that the word *calandruni,* besides designating a weevil, in Sicilian is also an epithet that means "idiot."

11. *Cornuto,* or cuckold, is a common and powerful insult in the Italian language.

12. A widow with no kids, La Pippitunna is considered a "used" woman in Sicilian society and thus can only play the role of a prostitute. The woman is a very sensual creature, and the suggestion that she might represent for Father Juffa what Mary Magdalene was for Christ is expressed by Don Tarralla: "Everyone knew that Father Juffa *si la faciva* with La Pippitunna, which was a Sicilian way of saying that he was making it with her. . . . It was accepted as another privilege for those who made the law. Then too, Don Tarralla let it be known that such talk against Juffa was blasphemy, a lie against a good man, as if to say that Christ was making it with Mary Magdalene. And, of course Pantaleone, encouraged by Tarralla's mocking tone, could not help but say in the noblemen's club that some scholars thought that that was just the case" (35).

13. The Allied Military Government of Occupied Territories was a government of military occupation ruled by American and British officers in charge of administrating the newly liberated territories in Italy during World War II.

14. For a discussion of the role that the Allies played in 1943 in the "rebirth" of the mafia, see Salvatore Lupo's 1993 *Storia della mafia: Dalle origini ai giorni nostri.*

15. Throughout the novel, Pantaleone/Sciascia appears in specific moments to express his own thoughts mostly in the form of asides on various issues of the "nature" of Sicilians, such as their suspiciousness, pessimism, and the like. In many cases, Morreale simply translates from Sciascia's works. While it is certainly worth mentioning the presence of these instances of a dialogue between Sicilian and Sicilian American literatures, I did not deem it necessary to delve further into Pantaleone's thoughts because I have extensively dealt with Sciascia's concept of *sicilitudine* in chapter 1 of this book.

16. Later in the novel, when Mimi is tricked by an attorney into investing his money on some shares, he returns home and proudly announces, "We have a piece of America" (146).

17. In his article "A Class Act," Gardaphé explores the figure of the Italian American gangster in relation to the question of class-based power and, therefore, as "a trope for signifying the gain of cultural power that comes through class mobility" (52).

Chapter 3. "Half-and-Half": Sicilianamericanità in Jerre Mangione's Memoirs

1. *Mount Allegro* was first published as *Mont'Allegro* in 1955 by SIAE and in 1983 by Franco Angeli Editore, while *Night Search* and *Reunion in Sicily* were published by Sellerio in 1987 and 1992, respectively. In 1971 Mangione also received the honorary title of "Commendatore dell'Ordine della Stella della Solidarietà italiana" from the Italian government for his literary merits.

2. In her 2009 study *A New Language, a New World*, Nancy Carnevale discusses this distinction from the perspective of language. As a second-generation child, Mangione was very much aware of the split between the public and the private spheres as reflected in the language spoken by his family inside the house and outside. Moreover, as Carnevale points out, the writer "manifested an acute sensitivity to the regional differences of Italian and the implications of their use" (97), realizing that most of his family spoke Sicilian, or a bastardized form of it, rather than standard Italian. In a 1996 interview, Mangione candidly described his relationship to both Italian and Sicilian as follows: "The best way perhaps of characterizing my relationship to the Italian language is to say that I speak bad Italian fluently. Mine is a mishmash of the Sicilian dialect, which my parents insisted upon at home, and of one year of college-taught Italian. Sicilian was my first language by edict" (Gardaphé, "An Interview with Jerre Mangione" 46).

3. In *An Ethnic at Large* first, and later in a footnote of the Finale added to the 1981 edition of *Mount Allegro*, Mangione explained that the publishers decided at the last moment to present the book as fiction instead of memoir for reasons of marketing. As a consequence of this editorial maneuver, the Mangiones became the Amoroso family, while the writer simply kept his real name in Italian, that is, Gerlando (*An Ethnic* 298–299). Finally, in the 1981 edition by Columbia University Press, the author could clarify the nature of his book by adding the subtitle *A Memoir of Italian American Life*.

4. The memoir is also the preferred genre of several Sicilian American women writers, such as Mary Cappello, Diane di Prima, Theresa Maggio, Karen Tintori, and Domenica Ruta. To the memoir, Mary Jo Bona also adds poetry as a means for second-wave Italian American women writers in general to establish "connections with familial and literary forbears" (*By the Breath* 145).

5. Mangione is also the author of the 1972 book *The Dream and the Deal: The Federal Writers' Project 1935–1943* (i.e., the WPA Federal Writers'

Project), in which he recounted his experience as the national coordinating editor of what in the author's words was "an extraordinary governmental enterprise" (ix). In 1965 he also published the pamphlet *Life Sentences for Everybody*, made up of a series of "modern satiric fables, each one told in a single sentence," a style he claims to have learned while working for a long time as a copywriter for the advertising agency Ayer (Gardaphé, "An Interview with Jerre Mangione" 52). Finally, in 1975, he published the educational booklet for children *Mussolini's March on Rome*.

6. It should not come as a surprise, then, that Mangione had decidedly unflattering words for Puzo's 1969 *The Godfather*, a novel he thought devoid of "any moral value whatsoever. Everybody in it, with the exception of the WASP wife of young Corleone, has no sense of ethics. They're all willing criminals or at least susceptible to criminality, even the police. Both the book and especially the movie have done tremendous damage to the image of Italians in this country" (Esposito 13).

7. I am here borrowing the expression "cultural grammar" from William Boelhower, by which he means "a metacritical organization of a culture into its constitutive structural norms and codes" (*Immigrant* 29, fn. 11).

8. In *Italian Signs, American Streets*, Fred Gardaphé places Mangione—together with John Fante and Pietro di Donato—in the "Early Mythic Stage" of the narrative development of Italian American literature. According to the literary mode peculiar to this stage, Mangione eventually "debunks the melting pot myth and replaces it with the myth that the two cultures can be synthesized into a new culture, Italian America. . . . He serves as a *diplomat* of the new world of Italian America that he fashions in his writing" (75, emphasis added).

9. In his article "Circles of the Cyclops," which focuses on the linguistic aspects of some Italian American texts, Robert Viscusi points to *Mount Allegro* as an example of "Cyclopean isolation" due to the language barriers experienced by the Italian immigrant characters with limited, if any at all, proficiency in English. The memoir, Viscusi argues, features many instances of what the critic terms "heteroglossolalia," or "an interruption in systems of communication that occurs as a result of large-scale migration into a nation with foreign language, customs, and political institutions" (*Buried Caesars* 113). In an attempt to overcome this linguistic isolation, the narrator, endowed with a double competence, functions as a purveyor of semiotic transactions between Sicilians and Americans. However, the narrator, Viscusi concludes on a pessimistic note, "mediates between these two discrete circles with the Homeric wit belonging to a veteran traveler who can accommodate comfortably conflicts that might inspire sadness in a more innocent mind or exhaustion in a less flexible spirit. His tone can accommodate, but not resolve, these conflicts" (122).

10. Every year, on March 19th, Sicilians celebrate St. Joseph's Day by offering large altars/banquets—or *tavolate*—in his honor everywhere the

diaspora has taken them, from Castelfranco Veneto in northern Italy to Toronto, through Brooklyn and New Orleans. A visual feast and guide to New Orleans's *tavolate* is Kerri McCaffety's 2003 *St. Joseph Altars*.

11. McBride also discusses the one-sided perspective offered by Mangione and wonders: "And what about the women? They tell no stories. They play no briscola or 'pochero' (poker). They reveal none of their inner thoughts, their psychological pain. Apparently, in Mangione's assessment, they had none. . . . One must wonder if Mangione's celebrative image of Sicilian life would remain unchallenged had the women of Mount Allegro told their stories" (112).

12. "As I grew up," the author recalls, "I developed a strong feeling that I had to leave home. As much as I loved my family and shared all their anxieties, I felt that unless I left I would never have much sense of what I was all about and what this country was all about" (Esposito, "Jerre Mangione" 8).

13. Only from various cues scattered throughout the text can the reader gather that the facts recounted in *Mount Allegro* took place in the 1920s.

14. From this experience, Mangione drew inspiration to write *The Dream and the Deal*.

15. Chapter 13 of *An Ethnic*, entitled "Concentration Camps—American Style" is based on Mangione's firsthand experience and personal visits to major internment camps. This chapter is also included in a study of the effects of internment on Italian Americans during World War II edited by Lawrence DiStasi, *Una Storia Segreta: The Secret History of Italian American Evacuation and Internment during World War II* (2001).

16. Mangione was also skeptical of Communism, an attitude that, to him, could be explained by his Sicilian heritage: "I could not bring myself to join the Communist Party. Some inner warning system, created perhaps by the weariness that Sicilians have developed through centuries of foreign invasions, made me chary of affiliating myself with a political organization that, like the Catholic Church I had rejected, handed down dogmas and orders which its membership was blindly expected to accept" (*An Ethnic* 121).

17. For the *New Masses*, Mangione also wrote a review of Ignazio Silone's *Fontamara*, an antifascist political novel, and published an interview with Luigi Pirandello that took place in New York, during the author's first visit to the states. Mangione managed to have an hour of the Nobel Prize winner's time by playing on the common heritage, being that both Pirandello and Mangione's parents hailed from Agrigento. From the interview, however, all that Mangione could get was the acknowledgment that the café where his father had worked as an apprentice pastry maker made the best cannoli in Sicily. As for Pirandello's stance toward fascism and Mussolini, which was Mangione's main reason for that interview, he could not get any satisfactory answer (see *An Ethnic* 126–129).

18. Mangione speculated on the mystery surrounding the assassination of the anarcho-syndicalist Carlo Tresca in his 1965 novel *Night Search*.

19. A much more politically mature antifascist statement is Mangione's first novel, *The Ship and the Flame* (1948).

20. On his second trip to Sicily, in 1947, Mangione had the possibility to reverse his opinion. He wrote: "On my first trip, both the scenery and the people had oppressed me with their sullen reticence. . . . Now, thanks to the spring of the season and of the new regime, everything seemed different. This was more like the Sicily, the God-graced garden, my Rochester relatives were so nostalgic about when I was a child" (*Reunion* 78).

21. Marcus Lee Hansen was an American historian of American immigration. In his now-famous 1938 essay "The Problem of the Third Generation Immigrant," Hansen argued that while children of immigrants tend to reject their parents' culture, the next generation wants to recover it. Hansen famously articulated his claims thus: "what the son wishes to forget the grandson wishes to remember" (206).

Chapter 4. "The Scum of the Scum of the Scum": Rose Romano's Search for Sisterhood

1. This is the last volume of the monumental *Biblioteca delle tradizioni popolari siciliane* (1871–1913), which Pitrè undertook to record all aspects pertaining to the life of the Sicilian people.

2. "Forte è nei siciliani il sentimento della famiglia. Il padre tiene il governo assoluto e indiscusso di essa; la madre governa la casa, ne prende il maggiore interesse e comanda sui figli, quasi per facoltà del marito, cui essa ubbidisce ed ama anche quando egli non lo meriti."

3. "Fa [al marito] sacrificio pieno di sé, della sua vita, dei suoi servigi, nei quali nessuno può eguagliarla, come non c'è cosa che possa eguagliare l'amore pei figli: *Amuri di matri, e sirvimentu di mugghieri.*"

4. In her 2006 memoir *The Skin between Us*, Kym Ragusa explores the meaning of a biracial identity by dissecting and reimagining her growing up split between her African American and her Italian American families. Sicily features prominently in this memoir as the place from where Ragusa's Italian family originally hailed. However, before moving to the United States, her paternal grandfather had established his family in Calabria. Thus, in the memoir, Ragusa's father and his family identify the region at the tip of the peninsula as their place of provenance.

5. Some Sicilian American authors have argued for a recovery of the ties between Africa and Sicily. In her 1993 study *Black Madonnas*, Lucia Chiavola Birnbaum suggests that the Marian figure with dark features represents a point of encounter between ancient and modern religiosity and embodies the transracial nature of the populations of the Mediterranean basin. A black Madonna is honored and venerated in Tindari, in the province of Messina. The sanctuary attracts many pilgrims and tourists who come to pay homage to the Byzantine Madonna statue whose inscription in Latin at the feet of

the statue reads "nigra sum sed formosa," or "I am black but beautiful." The black Madonna of Tindari is also celebrated in the United States. In fact, every year, on September 8th, a *festa* is held in New York in her honor with the goal of strengthening Italian Americans' connections to their spiritual and racially mixed past.

6. For a more complete discussion on the question of race in Italian American studies, see the essays that make up the 2003 *Are Italians White? How Race Is Made in America*, edited by Jennifer Guglielmo and Salvatore Salerno.

Chapter 5. Once upon a Place: Timpanelli and the Sicilian Storytelling Tradition

1. The first national storytelling festival took place in 1973 in Jonesborough, Tennessee, and it is still held annually in the same place, which is also the site of the International Storytelling Center. In fact, many national, regional, and local associations and organizations have sprouted in the past decades in the United States. In 1982, with fellow professional storytellers Diane Wolkstein, Laura Simms, and Lorraine Ackerman, Timpanelli founded the Storytelling Center of New York City, which is among the most prominent organizations of its kind in the United States for the promotion and advancement of the art.

2. Timpanelli actually started her career as a poet, authoring *Stones for the Hours of the Night*, a series of black and white pictures of stones accompanied by poems, published in 1978, when she was still known as Joyce Timpanelli. The author herself attributes the shift from poetry to story to her work in public TV, for which in the late 1960s she first hosted *Come, Read to Me a Poem*, a series of thirty programs on poetry. After that, Timpanelli completed another educational literature series, *African Anthology*, before she moved on to her most acclaimed one on stories and folktales, namely, the PBS series *Stories from My House*, which won an Emmy citation for content and format.

3. http://www.californiapoetics.org/interviews/1603/an-interview-with-gioia-timpanelli.

4. The collection of Pitrè's folktales has only recently become available to the English-speaking public thanks to the editing and translating efforts of Jack Zipes and Joseph Russo, who coedited *The Collected Sicilian Folk and Fairy Tales of Giuseppe Pitrè* (2009). Before tackling Pitrè, Zipes had already translated Gonzenbach's collected tales in two volumes entitled *Beautiful Angiola* and *The Robber with a Witch's Head*, which appeared in 2004 and 2005, respectively.

5. Fairy tales specialist Jack Zipes points out that the format is also characteristic of Eastern narratives, most famously the frame of *A Thousand and One Nights*, and how the parrot's phrase "becomes emblematic of the

power of oral storytelling to seduce, entertain, and support us" (*The Collected Sicilian Folk* 807).

6. When Edmundo shows up at the Green Palace to reclaim his parrot, through the peephole, Costanza "saw the most guileless beauty she had ever seen. She saw the dark olive face, from the blue-gray Sicilian eyes, with their dark lashes, separate and thick, to the curve of a full upper lip and no more. The expression in the soft eyes was compassionate and still" (43).

7. "Chi legge, non trova che la fredda, la nuda parola; ma la narrazione della Messia più che nella parola consiste nel muovere irrequieto degli occhi, nell'agitar delle braccia, negli atteggiamenti della persona tutta, che si alza, gira intorno per la stanza, s'inchina, si solleva, facendo la voce ora piana, ora concitata, ora paurosa, ora dolce, ora stridula, ritraente la voce de' personaggi e l'atto che essi compiono. Della mimica nelle narrazioni, specialmente della Messia, è da tenere molto conto, e si può esser certi che, a farne senza, la narrazione perde metà della sua forza ed efficacia."

8. According to the legend, Santa Rosalia chose to live in a cave on Monte Pellegrino in order to better serve God and to run away from an arranged marriage. There she died all alone, and barely in her thirties, in the twelfth century. In the first part of the seventeenth century, however, she was rediscovered by the inhabitants of Palermo, whom she helped survive the plague in return for a Christian burial of her bones, which had lain untouched for three centuries on the mountain. From then on, a *festa* in her honor has been held in Palermo—and other parts of the world as well, such as Bensonhurst, New York—every year on July 15th.

9. Rusina, which is Sicilian for "little Rose," gets her name from the flower that the young girl asks her father to bring her from his trip.

10. Because of its location roughly at the center of Sicily, the city of Enna is known as the navel (umbilicus) of Sicily.

11. In the novella, Rusina talks about Vincenzo Guarnaccia as her uncle. Guarnaccia was born in Pietraperzia in the province of Enna, which is also the hometown of Timpanelli's family. The question of whether Guarnaccia is really Timpanelli's, and not Rusina's, relative is open to speculation.

12. In Beaumont's tale, the climax is reached when the Beast finally transforms into a prince: "Beauty had scarcely uttered these words when the castle radiated with light. Fireworks and music announced a feast. But these attractions could not hold her attention. She returned her gaze toward her dear Beast, whose dangerous condition made her tremble. But how great was her surprise! The Beast had disappeared, and at her feet was a prince more handsome than Eros himself, and he thanked her for having put an end to his enchantment" (Zipes, "Beauty and the Beast" 815).

13. Exactly ten years after *Sometimes the Soul*, in 2008, Timpanelli published her first novel, *What Makes a Child Lucky*. This short novel spins off of a few stories, most notably the story of Joseph as narrated in the book of Genesis, as well as Sicilian folktales such as "Tridicinu," featured in the

first volume of Pitrè's of *Fiabe, novelle e racconti popolari siciliani*, and another one collected by Laura von Gonzenbach in her *Sicilianische Märchen*, namely, "Von Joseph: Der Auszog sein Glück zu Suchen." The Sicilian formula *si cunta e si ricunta*, or "it is told again and again," is used once more by Timpanelli at the beginning of the novel to remind the reader that her novel is, in fact, part of the collective oral Sicilian heritage. *What Makes a Child Lucky* reconfirms Timpanelli's self-appointed role as a translator of the aural medium of tales into the visual medium of books, from Sicilian into English, and from the old to the new world.

Bibliography

Aaron, Daniel. "A Giant Mirror for America." Rev. of *The Dream and the Deal: The Federal Writers' Project, 1935–1943*, by Jerre Mangione. *Reviews in American History* 1.2 (June 1973): 277–281.

———. "The Hyphenate Writer and American Letters." *Smith Alumni Quarterly* 55.2 (1964): 213–217.

Accardi, Joseph. "Giovanni De Rosalia: Playwright, Poet and 'Nofrio.'" *Italian Americana* 19.2 (Summer 2001): 176–186.

Albright, Carol Bonomo, and Joanna Clapps Herman, eds. *Wild Dreams: The Best of Italian Americana*. New York: Fordham UP, 2008.

Alighieri, Dante. *Paradiso*. Trans. Robert M. Durling. New York: Oxford UP, 2011.

Ancona, Vincenzo. *Malidittu la Lingua/Damned Language*. Mineola: Legas, 2010.

Anderson, Benedict. *Imagined Communities: Reflections on the Origin and Spread of Nationalism*. New York: Verso, 1991.

Anzaldúa, Gloria. *Borderlands/La Frontera*. San Francisco: Aunt Lute Books, 1987.

Anzaldúa, Gloria, and Cherríe Moraga, eds. *This Bridge Called My Back: Writings by Radical Women of Color*. Watertown: Persephone Press, 1981.

Aprile, Pino. *Terroni: All That Has Been Done to Ensure That the Italians of the South Became "Southerners."* Trans. Ilaria Marra Rosiglioni. New York: Bordighera Press, 2011.

Ardizzone, Tony. *The Evening News*. Athens: U of Georgia P, 1986.

———. *In the Garden of Papa Santuzzu*. New York: Picador USA, 1999.

———. *Taking It Home*. Champaign: U of Illinois P, 1997.

Ashton, Shirley. Rev. of *Mount Allegro*, by Jerre Mangione. *The Humanist* 42 (1982): 53.

Ashyk, Daniel, Fred Gardaphé, and Anthony Julian Tamburri, eds. *Shades of Black and White: Conflict and Collaboration between Two Communities*. New York: American Italian Historical Association, 1999.

Azpadu, Dodici. *Goat Song*. Iowa City: Aunt Lute Books, 1984.

———. *Living Room*. Albuquerque: Neuma Books, 2010.

————. *Saturday Night in the Prime of Life.* Iowa City: Aunt Lute Books, 1983.

Baldacchino, Godfrey. "The Coming of Age of Island Studies." *Tijdschrift Voor Economische en Sociale Geografie* 95.3 (2004): 272–284.

————, ed. *A World of Islands.* Charlottetown: Institute of Island Studies, 2007.

Banfield, Edward C. *The Moral Basis of a Backward Society.* New York: The Free Press of Glencoe, 1958.

Barolini, Helen. *Chiaroscuro: Essays of Identity.* Madison: U of Wisconsin P, 1999.

————. *A Circular Journey.* New York: Fordham UP, 2006.

————, ed. *The Dream Book: An Anthology of Writings by Italian American Women.* Syracuse: Syracuse UP, 2000 [1985].

————. *Umbertina: A Novel.* New York: Feminist Press at the City University of New York, 1999.

Barreca, Regina. *Don't Tell Mama! The Penguin Book of Italian American Writing.* New York: Penguin, 2002.

Beauty and the Beast. Screenplay by Linda Woolverton. Dir. Gary Trousdale and Kirk Wise. Walt Disney Pictures, 1991.

La belle et la bête. Dir. Jean Cocteau. DisCina, 1946.

Berger, Meyer. "The People of 'Little Italy.'" Rev. of *Mount Allegro*, by Jerre Mangione. *New York Times*, 17 Jan. 1943: BR5.

Bevilacqua, Piero. *Breve storia dell'Italia meridionale.* Roma: Donzelli Editore, 1993.

————. "Peter Kolchin's 'American South' and the Italian Mezzogiorno: Some Questions about Comparative History." *The American South and the Italian Mezzogiorno: Essays in Comparative History.* Ed. Enrico Dal Lago and Rick Halpern. New York: Palgrave, 2002. 60–69.

Bhabha, Homi. *The Location of Culture.* New York: Routledge, 1994.

Binni, Walter, and Natalino Sapegno. *Storia letteraria delle regioni d'Italia.* Firenze: Sansoni, 1968.

Birnbaum, Lucia Chiavola. *Black Madonnas: Feminism, Religion, and Politics in Italy.* Boston: Northeastern UP, 1993.

Boelhower, William. *Immigrant Autobiography in the United States: Four Versions of the Italian American Self.* Verona: Essedue, 1982.

————. "Immigrant Novel as Genre." *MELUS* 8.1 (Spring 1981): 3–13.

————. "The Making of Ethnic Autobiography in the United States." *American Autobiography: Retrospect and Prospect.* Ed. John Paul Eakin. Madison: U of Wisconsin P, 1991. 123–141.

————. *Through a Glass Darkly: Ethnic Semiosis in American Literature.* New York: Oxford UP, 1987.

Boelhower, William, and Rocco Pallone, eds. *Adjusting Sites: New Essays in Italian American Studies.* Stony Brook: Forum Italicum, 1999.

Bona, Mary Jo. "'But Is It Great?' The Question of the Canon for Italian American Women Writers." *Breaking Open: Reflections on Italian Ameri-*

can *Women's Writing*. Ed. Mary Ann Vigilante Mannino and Justin Vitiello. West Lafayette: Purdue UP, 2003. 239–264.

———. *By the Breath of Their Mouths: Narratives of Resistance in Italian America*. Albany: State U of New York P, 2010.

———. *Claiming a Tradition: Italian American Women Writers*. Carbondale: Southern Illinois UP, 1999.

———. "Gorgeous Identities: Gay and Lesbian Italian/American Writers." *Fuori: Essays by Italian/American Lesbians and Gays*. Ed. Anthony Julian Tamburri. West Lafayette: Bordighera Press, 1996. 1–12.

———, ed. *Italian American Literature*. Spec. issue of *MELUS* 28.3 (Fall 2003): 1–229.

———. "Learning to Speak Doubly: New Poems by Gianna Patriarca and Rose Romano." *VIA: Voices in Italian Americana* 6.1 (Spring 1995): 161–168.

———, ed. *The Voices We Carry: Recent Italian American Women's Fiction*. Toronto: Guernica, 1994.

Bordonaro, Tommaso. *La spartenza: La storia di tutta la mia vita da quando io rigordo ch'ero un bambino*. Palermo: Navarra Editore, 2013 [1991].

Brancati, Vitaliano. *Il borghese e l'immensità*. Milano: Bompiani, 1973.

———. *Don Giovanni in Sicilia*. Milano: Bompiani, 1973.

Brinklow, Laurie, Frank Ledwell, and Jane Ledwell, eds. *Message in a Bottle: The Literature of Small Islands*. Charlottetown: Institute of Island Studies, 2000.

Brown, Carol. "From Saracen to Iggy: The Novels of Ben Morreale." *Italian Americana* 5.2 (Spring/Summer 1979): 205–221.

Bufalino, Gesualdo. *Cere perse*. Palermo: Sellerio, 1985.

Bufalino, Gesualdo, and Nunzio Zago, eds. *Cento Sicilie: Testimonianze per un ritratto*. Scandicci: La Nuova Italia Editrice, 1993.

Bull, Anna Cento, and Mark Gilbert. *The Lega Nord and the Northern Question in Italian Politics*. New York: Palgrave, 2001.

Burch, Betty Ann. *The Assimilation Experience of Five American White Ethnic Novelists of the Twentieth Century*. New York: Garland, 1990.

Calvino, Italo. *Italian Folktales: Selected and Retold by Italo Calvino*. Trans. George Martin. New York: Harcourt Brace Jovanovich, 1980.

Caples, Garrett, Andrew Joron, and Nancy Joyce Peters, eds. *The Collected Poems of Philip Lamantia*. Berkeley: U of California P, 2013.

Capone, Giovanna, and Denise Leto, eds. *Il Viaggio Delle Donne*. Spec. issue of *Sinister Wisdom* 41 (Summer/Fall 1990).

Capone, Giovanna, Denise Leto, and Tommi Avicolli Mecca, eds. *Hey Paesan: Lesbians and Gay Men of Italian Descent*. Oakland: Three Guineas Press, 1999.

Caponeto, Gaetano, Sergio Collura, Salvatore Rossi, and Rita Verdirame, eds. *Novecento siciliano*. Catania: Editrice Tifeo, 1986.

Cappello, Mary. *Awkward: A Detour*. New York: Bellevue, 2007.

————. *Night Bloom*. Boston: Beacon, 1998.

Carnevale, Nancy. *A New Language, a New World: Italians in the United States*. Urbana: U of Illinois P, 2009.

Caronia, Nancy. "The Exilic Immigrant." *Italian Passages: Making and Thinking History*. Ed. John Paul Russo and Teri Ann Bengiveno. New York: American Italian Historical Association, 2010. 5–20.

Cassano, Franco. *Southern Thought and Other Essays on the Mediterranean*. Ed. and trans. Norma Bouchard and Valerio Ferme. New York: Fordham UP, 2012.

Cavalcanti, Pedro, and Paul Piccone, eds. *History, Philosophy and Culture in the Young Gramsci*. Saint Louis: Telos Press, 1975.

Cavalieri, Grace. *The Mandate of Heaven*. New York: Bordighera Press, 2014.

————. *Sounds Like Something I Would Say*. Bloomington: Casa Mendenez, 2010.

Cavallo, Diana. *A Bridge of Leaves*. Toronto: Guernica, 1997.

Cinel, Dino. Rev. of *La Storia: Five Centuries of the Italian American Experience*, by Jerre Mangione. *The American Historical Review* 98.4 (1993): 1311.

Cipolla, Gaetano. *Siciliana: Studies on the Sicilian Ethos*. Mineola: Legas, 2005.

Ciresi, Rita. *Blue Italian*. New York: Delta, 1997.

————. *Sometimes I Dream in Italian*. New York: Delacorte Press, 2000.

Colajanni, Napoleone. *Latini e anglosassoni: Razze inferiori e razze superiori*. Roma: Rivista Popolare, 1906.

Coppola, Marie Saccomando. "Breaking the Code of Silence Woman to Woman." *Oral History, Oral Culture, and Italian Americans*. Ed. Luisa Del Giudice. New York: Palgrave Macmillan, 2009. 55–67.

Corrao, Francesca Maria. *Giufà il furbo, lo sciocco, il saggio*. Milano: Mondadori, 1991.

————. *Le storie di Giufà*. Palermo: Sellerio, 2001.

Cosco, Joseph P. *Imagining Italians: The Clash of Romance and Race in American Perceptions, 1880–1910*. Albany: State U of New York P, 2003.

Cummins, Jane. "Romancing the Plot: The Real Beast of Disney's *Beauty and the Beast*." *Children's Literature Association Quarterly* 20.1 (Spring 1995): 22–28.

D'Acierno, Pellegrino, ed. *The Italian American Heritage: A Companion to Literature and Arts*. New York: Garland, 1999.

D'Agostino, Guido. *Olives on the Apple Tree*. New York. Doubleday, 1940.

Dainotto, Roberto M. *Place in Literature: Regions, Cultures, Communities*. Ithaca: Cornell UP, 2000.

————. "The Importance of Being Sicilian: Italian Cultural Studies, Sicilitudine, and Je Ne Sais Quoi." *Italian Cultural Studies*. Ed. Graziella Parati and Ben Lawton. Boca Raton: Bordighera Press, 2001. 201–219.

Dal Lago, Enrico, and Rick Halpern, eds. *The American South and the Italian Mezzogiorno: Essays in Comparative History*. New York: Palgrave, 2002.

De Mauro, Tullio. *Storia linguistica dell'Italia unita*. Bari: Laterza, 1999.

De Rosa, Tina. *Paper Fish*. New York: Feminist Press at the City University of New York, 2003.

De Stefano, George. *An Offer We Can't Refuse: The Mafia in the Mind of America*. New York: Farrar, Straus and Giroux, 2006.

deVries, Rachel Guido. *Gambler's Daughter*. Toronto: Guernica, 1991.

———. *How to Sing to a Dago*. Toronto: Guernica, 1996.

———. *Tender Warriors*. Ithaca: Firebrand Books, 1986.

———. "Until the Voices Came." *Breaking Open: Reflections on Italian American Women's Writing*. Ed. Mary Ann Vigilante Mannino and Justin Vitiello. West Lafayette: Purdue UP, 2003. 73–90.

Dickie, John. *Darkest Italy: The Nation and Stereotypes of the Mezzogiorno, 1860–1900*. New York: St. Martin's Press, 1999.

di Donato, Pietro. *Christ in Concrete*. New York: Signet Classic, 1993 [1939].

Di Gesù, Matteo. "Cent'anni di sicilitudine." *La Repubblica*, 1 Oct. 2000: http://ricerca.repubblica.it/repubblica/archivio/repubblica/2000/10/01/centanni-di-sicilitudine.html?ref=search. Accessed 5 Nov. 2014.

———. *Dispatrie lettere. Di Blasi, Leopardi, Collodi: Letterature e identità nazionali*. Roma: Aracne Editrice, 2005.

———. "La sicilitudine cancella la Sicilia." *La Repubblica*, 25 Jan. 2005: http://ricerca.repubblica.it/repubblica/archivio/repubblica/2005/01/25/la-sicilitudine-cancella-la-sicilia.html?ref=search. Accessed 5 Nov. 2014.

di Lampedusa, Giuseppe. *The Leopard*. New York: Pantheon Books, 2007.

DiPaolo, Marc. "Mass-Marketing 'Beauty': How a Feminist Heroine Became an Insipid Disney Princess." *Beyond Adaptations: Essays on Radical Transformations of Original Works*. Ed. Phyllis Frus and Christy Williams. Jefferson: McFarland, 2010. 168–180.

di Prima, Diane. *Recollections of My Life as a Woman: The New York Years. A Memoir*. New York: Viking, 2001.

Di Renzo, Anthony. *Trinàcria: A Tale of Bourbon Sicily*. Toronto: Guernica, 2013.

DiStasi, Lawrence, ed. *Una Storia Segreta: The Secret History of Italian American Evacuation and Internment during World War II*. Berkeley: Heyday Books, 2001.

Dufresne, Laura Rinaldi. "Women Warriors: A Special Case from the Fifteenth Century: *The City of Ladies*." *Women's Studies* 23.2 (March 1994): 111–131.

Durante, Francesco. *Italoamericana: Storia e letteratura degli italiani negli Stati Uniti, 1880–1943*. Milano: Mondadori, 2005.

Edwards, Andrew, and Suzanne Edwards. *Sicily: A Literary Guide for Travellers*. New York: I. B. Tauris, 2014.

Esposito, Michael D. "Jerre Mangione: Novelist, Scholar, Critic." *Ethnic Forum: Center for the Study of Ethnic Publications* 3.1–2 (Fall 1983): 7–22.

Ets, Marie Hall. *Rosa: The Life of an Italian Immigrant*. Minneapolis: U of Minnesota P, 1970.

Famà, Maria. "La Carta Parla." *Breaking Open: Reflections on Italian American Women's Writing*. Ed. Mary Ann Vigilante Mannino and Justin Vitiello. West Lafayette: Purdue UP, 2003. 109–135.

———. *Currents*. Chicago: Adams Press, 1988.

———. "I Am Not White." *Sweet Lemons: Writings with a Sicilian Accent*. Mineola: Legas, 2004. 217–218.

———. *Identification*. San Francisco: malafemmina press, 1991.

———. *Mystics in the Family*. New York: Bordighera Press, 2013.

Fanon, Frantz. *Black Skin, White Masks*. New York: Grove Press, 1967 [1952].

Fante, John. *Ask the Dust*. Santa Barbara: Black Sparrow Press, 1980.

———. *Wait Until Spring, Bandini!* Santa Barbara: Black Sparrow Press, 1983 [1938].

Farrell, Joseph. *Leonardo Sciascia*. Edinburgh: Edinburgh UP, 1995.

———. *Sicily: A Cultural History*. Northampton: Interlink Books, 2014.

———. "The Things That Make Sicily Sicily: Considerations on Sicilian Identity." *The Politics of Italian National Identity: A Multidisciplinary Perspective*. Ed. Gino Bedani and Bruce Haddock. Cardiff: U of Wales P, 2000. 72–97.

Fausty, Joshua, and Edvige Giunta. "Quentin Tarantino: An Ethnic Enigma." *Screening Ethnicity: Cinematographic Representations of Italian Americans in the United States*. Boca Raton: Bordighera Press, 2002. 210–221.

Fazio, Venera. "The Sacred Stories of Gioia Timpanelli." *Descant* 42.3 (Fall 2011): 155–160.

Fazio, Venera, and Delia De Santis, eds. *Sweet Lemons: Writings with a Sicilian Accent*. Mineola: Legas, 2004.

———. *Sweet Lemons 2: International Writings with a Sicilian Accent*. Mineola: Legas, 2010.

Ferlita, Salvatore, and Paolo Nifosì. *La Sicilia di Andrea Camilleri: Tra Vigata e Montelusa*. Palermo: Kalos, 2003.

Finley, Moses I. *A History of Sicily: Ancient Sicily to the Arab Conquest*. New York: The Viking Press, 1968.

Franzina, Emilio. *Dall'Arcadia in America: Attività letteraria ed emigrazione transoceanica in Italia (1850–1940)*. Torino: Edizioni della Fondazione Giovanni Agnelli, 1996.

Gabaccia, Donna. *From Sicily to Elizabeth Street: Housing and Social Change among Italian Immigrants, 1880–1930*. Albany: State U of New York P, 1984.

———. *Militants and Migrants: Rural Sicilians Become American Workers*. New Brunswick: Rutgers UP, 1988.

———. "Two Great Migrations: American and Italian Southerners in Comparative Perspective." *The American South and the Italian Mezzogiorno: Essays in Comparative History*. Ed. Enrico Dal Lago and Rick Halpern. New York: Palgrave, 2002. 215–232.

Gallo, Frank. Rev. of *La Storia: Five Centuries of the Italian American Experience*, by Jerre Mangione. *Annals of the American Academy of Political and Social Science* 534 (1994): 202.

Gambino, Richard. *Blood of My Blood: The Dilemma of the Italian-Americans*. Garden City: Doubleday, 1974.

———. *Vendetta: A True Story of the Worst Lynching in America, the Mass Murder of Italian-Americans in New Orleans in 1891, the Vicious Motivations behind It, and the Tragic Repercussions That Linger to This Day*. Garden City: Doubleday, 1977.

Gans, Herbert J. *The Urban Villagers: Group and Class in the Life of Italian-Americans*. New York: The Free Press, 1966 [1962].

Gardaphé, Fred. *The Art of Reading Italian Americana*. New York: Bordighera Press, 2011.

———. "A Class Act: Understanding the Italian American Gangster." *Screening Ethnicity:Essays on Italian American Film*. Ed. Anthony Julian Tamburri and Anna Camaiti Hostert. Boca Raton: Bordighera Press, 2002. 48–68.

———. *Dagoes Read*. Toronto: Guernica, 1996.

———. *From Wiseguys to Wise Men: The Gangster and Italian American Masculinities*. New York: Routledge, 2006.

———. "An Interview with Jerre Mangione." *Forkroads* 5 (1996): 43–55.

———. *Italian Signs, American Streets: The Evolution of Italian American Narrative*. Durham: Duke UP, 1996.

———. *Leaving Little Italy: Essaying Italian American Culture*. Albany: State U of New York P, 2004.

———. "Left Out: Three Italian American Writers of the 1930s." *Radical Revisions: Rereading 1930s Culture*. Ed. Bill Mullen and Sherry Lee Linkon. Urbana: U of Illinois P, 1996. 60–77.

———. "My House Is Not Your House: Jerre Mangione and Italian-American Autobiography." *Multicultural Autobiography: American Lives*. Ed. James Robert Payne. Knoxville: U of Tennessee P, 1992. 139–177.

———. "Re-Inventing Sicily in Italian American Writing and Film." *MELUS* 28.3 (2003): 55–71.

Gentile, Giovanni. *Il tramonto della cultura siciliana*. Firenze: Sansoni, 1985.

Gilbert, Sandra M. *Belongings: Poems*. New York: Norton, 2005.

———. *Blood Pressure*. New York: Norton, 1988.

———. *Emily's Bread: Poems*. New York: Norton, 1984.

———. *Ghost Volcano: Poems*. New York: Norton, 1995.

———. *Italian Collection: Poems of Heritage*. San Francisco: Depot Books, 2003.

———. *Kissing the Bread: New and Selected Poems, 1969–1999*. New York: Norton, 2000.

———. *Summer Kitchen*. Woodside: Heyeck Press, 1983.

Giordano, Paolo A., and Anthony Julian Tamburri, eds. *Beyond the Margin: Readings in Italian Americana*. Madison: Fairleigh Dickinson UP, 1998.

Giunta, Edvige. "Persephone's Daughters." *Women's Studies: An Inter-Disciplinary Journal* 33.6 (2004): 767–786.

———. "Speaking through Silences: Ethnicity in the Writings of Italian/ American Women." *Breaking Open: Reflections on Italian American Women's Writing*. Ed. Mary Ann Vigilante Mannino and Justin Vitiello. West Lafayette: Purdue UP, 2003. 279–300.

———. " 'Spills of Mysterious Substances' or Making One's Own History: Tina DeRosa, Louise DeSalvo, Sandra Gilbert, and Rose Romano." *A Tavola: Food, Tradition and Community among Italian Americans*. Ed. Edvige Giunta and Samuel J. Patti. Staten Island: American Italian Historical Association, 1998. 97–123.

———. *Writing with an Accent: Contemporary Italian American Women Authors*. New York: Palgrave, 2002.

Giunta, Edvige, and Kathleen Zamboni McCormick, eds. *Teaching Italian American Literature, Film, and Popular Culture*. New York: The Modern Language Association of America, 2010.

Glazer, Nathan, and Daniel P. Moynihan. *Beyond the Melting Pot: The Negroes, Puerto Ricans, Jews, Italians, and Irish of New York City*. Cambridge: MIT Press, 1963.

Goeller, Alison D. "Persephone Goes Home: Italian American Women in Italy." *MELUS* 28.3 (Fall 2003): 73–90.

Goethe, Johann Wolfgang von. *Italian Journey*. Princeton: Princeton UP, 1994.

Gramsci, Antonio. *Letteratura e vita nazionale*. Roma: Editori Riuniti, 1971.

———. *Opere di Antonio Gramsci*. Torino: Einaudi, 1950.

———. *La questione meridionale*. Ed. Franco De Felice and Valentino Parlato. Roma: Editori Riuniti, 1974.

———. *The Southern Question*. Trans. Pasquale Verdicchio. West Lafayette: Bordighera Press, 1995.

Granara, William. "Remaking Muslim Sicily: Ibn Hamdīs and the Poetics of Exile." *Edebiyat* 9 (1998): 167–198.

Green, Rose Basile. *The Italian-American Novel: A Document of the Interaction of Two Cultures*. Rutherford: Fairleigh Dickinson UP, 1974.

Grove, Lisa. "An Interview with Gioia Timpanelli." *California Journal of Poetics* (2001): http://www.californiapoetics.org/interviews/1603/an-interview-with-gioia-timpanelli/.

Guglielmo, Jennifer. "White Lies, Dark Truths." Introduction. *Are Italians White? How Race Is Made in America*. New York: Routledge, 2003. 1–14.

Guglielmo, Jennifer, and Salvatore Salerno, eds. *Are Italians White? How Race Is Made in America*. New York: Routledge, 2003.

Hansen, Marcus Lee. "The Problem of the Third Generation Immigrant." 1938. *Theories of Ethnicity: A Classical Reader*. Ed. Werner Sollors. New York: New York UP, 1996. 202–215.

Hay, Pete. "The Poetics of Island Place: Articulating Particularity." *Local Environment* 8.5 (October 2003): 553–558.

Hendin, Gattuso Josephine. *The Right Thing to Do*. New York: Feminist Press at the City University of New York, 1999.

Hobsbawm, Eric. *Nations and Nationalism since 1780*. Cambridge: Cambridge UP, 1990.

Hostert Camaiti, Anna, and Anthony Tamburri, eds. *Screening Ethnicity: Cinematographic Representations of Italian Americans in the United States*. Boca Raton: Bordighera Press, 2002.

Ignatiev, Noel, and John Garvey, eds. *Race Traitor*. New York: Routledge, 1996.

Iorizzo, Luciano J., and Salvatore Mondello. *The Italian Americans*. New York: Twayne, 1971.

Keahey, John. *Seeking Sicily: A Cultural Journey through Myth and Reality in the Heart of the Mediterranean*. New York: Thomas Dunne Books/St. Martin's Press, 2011.

King, Russell. "The Geographical Fascination of Islands." *The Development Process in Small Island States*. Ed. Douglas G. Lockhart, David Drakakis-Smith, and Patrick Schembri. New York: Routledge, 1993. 13–37.

Kolchin, Peter. "The American South in Comparative Perspective." *American South and the Italian Mezzogiorno: Essays in Comparative History*. Ed. Enrico Dal Lago and Rick Halpern. New York: Palgrave, 2002. 26–59.

Korneeva, Tatiana. "Desire and Desirability in Villeneuve and Leprince de Beaumont's 'Beauty and the Beast.'" *Marvels and Tales: Journal of Fairy-Tale Studies* 28.2 (2014): 233–251.

LaGumina, Salvatore J. *Wop! A Documentary History of Anti-Italian Discrimination in the United States*. Toronto: Guernica, 1999.

Landry, Donna, and Gerald MacLean, eds. *The Spivak Reader: Selected Works of Gayatri Chakravorty Spivak*. New York: Routledge, 1996.

Lane, Dorothy. *The Island as Site of Resistance: An Examination of Caribbean and New Zealand Texts*. New York: Peter Lang, 1995.

Lee, Charles. "The Bitter Dilemma of the D. P." Rev. of *The Ship and the Flame*, by Jerre Mangione. *New York Times*, 16 May 1948: BR5.

Lloyd, Susan Caperna. *No Pictures in My Grave: A Spiritual Journey in Sicily*. San Francisco: Mercury House, 1992.

Lowe, John. "Humor and Identity in Ethnic Autobiography: Zora Neale Hurston and Jerre Mangione." *Cultural Difference and the Literary Text: Pluralism and the Limits of Authenticity in North American Literatures*. Ed. Winfried Siemerling and Katrin Schwenk. Iowa City: U of Iowa P, 1996. 75–99.

Lupo, Salvatore. *Storia della mafia: Dalle origini ai giorni nostri*. Roma: Donzelli, 1993.

Mack Smith, Denis. *A History of Sicily: Medieval Sicily, 800–1713.* New York: Viking Press, 1968.

———. *A History of Sicily: Modern Sicily, after 1713.* New York: Viking Press, 1968.

Maggio, Theresa. *Mattanza: The Ancient Sicilian Ritual of Bluefin Tuna Fishing.* New York: Penguin Books, 2001.

———. *The Stone Boudoir: Travels through the Hidden Villages of Sicily.* Berkeley: Counterpoint, 2003.

Manfredi, Renée. *Above the Thunder.* San Francisco: MacAdam/Cage, 2004.

———. *Running Away with Frannie.* San Francisco: MacAdam/Cage, 2006.

———. *Where Love Leaves Us.* Iowa City: U of Iowa P, 1994.

Mangione, Jerre. *America Is also Italian.* New York: G. P. Putnam's Sons, 1969.

———. "A Double Life: The Fate of the Urban Ethnic." *Literature and the Urban Experience: Essays on the City and Literature.* Ed. Michael C. Jaye and Ann Chalmers Watts. New Brunswick: Rutgers UP, 1980. 169–183.

———. *The Dream and the Deal: The Federal Writers' Project 1935–1943.* Boston: Little, Brown, 1972.

———. *An Ethnic at Large: A Memoir of America in the Thirties and Forties.* New York: G. P. Putnam's Sons, 1978.

———. *Life Sentences for Everybody.* New York: Abelard-Schuman, 1965.

———. *Mont'Allegro: Una comunità siciliana in America.* Milano: Franco Angeli Editore, 1983 [1943].

———. *Mount Allegro: A Memoir of Italian American Life.* Syracuse: Syracuse UP, 1998.

———. *Mussolini's March on Rome.* London: Franklin Watts, 1975.

———. "My Experience as an Italian American Writer." *Rivista di studi anglo-americani* 3.4–5 (1984): 67–86.

———. *Night Search.* New York: Crown, 1965.

———. "On Being a Sicilian American." *Studies in Italian American Social History: Essays in Honor of Leonard Covello.* Ed. Francesco Cordasco. Totowa: Rowman & Littlefield, 1975. 40–49.

———. *A Passion for Sicilians: The World around Danilo Dolci.* New York: William Morrow, 1968.

———. "Remembrances and Impressions of an Ethnic at Large." *Writers Speak: America and the Ethnic Experience.* Ed. Alan Lelchuk, John Edgar Wideman, and Jerre Mangione. Amherst: Institute for Advanced Study in Humanities, 1984. 42–58.

———. *Reunion in Sicily.* New York: Columbia UP, 1984.

———. *Riunione in Sicilia.* Trans. Maria Anita Stefanelli. Palermo: Sellerio, 1992.

———. *The Ship and the Flame.* New York: A. A. Wyn, 1948.

———. "The Two Uncles: An Addendum to *Mount Allegro*." *Wild Dreams: The Best of Italian Americana.* Ed. Carol Bonomo Albright and Joanna Clapps Herman. New York: Fordham UP, 2008. 177–181.

Mangione, Jerre, and Ben Morreale. *La Storia: Five Centuries of the Italian American Experience*. New York: HarperCollins, 1992.

Mannino, Mary Ann. "Blurred Racial Borders in the Poetry of Maria Mazziotti Gillan and Rose Romano." *Shades of Black and White*. Ed. Dan Ashyk, Fred Gardaphé, and Anthony Julian Tamburri. Staten Island: American Italian Historical Association, 1999. 331–339.

———. *Revisionary Identities: Strategies of Empowerment in the Writing of Italian/American Women*. New York: Peter Lang, 2000.

Mannino, Mary Ann, and Justin Vitiello, eds. *Breaking Open: Reflections on Italian American Women's Writing*. West Lafayette: Purdue UP, 2003.

Marazzi, Martino. *Voices of Italian America*. New York: Fordham UP, 2012.

Marotta, Kenny. *A House on the Piazza*. Toronto: Guernica, 1998.

———. *A Piece of Earth*. New York: William Morrow, 1985.

Martelli, Matteo. "Leggere l'idiozia: Note sul ciclo narrativo di Giufà." *Strumenti critici* 1 (2011): 1–16.

Maso, Carol. *Ghost Dance*. Hopewell: The Ecco Press, 1986.

McBride, Paul W. Rev. of *Mount Allegro*, by Jerre Mangione. *Journal of American Ethnic History* 11.2 (Winter 1992): 112.

McCaffety, Kerri. *St. Joseph Altars*. Gretna: Pelican, 2003.

Morreale, Ben. *Down and Out in Academia*. New York: Pitman, 1972.

———. *A Few Virtuous Men (Li Cornuti)*. Plattsburgh: Tundra Books, 1973.

———. "Jerre Mangione: The Sicilian Sources." *Italian Americana* 7.1 (1981): 4–18.

———. *The Loss of the Miraculous*. Toronto: Guernica, 1997.

———. *Monday, Tuesday . . . Never Come Sunday*. Plattsburgh: Tundra Books, 1977.

———. "The Prince of Racalmuto." *Wild Dreams: The Best of Italian Americana*. Ed. Carol Bonomo Albright and Joanna Clapps Herman. New York: Fordham UP, 2008. 182–188.

———. *The Seventh Saracen*. New York: Coward-McCann, 1958.

———. *Sicily, the Hallowed Land: A Memoir*. Mineola: Legas, 2000.

Mulas, Franco, and Jerre Mangione. "A MELUS Interview: Jerre Mangione." *MELUS* 12.4 (1985): 73–83.

Muscarà, Sarah Zappulla, ed. *Narratori siciliani del secondo dopoguerra*. Catania: Maimone Editore, 1990.

Niceforo, Alfredo. *Italiani del nord, italiani del sud*. Torino: Fratelli Bocca Editori, 1901.

Olson, Ray. "What Makes a Child Lucky." Rev. of *What Makes a Child Lucky*, by Gioia Timpanelli. *Booklist* 105.3 (2008): 25.

Painter, Ronnie Mae, and Rosette Capotorto. "Italiani/Africani." *Are Italians White? How Race Is Made in America*. Ed. Jennifer Guglielmo and Salvatore Salerno. New York: Routledge, 2003. 250–258.

Peragallo, Olga. *Italian American Authors and Their Contribution to American Literature*. New York: S. F. Vanni, 1949.

Petraccone, Claudia. *Federalismo e autonomia in Italia dall'unità a oggi*. Bari: Laterza, 1995.

Pirandello, Luigi. *Short Stories*. Ed. and trans. Frederick May. London: Oxford UP, 1975.

Pitrè, Giuseppe. *Fiabe, novelle e racconti popolari siciliani*. Ed. Silvia Masaracchio. 2 vols. Collana Bacheca EBook, 2010: http://www.aiutamici.com/ftp/eBook/ebook/Giuseppe%20Pitre%20-%20Fiabe%20novelle%20e%20racconti%20popolari%20siciliani%20Vol%201.pdf. Accessed 5 Nov. 2014.

———. *Il Popolo siciliano, la famiglia e la casa*. Milano: Brancato Editore, 2002.

Prezzolini, Giuseppe. *I trapiantati*. Milano: Longanesi, 1963.

Provenzano, Antonino. *Tornu/The Return*. Mineola, NY: Legas, 2009.

———. *Vinissi . . . I'd Love to Come . . .* Mineola: Legas, 1995.

Puzo, Mario. *The Fortunate Pilgrim*. New York: Atheneum, 1964.

———. *The Godfather*. New York: G. P. Putnam's Sons, 1969.

———. *The Last Don*. New York: Random House, 1996.

———. *Omerta*. New York: Random House, 2000.

———. *The Sicilian*. New York: Simon and Schuster, 1984.

Quasimodo, Salvatore. *Tutte le poesie*. Milano: Mondadori, 1984.

Quinn, Roseanne. "Sorelle delle Ombre: Confronting Racism and Homophobia in Literature by Contemporary Italian-American Women." *Italian Americans in a Multicultural Society*. Ed. Jerome Karase and Judith DeSena. Stony Brook: Forum Italicum, 1994. 236–246.

Radner, Jo, Joseph Sobol, David Novak, Karen Dietz, Gioia Timpanelli, and Doug Lipman. "Visions for Storytelling Studies: Why, How, and for Whom?" *Storytelling, Self, Society* 1.1 (Fall 2004): 8–27.

Ragusa, Kym. *The Skin between Us: A Memoir of Race, Beauty, and Belonging*. New York: Norton, 2006.

Raptosh, Diane. *Just West of Now*. Toronto: Guernica, 1995.

———. *Labor Songs: Poems*. Toronto: Guernica, 1999.

———. *Parents from a Different Alphabet*. Toronto: Guernica, 2008.

Reinburg, Virginia. " 'For the Use of Women': Women and Books of Hours." *Early Modern Women: An Interdisciplinary Journal* 4 (Fall 2009): 235–240.

Renda, Francesco. *L'emigrazione in Sicilia*. Palermo: Ed. Sicilia al Lavoro, 1963.

———. *I fasci siciliani, 1892–1894*. Torino: Einaudi, 1977.

Rev. of *Tales from the Roof of the World*, by Gioia Timpanelli. *Bulletin of the Center for Children's Books* 38 (September 1984): 17.

Rich, Adrienne. "Compulsory Heterosexuality and Lesbian Existence." *Journal of Women's History* 15.3 (2003): 11–48.

Roberts, Alfred. Rev. of *An Ethnic at Large: A Memoir of America in the Thirties and Forties*, by Jerre Mangione. *MELUS* 6.4 (Winter 1979): 86–88.

Roediger, David D. *The Wages of Whiteness: Race and the Making of the American Working Class*. London: Verso, 1999.

Romano, Rose, ed. *la bella figura, 1988–1992: A Choice*. San Francisco: mala-femmina press, 1993.

———. "Coming Out Olive in the Lesbian Community: Big Sister Is Watching You." *Social Pluralism and Literary History: The Literature of the Italian Emigration*. Ed. Francesco Loriggio. Toronto: Guernica, 1996. 161–175.

———. *Vendetta*. San Francisco: malafemmina press, 1990.

———. "Where Is Nella Sorellanza When You Really Need Her?" *New Explorations in Italian American Studies*. Ed. Richard N. Juliani and Sandra P. Juliani. Staten Island: American Italian Historical Association, 1994. 147–154.

———. *The Wop Factor*. Brooklyn: malafemmina press, 1994.

Rose, Peter. Rev. of *Mount Allegro: A Memoir of Italian American Life*, by Jerre Mangione. *Contemporary Sociology* 12.2 (1983): 222–223.

———. Rev. of *La Storia: Five Centuries of the Italian American Experience*, by Jerre Mangione and Ben Morreale. *International Migration Review* 27.4 (Winter 1993): 900–901.

Rosemont, Franklin. "Surrealist, Anarchist, Afrocentrist: Philip Lamantia Before and After the 'Beat Generation.'" *Are Italians White? How Race Is Made in America*. Ed. Jennifer Guglielmo and Salvatore Salerno. New York: Routledge, 2003. 124–143.

Royle, Stephen A. *A Geography of Islands: Small Island Insularity*. New York: Routledge, 2001.

Runciman, Steven. *The Sicilian Vespers*. London: Cambridge UP, 1958.

Russo, John Paul. "Giuseppe Pitrè and the Sicilian Folk Tradition." *Sweet Lemons 2: International Writings with a Sicilian Accent*. Ed. Venera Fazio and Delia De Santis. Mineola: Legas, 2010. 76–79.

Ruta, Domenica. *With or Without You*. New York: Random House, 2013.

Said, Edward. *Culture and Imperialism*. New York: Knopf, 1993.

———. *Orientalism*. New York: Pantheon Books, 1978.

Santangelo, Giorgio. *Letteratura in Sicilia da Federico II a Pirandello*. Palermo: Flaccovio, 1975.

Scammacca, Nat, ed. *Antigruppo 1975: Trapani 3ª pagina*. Trapani: Ed. Trapani Nuova, 1975.

———. *Bye Bye America: Memories of a Sicilian-American*. Merrick/Trapani: Coop. Ed. Antigruppo Siciliano & Cross-Cultural Communications, 1986.

———. *Bye bye America: Ricordi di un wop*. Palermo: Libri siciliani, 1972.

———. *Due mondi*. Trapani: Coop. Ed. Antigruppo Siciliano, 1979.

———. *Ericepeo I*. Merrick/Trapani: Coop. Ed. Antigruppo Siciliano & Cross-Cultural Communications, 1990.

———. *Ericepeo II*. Merrick/Trapani: Coop. Ed. Antigruppo Siciliano & Cross-Cultural Communications, 1990.

———. *Ericepeo III*. Merrick/Trapani: Coop. Ed. Antigruppo Siciliano & Cross-Cultural Communications, 1990.

———. *Glenlee*. Catania: Cooperativa Operatori Grafici, Giuseppe Di Maria Editore, 1971.

———, trans. *A Meeting with Disma Tumminello and William Stafford*. Merrick/ Trapani Coop. Ed. Antigruppo Siciliano & Cross-Cultural Communications, 1978.

———. *Schammachanat: Poesie in italiano e inglese*. Merrick/Trapani: Coop. Ed. Antigruppo Siciliano & Cross-Cultural Communications, 1985.

———. *Sikano l'amerikano!* Merrick/Trapani: Coop. Ed. Antigruppo Siciliano & Cross-Cultural Communications, 1989.

———. *Una possibile poetica per un Antigruppo*. Trapani: Editore Celebes, 1970.

Scarpaci, Vincenza. "Walking the Color Line: Italian Immigrants in Rural Louisiana, 1880–1910." *Are Italians White? How Race Is Made in America*. Ed. Jennifer Guglielmo and Salvatore Salerno. New York: Routledge, 2003. 60–76.

Scelsa, Joseph V. "They Triumphed in 'La Merica.'" Rev. of *La Storia: Five Centuries of the Italian American Experience*, by Jerre Mangione and Ben Morreale. *New York Times Book Review*, 27 Sept. 1992, sec. 142: 12.

Schneider, Jane, ed. *Italy's "Southern Question": Orientalism in One Country*. Oxford: Berg, 1998.

Schneider, Jane, and Peter Schneider. *Reversible Destiny: Mafia, Antimafia, and the Struggle for Palermo*. Berkeley: U of California P, 2003.

Sciascia, Leonardo. *La corda pazza: Scrittori e cose della Sicilia*. Milano: Adelphi, 1991 [1970].

———. *Le parrocchie di Regalpetra*. Milano: Adelphi, 2003 [1956].

———. *Pirandello e la Sicilia*. Milano: Adelphi, 1996.

———. *La Sicilia come metafora: Intervista di Marcelle Padovani*. Milano: Mondadori, 1989.

———. *The Wine-Dark Sea*. New York: New York Review Books, 2000.

Sciascia, Leonardo, and Salvatore Guglielmino, eds. *Narratori di Sicilia*. Milano: Mursia, 1967.

Sciorra, Joseph. "Locating Memory: Longing, Place, and Autobiography in Vincenzo Ancona's Sicilian Poetry." *Italian Folk: Vernacular Culture in Italian-American Lives*. Ed. Joseph Sciorra. New York: Fordham UP, 2011. 107–131.

Scott, Dorothea Hayward. Rev. of *Tales from the Roof of the World*, by Gioia Timpanelli. *School Library Journal* 31.1 (1984): 124.

Serra, Ilaria. "Narratives That Heal: An Interview with Gioia Timpanelli." *FACS: Florida Atlantic Comparative Studies* 7 (2004): 1–11.

Signorile, Michelangelo. *Queer in America: Sex, the Media, and the Closets of Power*. Madison: U of Wisconsin P, 2003.

Simeti, Mary Taylor. *On Persephone's Island: A Sicilian Journal*. London: Penguin Books, 1988.

Sollors, Werner. *Beyond Ethnicity: Consent and Descent in American Culture*. New York: Oxford UP, 1986.

———. *Theories of Ethnicity: A Classical Reader*. Washington Square: New York UP, 1996.

Sori, Ercole. *L'emigrazione italiana dall'unità alla II guerra mondiale*. Bologna: Il Mulino, 1979.

Spivak, Gayatri. "Can the Subaltern Speak?" *Colonial Discourse and Post-Colonial Theory*. Ed. Patrick Williams and Laura Chrisman. New York: Columbia UP, 1994. 66–111.

Steinberg, Stephen. *The Ethnic Myth: Race, Ethnicity, and Class in America*. Boston: Beacon Press, 1982.

Talese, Gay. *Honor Thy Father*. New York: HarperCollins, 2009.

Tamburri, Anthony Julian. *A Semiotic of Ethnicity: In (Re)cognition of the Italian/American Writer*. Albany: State U of New York P, 1998.

———. "Beyond 'Pizza' and 'Nonna'! Or, What's Bad about Italian/American Criticism? Further Directions for Italian/American Cultural Studies." *MELUS* 28.3 (2003): 149–174.

———, ed. *Fuori: Essays by Italian/American Lesbians and Gays*. West Lafayette: Bordighera Press, 1996.

———. *To Hyphenate or Not to Hyphenate? The Italian/American Writer: An Other American*. Toronto: Guernica, 1991.

Tamburri, Anthony Julian, Paolo A. Giordano, and Fred L. Gardaphé, eds. *From the Margin: Writings in Italian Americana*. 2nd ed. West Lafayette: Purdue UP, 2000.

Teti, Vito, ed. *La razza maledetta: Origini del pregiudizio antimeridionale*. Roma: Manifestolibri, 1993.

Timpanelli, Gioia. "Notes and Pieces on Speaking Poems and Stories, Learning by Heart." *Robert Bly in This World*. Ed. Thomas R. Smith and James P. Lenfestey. Minneapolis: U of Minnesota P, 2011, 149–159.

———. *Sometimes the Soul: Two Novellas of Sicily*. New York: Vintage Books, 1998.

———. *Stones for the Hours of the Night*. New York: Droll Kolbert Gallery, 1978.

———. "Stories and Storytelling, Italian and Italian American." *The Italian American Heritage: A Companion to Literature and Arts*. Ed. Pellegrino d'Acierno. New York: Garland, 1999. 131–148.

———. *Tales from the Roof of the World: Folktales of Tibet*. New York: Viking Press, 1984.

———. *What Makes a Child Lucky*. New York: Norton, 2008.

Tintori, Karen. *Unto the Daughters: The Legacy of an Honor Killing in a Sicilian-American Family*. New York: St. Martin's Griffin, 2007.

Valerio, Anthony. *Conversations with Johnny: A Novel*. Toronto: Guernica, 1997.

———. *The Mediterranean Runs through Brooklyn*. New York: H. B. Davis, 1982.

———. *Toni Cade Bambara's One Sicilian Night: A Memoir*. New York: Bordighera Press, 2007.

Vecoli, Rudolph. "Are Italian Americans Just White Folks?" 1994. *Italian and Italian/American Images in the Media*. Ed. Mary Jo Bona and Anthony J. Tamburri. Staten Island: American Italian Historical Association, 1996. 3–17.

Vellon, Peter. "Between White Men and Negroes: The Perception of Southern Italian Immigrants through the Lens of Italian Lynchings." *Anti-Italianism: Essays on a Prejudice*. Ed. William J. Connell and Fred Gardaphé. New York: Palgrave, 2010. 23–32.

Verdicchio, Pasquale. *Bound by Distance: Rethinking Nationalism through the Italian Diaspora*. Madison: Fairleigh Dickinson UP, 1997.

Verga, Giovanni. *I Malavoglia*. Milano: Mondadori, 1989.

———. *Novelle*. Ed. Gabriella Ravizza. Milano: Mondadori, 1991.

———. *Mastro Don Gesualdo*. Milano: Rizzoli, 1979.

———. *Vita dei campi*. Firenze: Le Monnier, 1987 [1880].

Viscusi, Robert. *Buried Caesars, and Other Secrets of Italian American Writing*. Albany: State U of New York P, 2006.

Vitiello, Justin. "Beyond Tautologies? Poetics of Female and Feminist 'Italianità' in Four Anthologies of Italian American Women's Literature." *Breaking Open: Reflections on Italian American Women's Writing*. Ed. Mary Ann Vigilante Mannino and Justin Vitiello. West Lafayette: Purdue UP, 2003. 323–357.

———. *Poetics and Literature of the Sicilian Diaspora: Studies in Oral History and Storytelling*. San Francisco: Mellen Research UP, 1993.

———. "Sicilian Folk Narrative versus Sicilian-American Literature: Mangione's *Mount Allegro*." *MELUS* 18.2 (1993): 61–75.

———. "What I Wanted to Ask and Say." *Breaking Open: Reflections on Italian American Women's Writing*. Ed. Mary Ann Vigilante Mannino and Justin Vitiello. West Lafayette: Purdue UP, 2003. 19–28.

Vittorini, Elio. *Conversations in Sicily*. New York: New Directions, 2000.

Warrington, Edward, and David Milne. "Island Governance." *A World of Islands*. Ed. Godfrey Baldacchino. Charlottetown: Institute of Island Studies, 2007. 379–427.

Washington, Booker T. *The Man Farthest Down: A Record of Observation and Study in Europe*. New Brunswick: Transaction Books, 1984.

Weale, David. "Islandness." *Island Journal* 8 (1991): 81–82.

Weisberger, Bernard A. "Jerre Mangione: The Man and His Work." *VIA—Voices in Italian Americana* 4.2 (1993): 5–17.

Zipes, Jack, trans. *Beautiful Angiola: The Great Treasury of Sicilian Folk and Fairy Tales Collected by Laura Gonzenbach*. New York: Routledge, 2004.

———, trans. "Beauty and the Beast." *The Great Fairy Tale Tradition: From Straparola and Basile to the Brothers Grimm*. Ed. Jack Zipes. New York: Norton Critical Editions, 2001. 805–815.

———, trans. *The Robber with a Witch's Head: More Stories from the Great Treasury of Sicilian Folk and Fairy Tales Collected by Laura Gonzenbach*. New York: Routledge, 2005.

Zipes, Jack, and Joseph Russo, eds. *The Collected Sicilian Folk and Fairy Tales of Giuseppe Pitrè*. New York: Routledge, 2009.

Index

beliefs, magical; Catholicism;
Christianity; pagan customs
Renda, Francesco: *L'emigrazione in
Sicilia*, 31; *I fasci siciliani*, 27
Repubblica, La, 25
Rich, Adrienne, 103
Rizzotto, Giuseppe: *I mafiusi della
Vicaria*, 36
Rochester (New York), 70, 73–76,
80, 82–83, 86–89, 92, 149n31,
156n20
romanticization, 32, 50
Roman Empire, 23, 83–84, 89
Romano, Rose, x, 1–2, 14, 15,
16–17, 32, 36, 68, 74, 95–111,
113, 138, 139–140; *Vendetta*,
16–17, 96, 97–98, 102–105,
109, 110; "Where Is Nella
Sorellanza When You Really
Need Her?," 103; *The Wop
Factor*, 16–17, 96, 100–102,
108–110
Rome, 3, 46
Roosevelt, Franklin D., 88, 92
Rosemont, Franklin, 10
Rossi, Salvatore: *Novecento siciliano*,
149n27
Runciman, Steven: *The Sicilian
Vespers*, 26
rural life, Italian, 12, 131, 148n25
Russian Americans. *See* Jewish
Americans
Russo, Joseph: *The Collected Sicilian
Folk and Fairy Tales of Giuseppe
Pitrè*, 157n4
Ruta, Domenica, 140–141, 153n4;
With or Without You, 14
Ruvoli, JoAnne, 12

SageWoman, 107
Said, Edward: *Culture and
Imperialism*, 28
Saint Joseph, 84; *festa* altars, 84,
154n10

Saint Rosalie, 124, 158n8; *festa*,
124, 158n8
saints, 44, 84, 91, 124. *See also*
Catholicism
Salerno, Salvatore: *Are Italians
White?*, 157n6
San Francisco Renaissance, 9–10
Sanskrit, 118
Santangelo, Giorgio: *Letteratura in
Sicilia da Federico II a Pirandello*,
149n27
Sapegno, Natalino: *Storia letteraria
delle regioni d'Italia*, 149n27
Saracens, 43, 50
Sardinia, 3, 20, 21, 146n2, 148n24
satire, 154n5
Savoy, House of, 3
Scammacca, Nat, x, 13, 14, 32–33,
139, 147n12, 150n32; *Bye Bye
America*, 14, 139; *Due Mondi*,
14, 139; *Sikano l'Amerikano*,
14, 139
Scammacca, Nina, 150n32
Scarpaci, Vincenza: "Walking the
Color Line," 100
scholarship, 3, 17, 18, 21, 30, 72,
90, 97, 114, 116, 141, 143n1
Sciascia, Leonardo, ix–x, 25, 28–29,
41–42, 43, 60, 137, 150n31,
152n15: *La corda pazza*, 23–24;
Il giorno della civetta, 42, 62;
Narratori di Sicilia, 24, 32,
149n27, 150n31; *Le parrocchie
di Regalpetra*, 41, 42, 49, 151n2,
151n5; *Pirandello e la Sicilia*, 24;
La Sicilia come metafora, 24–25;
Gli zii di Sicilia, 42
Scott, Dorothea Hayward, 115
self-discovery, 69, 71–72, 131
Sellerio (publisher), 153n1
Senghor, Léopold, 24
Sergi, Giuseppe, 5, 106
sexism, 95–96, 139–140. *See also*
heteropatriarchy; misogyny